Praise for *SLUT!* by Leora Tanenbaum

"Leora Tanenbaum is one of the most astute and thoughtful of the new generation of feminist writers."
—Elizabeth Wurtzel, author of
Prozac Nation and *Bitch*

"Tanenbaum has written an important and alarming book; it deserves serious attention and should encourage serious action."
—*Women's Review of Books*

"Through bitter experience, either their own or a friend's, [young women] know that Leora Tanenbaum is right."
—*Washington Post*

"Tanenbaum [has made a] bold step into the literary world to start a bold discussion."
—*Newsday*

"An eye-opening book."
—*Redbook*

"A brisk and straightforward analysis of sexual harassment among preteens and adolescents. . . . An especially good resource for young women and their parents."
—*Publishers Weekly*

"Author Leora Tanenbaum makes an alternately powerful and touching case for the abolition of the use of the word slut. . . . An excellent resource."
—*New York Amsterdam News*

"*Slut!* is a powerful book. . . . It has potential as an instructional tool (and a cautionary tale) for educators."
—*Seattle Times*

"As Tanenbaum persuasively shows, slut-bashing has enormous consequences for everyone, not only for the girls who are harassed."
—*San Francisco Bay Times*

"Tanenbaum's argument is as sharp as the tongue of a ninth-grade girl."
—*BUST* Magazine

"Tanenbaum deserves praise for addressing the complications of sluttiness. . . . She makes interesting connections between sluttiness and braininess, gutsiness and independence. . . . This is refreshing stuff in light of the recent attention given to books such as *A Return to Modesty* by Wendy Shalit."
—*Nerve*

"Highly recommended for anyone who has ever judged or been judged—which means pretty much everyone."
—*Bitch* Magazine

SLUT!

SLUT!

GROWING UP
FEMALE WITH A
BAD REPUTATION

LEORA TANENBAUM

Perennial

An Imprint of HarperCollinsPublishers

Reprinted by arrangement with Seven Stories Press.

HarperCollins books may be purchased for educational business, or
sales promotional use. For information please write: Special Markets
Department, HarperCollins Publishers Inc., 10 East 53rd Street, New
York, NY 10022.

FIRST PERENNIAL EDITION PUBLISHED 2000.

Printed on acid-free paper

Library of Congress Cataloging-in-Publication Data

Tanenbaum, Leora.
   Slut! : growing up female with a bad reputation / Leora Tanen-
baum.—1st ed.
    p. cm.
   Originally published: New York : Seven Stories Press, 1999.
   Includes index.
   ISBN 0-06-095740-9
    1. Girls—United States—Social conditions.   2. Teenage girls—
United States—Social conditions.   3. Sex discrimination against
women—United States.   4. Sex in popular culture—United States.
I. Title

HQ798 .T36 2000
305.23—dc21   00-038516

09 10 11 ❖ 20 19 18

In memory of Sassi Lonner

CONTENTS

Positive Expressions For a Sexually Active Man	Positive Expressions For a Sexually Active Woman
stud	hot
player	sexy
stallion	
ladies' man	
the man	
Romeo	
Don Juan	
Casanova	
bounder	
gigolo	
lover	
lover man/boy	

Negative Expressions For a Sexually Active Man	Negative Expressions For a Sexually Active Woman
womanizer	slut
wolf	whore
"can't keep it in his pants"	tramp
	ho
	bitch
	hoochie mama
	pig
	prostitute
	hooker
	nympho
	harlot
	hussy
	tart
	bimbo
	floozy
	vixen
	minx
	loose woman
	fallen woman
	vamp
	wench
	slattern
	Jezebel
	strumpet
	skank
	sleaze
	slag
	sexpot

Note: Many of the girls and women whose stories follow asked me to disguise their names. Several also asked me to change the names of the cities or towns where they grew up. All changed locales are equivalent to the original ones (one northeastern city substituted for another, for instance). All ages, ethnicities, and occupations are unchanged.

INTRODUCTION

Julie arrives for our meeting, at a diner across the street from her college campus, dressed for comfort: faded jeans, untucked denim shirt, olive-green army-surplus jacket. She slides opposite me into the windowed booth. I offer her a menu, but she shakes it away: she already knows she wants the French fries. Julie's face is round and friendly, her manner relaxed. But as Julie unfolds her story, I learn that she wasn't always as self-assured as she is today, at nineteen. Back in junior high in New Jersey, she was easily intimidated. Her greatest ambition in life was just to fit in. But she didn't fit in. Julie was something of an outsider in her solidly Catholic, Irish-Italian neighborhood. Her family was the only one in town that didn't attend church. She hadn't gone to the same middle school her friends had attended. And she was pudgy, a bit overweight. Too eager to conform yet too different, Julie was an easy target.

One evening when she was thirteen, Julie tells me, her soft brown eyes meeting mine squarely, she and her friends were hanging out as usual at one of their houses. They were drinking beers. Julie had recently begun to drink more and more: Alcohol enabled her to push aside the fact that her parents were sleeping in separate beds and not talking to each other. Besides, some older guys had joined them this evening, and Julie figured that it made her seem cool if she drank. That night she drank until she passed out unconscious. When she regained consciousness semiclothed and with a dull pain, she realized that someone had had sex with her. Julie pulled herself together and asked one of her friends what had happened. The guy who did it, she was informed, had been drinking with the group that night—a classmate she only slightly knew. Julie understood that she had been raped.

By Monday morning a friend of the rapist, who had witnessed the event, had spread the news that his friend and Julie had had sex. In a matter of hours, Julie tells me, she was known as a slut. "They'd call out 'slut' to me in the halls. There was graffiti. I got calls in the middle of the night, at four A.M.: 'Fat slut.' Behind the junior high school there was a playground with a handball court, and people would write graffiti there in shaving cream." Everybody in school knew about her. Even today, years later, Julie's reputation as a slut is known to each new crop of incoming high school students.

Julie's story of being singled out as a slut is much more common than you might think. Indeed, you would be hard-pressed to find a high school in the United States in which there is no designated slut. Two out of five girls nationwide— 42 percent—have had sexual rumors spread about them, according to a 1993 poll conducted for the American Association of University Women (AAUW) on sexual harassment in schools.[1] ("Sexual rumor" sometimes means speculation that a classmate is gay, but more often it is a polite way of saying "slutty reputation.") Three out of four girls have received sexual comments or looks, and one in five has had sexual messages written about her in public areas.

Slut-bashing—as I call it—is one issue that affects every single female who grows up in this country because any pre-

the slut label has
nothing to do with
sex ↓

Introduction / xv

teen or teenage girl can become a target. "Slut" is a pervasive
insult applied to a broad spectrum of American adolescent
girls, from the girl who brags about her one-night stands to
the girl who has never even kissed a boy to the girl who has
been raped. Some girls are made fun of because they appear
to have a casual attitude about sex (even if, in reality, they are
no more sexual than their peers). Many others are picked on
because they stand out in some way—being an early developer, new in school, an ethnic or class minority, overweight, or
just considered "weird" for whatever reason. Some are called
"sluts" because other girls dislike or envy them, and spread a
sexual rumor as a form of revenge. While a girl can almost
instantly acquire a "slut" reputation as a result of one well-
placed rumor, it takes months, if not years, for the reputation
to evaporate—if it does at all.

Being called a slut sounds like a sexy topic: All of my male
friends joked that they wanted to help me with the research
for this book. But in truth the "slut" label doesn't necessarily
have anything to do with sex. Very often the label is a stand-
in for something else: the extent to which a girl fails to conform to the idea of "normal" appearance and behavior.

A girl's sexual status is a metaphor for how well she fits
into the American ideal of femininity. Boys who don't conform to the masculine role are similarly judged on a phantom
sexual scale—the short boy with a slight build who strikes out
whenever he's up to bat is called a fag, even though his ability in sports says nothing about his sexual orientation. Yet a
"fag" can overcome his status through bench-pressing; there
is little a "slut" can do to erase her stigma. Magnified by sexual metaphor, her social difference defines everything about
her. She represents soiled femininity.

Looking and behaving and dressing like everyone else is a
classic American tradition, possibly attributable to the melt-
ing-pot ideal for ethnic groups, the Protestant work ethic, and
the capitalist drive to be accepted into the centrist middle
class. Fitting into America requires adherence to gender roles:

Girls and women must act one way, boys and men must act another way. Girls and women are expected to lack sexual desires; boys and men are presumed to be ruled by them. Sexuality and gender roles, then, become intertwined—and easily confused.

The "slut" label carries a set of class associations. Regardless of her family's actual economic status, the "slut" is thought to be "low-class" and "trampy," the kind of girl who wears gobs of makeup and whose voluptuous curves threaten to explode the fabric of her tight clothes. She lacks the polish of the "good" girl, who keeps her sexuality reigned in and discreet (beneath a blazer, a belt, some nude pantyhose), and who will no doubt one day marry a nice middle-class man and raise a nice middle-class family. The "slut" is thought to be a girl without a future.

Being known as the school slut is a terrifying experience. In school, where social hierarchy counts for everything, the school "slut" is a pariah, a butt of jokes, a loser. Girls and boys both gang up on her. She endures cruel and sneering comments—*slut* is often interchangeable with *whore* and *bitch*—as she walks down the hallway. She is publicly humiliated in the classroom and cafeteria. Her body is considered public property: She is fair game for physical harassment. There is little the targeted girl can do to stop the behavior. I was surprised to learn that teachers, generally speaking, do not intervene; they consider this behavior normal for teenagers.

I know what it feels like. I, too, was a "slut" in my high school. In the spring of 1984, when I was in the ninth grade, I fooled around with a guy whom a popular friend of mine had her eye on. In retaliation, she spread the word that I was a "slut." For many months I was snubbed by girls as well as guys, called names to my face, and whispered about behind my back. Gossip shadowed me through the rest of my high school years, and I felt alienated and insecure up until the day of graduation. For years afterward I thought that I alone had been called a slut, and I never discussed it with anyone. I sliced off the experience from my memory when I went away to college, where no one knew.

It was only in 1993, when the AAUW poll revealed the prevalence of hurtful sexual rumors about teenage girls, that I came to terms with my own history. It was then that the enormity of slut-bashing really sank in. I understood that slut-bashing is a form of verbal sexual harassment and a classic illustration of the sexual double standard: the idea that there is one set of sexual rules for men and boys, and another, unequal one for women and girls. Realizing that my experience was hardly unique infused me with the determination to find others who had been similarly shamed. I decided to seek out and talk with former "sluts" like myself, to find out if their experience molded their attitudes and lives, as my experience has shaped me. I also spoke with teenage girls currently in the thick of their "slut" reputations. Their confessional narratives are interspersed throughout the book.

Several of these "sluts" came of age in the 1950s and 1960s, before the sexual and feminist revolutions. They provide us with a benchmark of the old sexual rules, enabling us to compare the situation of "sluts" today with their historical counterparts. Most of the stories in this book, however, are those of women and girls who were ostracized in more recent years, during a time when girls and women have been told that they have the same freedoms as boys and men.

In all, I interviewed fifty girls and women, ages fourteen through sixty-six, who had been targeted as "sluts" in junior high or high school. I spoke with black, Asian, white, and Latina girls and women from twelve different states around the country. They grew up with different economic levels and with different values in cities, suburbs, and rural towns. On the surface, then, these girls and women have absolutely nothing in common. But there is one uniting characteristic: They were all stigmatized in sexual terms.

How did I find these girls and women? I placed classified

ads explaining my research and asking for participants in several college newspapers, as well as alternative weekly papers such as *The Village Voice* and *The Boston Phoenix*. I posted a query in an Internet newsgroup on female sexuality. I wrote about my own high school experiences in *Ms.* and *Seventeen*, which prompted many teenage girls and young women to respond with letters to the editor; I contacted those who provided an address and number. I also reached out to some of the excellent teenage writers for the New York–based newspaper *New Girl Times* and the Boston-based magazine *Teen Voices* who had written about sexual harassment in their schools. Finally, I was introduced to several women through plain, old-fashioned word of mouth.

I asked each interviewee the specifics of her upbringing and school social life, and about the development of her reputation. I then directed her to reflect on several primary questions:

- How did she acquire a "slut" reputation?
- Were her friends less sexually active? Equally sexually active? More sexually active?
- How did she cope with her reputation? Did she behave any differently than she had before she acquired the reputation?
- Did she receive any support from a friend, teacher, or parent?
- How did others regard her and how did she regard herself?
- How did girls treat her and how did that compare with the way boys treated her?
- Did the experience change her outlook on dating, sex, female friendships, being female, or being "different"?

I did not attempt to conduct a scientific survey. My interviewees, as self-selected individuals, do not constitute a random selection of American girls and women labeled sluts. They do provide us, however, with a graphic illustration of the experience of being called a slut. Their answers to my questions illuminate a far-reaching phenomenon that speaks to our societal attitudes about women and sexuality, as it points out the presence of adolescent vindictiveness.

Adolescence, we can all recall, is perhaps more than anything else a time of social jostling and petty cruelties. Isn't slut-bashing, then, just part of the fabric of adolescence? Isn't it, to some extent, normal and therefore acceptable? No. Slut-bashing is uniquely damaging—and not only to teenage girls but to all women. Fearful of being considered a "slut," many girls and women don't carry or use contraception, leading to unplanned and unwanted pregnancies and life-threatening diseases. Worried about seeming sexually aggressive, many girls and women remain silent in ambivalence rather than say yes or no, which leads to murky sexual scenarios that are neither completely consensual nor completely coerced but somewhere in between. The cultural assumptions behind slut-bashing implicate us all: Knowing that being sexually promiscuous stigmatizes a girl, many of us assume that a girl who reports that she was raped is lying in order to cover up a regretted sexual encounter.

Slut-bashing shows us that sexism is still alive and that as boys and girls grow up, different sexual expectations and identities are applied to them. Slut-bashing is evidence of a sexual double standard that should have been eliminated decades ago, back when abortions were illegal, female office assistants were called "gal Fridays," and doctors were men and nurses were women. Slut-bashing sends the message to all girls, no matter how "pure" their reputations, that men and boys are free to express themselves sexually, but women and girls are not.

SLUT!

CHAPTER 1

INSULT OF INSULTS

evaluated / punished for sexuality

Women living in the United States are fortunate indeed. Unlike women living in Muslim countries, who are beaten and murdered for the appearance of sexual impropriety, we enjoy enormous sexual freedom.[1] Yet even we are routinely evaluated and punished for our sexuality. In 1991, Karen Carter, a twenty-eight-year-old single mother, lost custody of her two-year-old daughter in a chain of events that began when she called a social service hot line to ask if it's normal to feel sexual arousal while breast feeding. Carter was charged with sexual abuse in the first degree, even though her daughter showed no signs of abuse; when she revealed in court that she had had a lifetime total of eight (adult male) lovers, her own lawyer referred to her "sexual promiscuity."[2] In 1993, when New Mexico reporter Tamar Stieber filed a sex discrimination lawsuit against the newspaper where she worked because she was earning substantially less than men in similar positions, defense attorneys deposed her former lover to ask him how often they'd had sex.[3] In the 1997 sexual-harassment lawsuits against Mitsubishi Motor

Manufacturing, a company lawyer asked for the gyne-
cological records of twenty-nine women employees charging
harassment, and wanted the right to distribute them to company executives.[4] And in 1997 a North Carolina woman sued
her husband's secretary for breaking up their nineteen-year-
marriage and was awarded $1 million in damages by a jury.
During the seven-day trial the secretary was described as a
"matronly" woman who deliberately began wearing heavy
makeup and short skirts in order to entice the husband into
an affair.[5]

It's amazing but true: Even today a common way to damage a woman's credibility is to call her a slut. Look at former
CIA station chief Janine Brookner, who was falsely accused of
being a drunken "slut" after she reprimanded several corrupt
colleagues in the early 1990s.[6] Consider Anita Hill, whose
accusation that Clarence Thomas sexually harassed her was
dismissed by the Senate because, in the memorable words of
journalist David Brock, she was "a bit nutty and a bit slutty."[7]
Clearly, slut-bashing is not confined to the teenage years.

Nor is it a new phenomenon. If anything, it is the continu-
ation of an old tradition. For girls who came of age in the
1950s, the fear of being called a slut ruled their lives. In that
decade, "good" girls strained to give the appearance that they
were dodging sex until marriage. "Bad" girls—who failed to
be discreet, whose dates bragged, who couldn't get their dates
to stop—were dismissed as trashy "sluts." Even after she had
graduated from high school, a young woman knew that submitting to sexual passion meant facing the risk of unwed
pregnancy, which would bar her entrée to the social
respectability of the college-educated middle class. And so, in
addition to donning cashmere sweater sets and poodle skirts,
the 1950s "good" girl also had to hone the tricky talent of
doling out enough sexual preliminaries to keep her dates
interested while simultaneously exerting enough sexual control to stop before the point of no return: intercourse. The
twin fears of pregnancy and loss of middle-class respectability

kept her desires in check. The protagonist of Alix Kates Shulman's novel *Memoirs of an Ex-Prom Queen* summed up the prevailing attitude: "Between me and Joey already one thing had led to another—kissing had led to French kissing, French kissing to necking, necking to petting, petting to bare-titting, bare-titting to dry humping—but somehow, thank God, I had always managed to stop at that penultimate step."[8]

No wonder that obtaining a reputation was even more frightening than becoming pregnant. An unwanted pregnancy could be taken care of—somehow, somewhere. A reputation, however, was an indelible stamp. "Steve's finger in my cunt felt good," reminisced Erica Jong's alter ego, Isadora Wing, about her 1950s high school boyfriend in *Fear of Flying*. "At the same time, I knew that soft, mushy feeling to be the enemy. If I yielded to that feeling, it would be goodbye to all the other things I wanted. 'You have to choose,' I told myself sternly at fourteen. Get thee to a nunnery. So, like all good nuns, I masturbated...at fourteen all I could see were the disadvantages of being a woman.... All I could see was the swindle of being a woman."[9] The maneuvering was so delicate that pretty girls, the ones most sought after by the boys, sometimes secretly wished they were ugly just to avoid the dilemma altogether.

In the realm of sexual choices we are light-years beyond the 1950s. Today a teenage girl can explore her sexuality without getting married, and most do. By age eighteen over half of all girls and nearly three quarters of all boys have had intercourse at least once.[10] Yet at the same time, a fifties-era attitude lingers: Teens today are fairly conservative about sex. A 1998 *New York Times*/CBS News poll of a thousand teens found that 53 percent of girls believe that sex before marriage is "always wrong," while 41 percent of boys agree.[11] Teens may be having sex, but they also look down on others, especially girls, who are sexually active. Despite the sexual revolution, despite three decades of feminism, despite the Pill, and despite legalized abortion, teenage girls

defined by our sexuality

today continue to be defined by their sexuality. The sexual double standard—and the division between "good" girls and "bad" or "slutty" ones—is alive and well. Some of the rules have changed, but the playing field is startlingly similar to that of the 1950s.

Skeptical? Just take a look at teenage pop culture. On the TV show *Dawson's Creek*, which chronicles the lives of four hip, painfully self-aware teens, an episode is devoted to Dawson's discovery that his girlfriend Jen is not only not a virgin, she's had sex with a number of guys. Dawson is both disappointed and disapproving, and before long the relationship ends. An ad for Converse sneakers, appearing in a 1995 issue of *Seventeen*, depicts two girls, one white and the other black, sharing self-satisfied smirks as a busty girl in a short, tight dress lingers nearby. The caption reads, "Carla and Rachel considered themselves open-minded, nonjudgmental people. Although they did agree Brenda was a tramp." In the 1996 movie *Jerry Maguire* you just know that Tom Cruise's girlfriend is a good-for-nothing tramp the moment you lay eyes on her: She makes her first appearance in a torrid, sweaty sex scene. (If it were a horror movie, she'd be murdered within ten minutes.) Indeed, her heartlessness is later revealed when she berates Cruise for allowing conscience rather than greed to guide his career as a sports agent.

But forget about make-believe characters in TV shows, ads, and movies: real life has enough examples. In Kentucky in 1998, two high school students were denied membership in the National Honor Society because they were pregnant—even though boys who engaged in premarital sex faced no such exclusion.[12] One Georgia teen wrote anxiously to *Seventeen*: "A few months ago, when my mom saw me hugging my boyfriend outside my house, she called me a slut and said we were 'putting on a show for the whole neighborhood.' I've never been so hurt in my life. I had done nothing to be called such an awful word other than display affection for someone I love very much. The word 'slut' doesn't need a definition; it needs to be abolished."[13]

agreed

Teenage model Jamie Messenger sued *YM* magazine for $17.5 million because the magazine ran her photo, without her permission, alongside an advice-column letter that had no connection to her. The headline was I GOT TRASHED AND HAD SEX WITH THREE GUYS. After the magazine's two million readers received their issue in the mail, Messenger got a quick course in slut-bashing. The football team bet on who would sleep with her first; her best friend's parents wouldn't allow their daughter to visit anymore. Her brother was caught in a fight after someone called the model a whore. "She wanted to go to the prom, she wanted to go to the homecoming," her mother said. "She wanted to be part of that. But unfortunately, she couldn't."[14]

Jamie Messenger isn't the only girl who has turned to the courts. A number of high school students around the country have sued their school districts for sexual harassment because teachers and administrators allowed slut-bashing to flourish. In 1996 alone there were three well-publicized cases, all involving junior high school students. In upstate New York, Eve Bruneau was called "whore" and "dog-faced bitch" by the boys in her sixth-grade class and became so depressed that she transferred schools; her harassment complaint against the South Kortright School District was rejected.[15] But Tianna Ugarte, a fourteen-year-old girl living near San Francisco, won a $500,000 award from a jury that found school officials had ignored her complaints of verbal abuse from a male sixth-grade classmate.[16] And in another northern California case, a girl identified only as Jane Doe from Petaluma won a settlement of $250,000 because the faculty at Kenilworth Junior High did nothing to stop students from hounding her for a year and a half with rumors that she had sex with hot dogs. (It got so bad that one day a boy felt free to stand up in class and say, "I have a question. I want to know if Jane Doe has sex with hot dogs.")[17]

In 1988, educators Janie Victoria Ward and Jill McLean Taylor surveyed Massachusetts teenagers across six different

understate
sexual
experience

ethnic groups—black, white, Hispanic, Haitian, Vietnamese, and Portuguese—and found that the different groups upheld different sexual values. But one thing was universal: The sexual double standard. Regardless of race or ethnicity, "boys were generally allowed more freedom and were assumed to be more sexually active than girls." Ward and Taylor found that "sexual activity for adolescent males usually met cultural expectations and was generally accepted by adults and peers as part of normal male adolescence.... In general, women are often seen in terms of their sexual reputation rather than in terms of their personal characteristics."[18]

The double standard, we know, does not vaporize after high school. Sociologist Lillian Rubin surveyed six hundred students in eight colleges around the country in the late 1980s and found that 40 percent of the sexually active women said that they routinely understate their sexual experience because "my boyfriend wouldn't like it if he knew," "people wouldn't understand," and "I don't want him to think I'm a slut." Indeed, these women had reason to be concerned. When Rubin queried the men about what they expected of the women they might marry, over half said that they would not want to marry a woman who had been "around the block too many times," that they were looking for someone who didn't "sleep around," and that a woman who did was a "slut."[19]

Similarly when sex researcher Shere Hite surveyed over 2,500 college men and women, 92 percent of the men claimed that the double standard was unfair. Yet overwhelmingly they themselves upheld it. When asked, "If you met a woman you liked and wanted to date, but then found out she had had sex with ten to twenty men during the preceding year, would you still like her and take her seriously?," 65 percent of the men admitted that they would not take her seriously. At the same time only 5 percent said they would lose respect if a male friend had had sex with ten to twenty women in one year.[20]

double standard

Teenage girls who are called sluts today experience slut-bashing at its worst. Caught between the conflicting pressures to have sex and maintain a "good" reputation, they are damned when they do and damned when they don't. Boys and girls both are encouraged to have sex in the teen years—by their friends, magazines, and rock and rap lyrics—yet boys alone can get away with it. "There's no way that anyone who talks to girls thinks that there's a new sexual revolution out there for teenagers," sums up Deborah Tolman, a developmental psychologist at the Wellesley College Center for Research on Women. "It's the old system very much in place." It *is* the old system, but with a twist: Today's teenage girls have grown up after the feminist movement of the late 1960s and 1970s. They have been told their whole lives that they can, and should, do anything that boys do. But soon enough they discover that sexual equality has not arrived. Certain things continue to be the privilege of boys alone.

With this power imbalance, it's no wonder high school girls report feeling less comfortable with their sexual experiences than their male counterparts do. While 81 percent of adolescent boys say that "sex is a pleasurable experience," only 59 percent of girls feel the same way.[21] The statistical difference speaks volumes. Boys and girls both succumb to early sex due to peer and media pressures, but boys still get away with it while girls don't.

power imbalance

WHO GETS PICKED ON

Girls who are singled out for being "sluts" are by no means a monolithic group. And contrary to what most people think of when they visualize a "slut," many have no more sexual experience than their peers do, and some have no sexual experience at all. Whether or not a girl is targeted because of her sexual behavior, the effect is nonetheless to police her sexuality.

looks not brhaues

"SHE'S SO LOOSE": THE SEXUAL GIRL—One type of girl is picked on because she appears to flaunt a casual attitude about sexuality: She is either sexually active or is perceived to be sexually active.

Pamela Spring, from Massachusetts, was a sexual girl who was taught a lesson. When she was discovered to have had intercourse with two different boys the summer before ninth grade, a girl on the basketball team called her over during lunch. "Pam," she asked before a packed table, "did you fuck Andy and John?" Everyone laughed. People talked about her in school and at parties. When she was a senior, someone spray-painted "Pam is a slut" on the school building.

On the other end of the spectrum, some girls who aren't sexually active at all are presumed to be so because of their physique. When everyone else in the class is wearing training bras, the girl with breasts becomes an object of sexual scrutiny. Yet when boys develop early, they are not similarly stigmatized. A girl with visible breasts becomes sexualized because she possesses a constant physical reminder of her sexual potential, whereas height, the marker of boys' development, does not carry sexual meanings, notes sociologist Barrie Thorne.[22] (Boys generally don't develop in build or grow facial hair until they're in high school.) In other words, a girl can become known as possessing a sexual persona simply because of the way she looks, not the way she behaves.

Eighteen-year-old Paula Pinczewski, from northwestern Wisconsin, got her period in the fifth grade and by seventh grade wore a 36C. In eighth grade, classmates called Paula, a virgin, a "five-cent whore," "hooker," and "slut." They took her notebook and wrote things in it like, "You're not worth shit" and "You're a bitch." "If I didn't get one of my daily insults," Paula tells me, "it was not worthy of being a school day." For her part, Julie, the girl who was raped when she passed out from drinking, was singled out as a "slut," she suspects, "because I was chesty. I was wearing a C bra in ninth

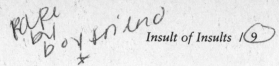

grade. Even my girlfriends would make comments about my chest. It made the stories about me easier to believe. I fit into a stereotype."

"SHE ASKED FOR IT": THE RAPED GIRL I never expected to find so many "sluts" who had been raped or attempted-raped. In fact, when I first thought about why certain girls might be singled out as "sluts," the issue of sexual coercion did not occur to me, nor did I ask a single interviewee if she had been assaulted or raped. And yet over and over again my interviewees volunteered that they had been raped by a date, acquaintance, or stranger, or that the boys in school assumed they were "easy" and therefore gang-raped or tried to gang-rape them. (Others mentioned that they had been sexually abused by a relative or baby-sitter.) Not one reported her assault to the police or school.

The parenthetical way some of the girls and women told me these stories made me wonder how reliable rape statistics are, especially for teenagers. According to a 1997 Commonwealth Fund survey, one in five high school girls has been physically or sexually abused, with nearly one in ten of the older girls reporting abuse by a date or boyfriend.[23] But I wouldn't be surprised if the real numbers are much higher. The fact is that most people refuse to believe that a teenage girl has been raped, especially if she knows her attacker. They assume that the sex was consensual, not forced.

 The "slut" reputation protects rapists because it makes the victims believe that they are partly to blame. Julie, for instance, did not press charges against her rapist. "I knew no one would believe me," she explained to me. "And I didn't want to tell my parents because they'd be mad that I was out drinking." She did confide in a few of the girls at school, but as expected, they thought she was making the rape up. "They felt, 'Oh, she's just saying it because she has a bad reputation.'"

Two of Julie's friends heard from another friend that the

couldn't help it [handwritten note]

sex was in reality a rape. But Julie sensed that they didn't really believe it. "They never came out and said they thought I was lying, but if we'd be talking about past boyfriends, they would bring up the rapist's name, as if he were a boyfriend. In their minds they believed the rumors. My friend Liz, who had seen me passed out, would stand by me in those cases. She was like, 'Well, that was a different situation; Julie couldn't help that. She was raped.' But the group always liked to have someone to make fun of, and I was the butt of jokes at times. Even though they were my friends, it stopped being funny."

"NOT ONE OF US": THE OUTSIDER—Adolescents label everybody. When they are confronted with someone who doesn't fit their idea of how a girl should act or look, they grasp for an insulting label. Typically the girl with the "slut" reputation fails to conform in some way. "Slut" becomes an insult like any other, with sexual implications thrown in for added measure.

Jaclyn Geller is a tall, striking-looking woman with defined cheekbones and penetrating blue-green eyes. Born in 1963, she is currently an essayist and doctoral candidate in English literature. She was called a "slut" in junior high. "I didn't have sexual relations with people aside from playing Spin the Bottle," she says, "so I knew it was a crazy thing." Jaclyn was taller and older-looking than the other kids. She read books while everyone else went to football games. She always sensed that somehow she was different.

Jaclyn grew up in the leafy suburb of Scarsdale, New York, where "popularity did not necessarily mean wealth—everyone was affluent. Popularity meant conformity." During the seventh grade, boys called her a slut when she walked down the halls. The jokes turned into violence when she was in the eighth grade walking to the cafeteria: Five boys pushed her down on the ground and climbed on top of her; Jaclyn had to fight them off. They were all boys who lived in her neighborhood.

Janice, now thirty-six, was a new student when she entered seventh grade: her father was in the military and the family had just moved to town. Almost immediately the boys in her Illinois junior high school started a rumor that she stuffed her bra. "I was very embarrassed. I changed my seat to get away from the boys who were talking about me, but my teacher made me go back. When my mother found out, she said, 'Don't you care about your reputation?'" This was already her third school, and in eighth grade she moved again. Each time she was a new student, the boys looked her over. Even though Janice was not sexually active, the boys reinforced the idea that she had no right to be sexual. Janice began to hunch her shoulders and wear a coat whenever possible. "I never really felt comfortable with my body," she says. "To this day I don't like people to hug me or feel my body."

GIRLS SLUT-BASHING GIRLS—A refrain throughout the interviews was how cruel girls could be. Nearly every "slut" told me that girls either had engineered the ostracism themselves or were more hurtful than boys. In some cases a girl spread a rumor about another girl whom she envied or resented.

Janet Jones, twenty-four, has radiant brown skin and deep brown eyes. In her South Carolina high school, she was captain of the cheerleading squad. "I don't mean to sound conceited," says Janet, now a student at a black women's college in Atlanta. "My immediate friends in my circle—I ain't gonna say they weren't *as* attractive—but they weren't. And girls can be extremely vengeful and extremely jealous when it comes to things like that. Friends that I thought were friends turned out not to be at all. That was my first important lesson in life. I found out that people I thought I could count on would turn on me."

One Sunday, Janet spent the afternoon with a close male friend, talking and hanging out. The next day everyone was buzzing about how the two of them had slept together. "What really hurt is that no one came back to me and asked me,

bra snapping

'Janet, is this true?' They just accepted it." It was girls, not boys, who made the rest of her high school years miserable. Even her best friend from elementary school stopped talking to her.

Boys and girls both can inflict emotional harm, but when girls are involved, the harassment tends to become more personal. Julie, the girl who was raped, says that it hurt more when girls judged her than when guys did. "If a girl gets a reputation and then does something that gets on another girl's nerves, that girl is going to immediately mention the reputation. Like, 'Not only did she do better than me on that test but she's also a slut.'"

Because girls rather than boys are often on the front lines of slut-bashing, teachers rarely identify the behavior as a form of sexual harassment. Americans seem to care more about harassment when it involves a male and female than when both harasser and victim are the same gender. Yet, as we will see, girls can bring enormous pain to other girls, leading them to engage in a number of self-destructive behaviors.

MY STORY

My breasts started to grow in the fifth grade, and by the time I was in the seventh grade, I was wearing a C cup. That's when I became known in my suburban New York private school for something other than my sterling report cards. Before, I had been someone who kids turned to for help when they were stumped with vocabulary homework. Now I was the number-one target for bra-snapping.

Jeremy, Joe, and Ivan were the leaders. They snapped my bra, and even tried to unhook it, during the four-minute lulls between classes as one teacher left and the next came in. They knew when to dash back to their seats because one student stood guard at the door and ran in to report the imminent arrival of the teacher. My girlfriends, meanwhile, were nervous about their own sprouting breasts. They couldn't wait to grow out of their AA cups, of course, but they also knew that once they hit the big time (an A or a B), they would themselves become targets. So they decided not to interfere and draw attention to themselves. I understood and didn't hold it against them. I was on my own.

In the beginning I was terrified that sooner or later I would have to run to the bathroom to rehook my bra, breasts bouncing as I sprinted down the hall. It seemed like such a humiliating scenario that I strategized at great lengths how to avoid it. I vigilantly guarded my personal space, holding my arms stiffly at my sides and constantly darting my eyes around me, ensuring that no boy could get directly behind me for more than a few seconds. They caught onto this pretty quickly, though, and would work in pairs: One would divert my attention by, say, asking to borrow a pen while another would sneak behind me. Like a cartoon character involved in a cat-and-mouse chase, I became preoccupied with every object within a 360-degree radius and would always whip my head around just in the nick of time.

The boys of course had a blast. And I, too, joked around and laughed about it. At first my reaction was a form of self-protection: If the boys believed that they weren't flustering me, maybe they would stop. But soon my laughter became quite genuine. To be honest, I wasn't completely upset about the bra-snapping: it wasn't done entirely against my will. If I had really wanted it to stop, I could have done so easily by reporting it to a teacher. But I chose not to.

In truth I was sort of flattered that the boys had chosen me as their target. For me the bra-snapping was, in a way, a compliment: The boys were indirectly telling me that they found me attractive, interesting, and fun. The boys did not consider me inferior to the other girls or to themselves. I was their equal, but different. No one called me names like "slut" or "bitch" or told me that because I wasn't a boy, I was worthless; I never felt that there was anything sexist about their behavior. My body was simply new territory; the boys were curious about it, just like all boys are. In any event the boys didn't regard me *only* as a pair of breasts. They still gossiped with me about the two single teachers we all thought would make a cute couple and groaned to me about the awful smell of formaldehyde in the science lab. In short they treated me like a peer. They didn't equate me with my body—they just *liked* my body.

Besides, though I was embarrassed, there was also a compelling element of sexual danger. School was no longer the safe, boring, same-old, same-old place it had been before. I liked being this new Leora, who was much more exciting than my old self—a Goody-Two-Shoes with glasses, neatly printed homework, and an arm shooting up with an answer before the teacher had even finished the question. I didn't stop excelling in school, but I did begin to experiment with clothes that hugged my body rather than hid it. I spent hours each evening in front of the mirror, checking out which outfits most flattered the new me. In addition to the eyeliner and lip gloss that all the other girls wore, I started to put on mascara that I'd found in my mother's medicine chest. I began to practice flirting—to seem at once aggressive and coy, daring and demure. The minute calculations of when to look a guy in the eye, when to look away, and when to toss my hair became more engrossing than the beloved algebra problems weighing down my book bag.

By the time the boys had matured enough to give up the bra-snapping, junior high was over. I had just begun to like the way my breasts curved in my T-shirts. I was also beginning to feel comfortable with my desire to hook up with guys, but it was time to graduate to high school, where I was soon to have an entirely different kind of sexual identity.

I was accepted into a private religious high school in New York City, and I quickly began to miss many of my friends from junior high (only a few continued on with me). I was no longer a member of the graduating class; now I was among a group of first-year students who kept forgetting whether the library was on the fourth floor or the sixth. But even among the first-years, there were clear social distinctions. Most of my new classmates came from wealthy and high-powered families, and there was a lot of competition to be popular. Clothes, attitude, and address (Manhattan's East Side or West Side) were key. Before, I had been perceived as smart and was respected for getting good grades. But in high school no one popular cared about getting A's; they just wanted to party. If you weren't good-looking, smooth, and trendy (within the constraints of the school's dress code, which dictated that girls wear skirts), you weren't a candidate for entry into the popular crowd. All of a sudden I felt very young and immature. I was surrounded by a lot of girls who wore underwire bras, could insert a tampon with their eyes closed, and had boys lining up to call them—a situation that both relieved and disappointed me. I no longer stood out as anything special.

One of the first friends I made freshman year, Michelle, was very sophisticated for a fourteen-year-old. She got me automatically accepted into the popular crowd. Michelle went to parties with seniors and smoked pot. She took me under her wing, instructing me on how to meet boys from other schools by getting a fake ID and hanging out at certain bars. It was a trade-off more than sisterly bonding: I helped her with homework, she improved my social life. Both of us felt we had made a good deal.

In the spring of ninth grade Michelle told me about a senior named Andy from another of the private schools in the city. She was interested in him but couldn't tell if he liked her. Would I talk to him, she asked, to find out what his feelings really were? After all, I was so good at that sort of thing. I said okay, and gave Andy a call one evening, sprawled stomach-down on my canopy bed with my geometry book open beside me, not too pleased with playing the mediator role. Andy had a deep, older-boy voice. He didn't want to talk about Michelle, though. Andy immediately asked me questions about myself—my age, where I lived, what kind of music I liked, what I looked like. He told me he thought I had a sexy voice. Then he asked me out. Thrilled that a senior would have anything to do with me, I flirted back and agreed to meet him Friday after school for a date. When Michelle asked me the next day about the call, I lied and said that I wasn't able to get through.

The day of the date, I brought a new pair of jeans to school and changed into them the moment the last bell rang. Then I ran for the subway, constantly keeping an eye out to make sure that I wouldn't bump into Michelle. I finally got to Andy's apartment building and took the elevator up, flushed and eager. When I saw his face, I was disappointed: It was rather unremarkable. But he did have a nice body. It was hard and muscular, clad in jeans and a white T-shirt.

Andy said he didn't want to go anywhere: he wanted to stay in his bedroom and fool around. I figured, why not? It didn't occur to me to be insulted; I was flattered and curious. I knew he was using me, that he didn't care about me as a person at all, and that he would probably never want to see me again. But I decided to use him too. I worried that Michelle would feel jealous and upset, but I rationalized that she wouldn't be hurt because I wouldn't tell her. So we went to his room and made out for about twenty minutes. Then Andy decided he'd had enough, and showed me to the door.

As I walked down the hall to the elevator, I instantly regretted the whole encounter. I didn't feel that I had done anything wrong by fooling around, but I was annoyed with Andy's behavior. By cutting short our make-out session when *he* felt like it, Andy had taken control and made me feel cheap, like I was nothing but his toy. He had used me more than I had used him. Even worse, I felt that I was a bad, immoral person who had betrayed a friend. I spent the next two days trying to forget what had happened. Little did I know that Andy called Michelle and told her everything.

Monday morning my date was the number-one item of

gossip, not only for the freshman class but for the entire school. Every face I encountered wore a smirk. No one came over to say hi. Girls standing in the hall in a cluster, animatedly whispering among themselves, became silent the moment I walked by. Michelle, I knew, had good reason to be angry, because she felt betrayed. But I couldn't figure out why on earth everyone *else* cared about my date. It turned out that most of them, in fact, didn't know a thing about the betrayal. I was amazed when it dawned on me that people were interested solely in the story of my sexual activity.

I knew that seeing Andy had been selfish. Michelle had every right to lash out at me, every right to make me feel guilty. But Michelle never confronted me. Instead she transplanted a private issue between the two of us into a public arena. And she did so in a way that could only be done to a girl, never to a boy.

In the space of a few hours I had become a "slut." I had obtained a reputation that followed me for my remaining three and a half years of high school, and probably follows me still today in the minds of some of my former classmates: I was a loose girl who had fooled around with a random guy and who therefore was worthy of scorn and ridicule. And since I felt guilty about my behind-the-scenes flirtations, I felt that I deserved it. Every time someone would look at me with that knowing, "you're such a slut" look, I felt like garbage. I started to suspect that maybe there really *was* something wrong with me. Maybe I really *was* garbage.

The first few days were the roughest. Students with whom I had never exchanged a word—girls as well as guys—came up to me to look at me with pity or to joke at my expense. My image was beyond my control, and the more it was taken out of my hands, the more tarnished it became. And my big breasts didn't help; they became "Exhibit A" rather than biological circumstance.

Slut. Hey Leora, who are you going out with tonight?

What hurt me most is that girls were the first ones to point

never thought about it that way

a finger at me. Looking back, I realize that for them it was a way to deflect attention from themselves: If they called me a "slut," it meant that they themselves (girls who had actually done the same thing, or who had considered doing the same thing) were pure and good. Besides, I had broken an unspoken code—that it was fine to flirt and lead a guy on, but "slutty" to be out-and-out sexual. In fooling around with Andy, I had made a statement that being sexual was okay, that I felt comfortable with guys. Hesitantly discovering sex themselves, the girls were probably jealous that I felt free to act on my desires. Along with the boys, they felt entitled to comment on my sexuality, to maliciously mock me and try to make me feel subhuman. And the intimidation worked: I felt utterly humiliated.

The comments lasted for the rest of the year, spilling into the beginning of the next. My friends from junior high stuck by me, though none of them actively dispelled the rumors. As for my parents, they saw that every night I glumly sequestered myself in my room the minute dinner was over, but since I was bringing home terrific grades, things seemed fine enough to them. Besides, en route to a divorce, they were too engrossed in their own battle with each other to notice much else.

The differences between the bra-snapping of junior high and the "slut" rumors of high school were significant. With the bra-snapping, no one thought I was "cheap" or "loose." It was just my physique, not me as a person, that was being judged. I was therefore able to remain the kind of girl whom parents thought of as a good influence for their children. In high school, though, there was only one identity attached to me: "slut." Nothing else about me seemed to matter. The two events were also as far apart as you could get in terms of how I came to regard myself. The bra-snapping did not cause me to doubt my abilities: I understood, and even identified with, the boys' motives. The "slut" label, on the other hand, made me doubt my own worth.

I wasn't a prude who couldn't handle a dirty joke. I was caught in the sexual double standard. I was told that my value was measured in sexual terms only, and for a while I even began to believe it.

SHAME

Public humiliation is in vogue. Former independent Whitewater Counsel Kenneth Starr publicized all the details of Bill Clinton's sexual affair with Monica Lewinsky, it seems, mainly to embarass the president. When a thirty-six-year-old Dallas woman was arrested recently for stealing three cartons of cigarettes, she was given a "shaming sentence": Judge Ted Poe of the 228th State District ordered her to stand before a supermarket carrying a sign reading, "I Stole From This Store. Do Not Steal! This Could Be You!" Judge Poe has similarly required welfare cheats to take out ads in local newspapers detailing their frauds.[24] In La Mesa, California, men convicted of soliciting prostitutes find their names and photos published in *The Daily Californian*, right next to the winning lottery numbers.[25] And in Kansas City, the television show *John TV* broadcasts on cable the names, mug shots, birth dates, and hometowns of men arrested for trying to buy sex and of women arrested for trying to sell it. The show is so popular that it runs four times every Wednesday.[26]

Newt Gingrich is so nostalgic for the days when criminals were paraded in the town square that he wants to extend the punishment of shame to anyone he feels deserves a good embarrassment. In 1995 Gingrich, then Speaker of the House, declared that he wanted to institute the public stigmatization of sexually active, unwed girls. Gingrich told Congress that in Victorian England "they reduced the number of children born out of wedlock by almost 50 percent. They changed the whole momentum of their society. They didn't do it through a new bureaucracy. They did it by reestablishing values, by moral leadership, and by being willing to look at people in the face and say, 'You should be ashamed when you get drunk in public; you ought to be ashamed if you're a drug addict.'[27]

But even without the intervention of Congress, girls who are sexually active (or believed to be sexually active) are disgraced every day. The "slut" label makes them feel very ashamed indeed. Over and over, girls and women told me about the disgust, guilt, and squeamishness they felt about sex for years. Some adult women, former "sluts," continue to feel uncomfortable with sex to this day.

As for myself, I was depressed for many months in the aftermath of the gossip. I saw a therapist, but was too mortified to spill out the true cause of my depression, instead sidetracking her with discussions of minor issues. At the time, I knew nothing about sexual freedom for women and the unfairness of the sexual double standard. Feminism was a very vague concept for me: it conjured up images of Geraldine Ferraro as a vice presidential candidate and Bella Abzug in a hat and maybe, if I really thought about it, Gloria Steinem as an undercover Playboy bunny. I had not yet learned about the feminists who had crowned a live sheep at the 1968 Miss America pageant to protest beauty contests or about Lonnie Barbach and Barbara Seaman, who had encouraged women to masturbate and examine their *labia minora* with the aid of a mirror. If I had been armed with a feminist understanding that no girl deserves to be called a slut, perhaps I would have fought back by reporting the harassment to my school's headmistress or another school authority, or at least I might have had the strength to tell off the name-callers on my own. But at the time, all I knew was that if I avoided eye contact, it was a hell of a lot easier to get through my days.

I did luck out, though: I made some new friends who didn't care about the rumors, and strengthened old relationships from my elementary school days. In my junior year a boyfriend convinced me that the reputation was absurd and that anyone who looked down on me because of it was a fool.

(He is now my husband.) Yet my sexuality remained in limbo: haunted by the association of sex with shame, I avoided sexual scenarios for several years.

In general I reacted to my sense of shame in benign ways. Mostly I tried to hide. I stopped going to lunch, because the thought of walking through the cafeteria door, all eyes turned toward me, paralyzed me. Instead I hung out in the school library. When I wasn't crying, I was studying. I began to tackle each assignment with vigorous determination. I double-checked math answers, prepared for tests a week in advance when one day would have been plenty of time, and peppered my essays with the new SAT words I was learning. Since I couldn't stand being identified by my sexuality, I retaliated by insisting that people regard me for my intellectual worth. My intellect became a form of damage control.

I also began wearing baggy clothes—large T-shirts and sweaters over long, elastic-waist prairie skirts. Fitted clothes accentuated my waist, which called attention to my breasts; so I never wore anything tucked in or belted. In fact for the next ten years I don't think I even owned a belt. When I wore jeans or pants, I always made sure that my top covered my waistband. I looked dumpy, but I didn't care: that was the least of my problems.

Abstaining from sex, hitting the books, and wearing loose-fitting clothes are common ways that girls try to molt their "slutty" image. But more often their shame leads them to self-destructive behavior. They become willing to do things that they wouldn't have dreamed of doing before they were scandalized because they now feel they have so little to offer. Some girls do drugs or drink to excess in an attempt to blot away their stigma. Others become depressed and anorexic. And others think so little of themselves that they date boys who insult or beat them.

Carmen, the daughter of Ecuadorian immigrants, felt it was important to study hard and be a "good" girl to make her parents proud. But in her school's hierarchy of popularity, her honor-student image placed her squarely at the bottom. She felt like an outsider. Longing both to fit in and let loose, she went on her school's senior ski trip in Vermont, intending to get drunk and fool around with the boys. Her best friend helped her pour vodka into empty shampoo bottles so that she wouldn't get caught. Over the course of the weekend, she did indeed get very drunk. And while she was still a virgin when she returned home, she had experimented sexually with several different classmates.

Back in school Monday morning, everybody was talking. "Behind my back I was called a slut and a sex maniac," she remembers. One classmate boasted that he had "fucked Carmen four times" the night before. The story spun so much out of control that Carmen was rumored to have had two abortions. Miserable and ashamed, she began to drink regularly, smoke, and cut classes. She failed two classes that semester.

Carla Karampatos, a high school senior in the Northeast, was always made fun of because of her Greek name and complexion. In seventh grade the girls seethed with resentment when twelfth-grade boys called Carla cute. When she turned down the advances of a tenth-grade boy, he called her a slut, an insult that pleased the girls. Before long the girls were picking fights with her. In the beginning of eleventh grade, Carla was so despondent that she ingested an entire bottle of sleeping pills. She would have died if her mother hadn't found her on the kitchen floor and rushed her to the hospital, where her stomach was pumped.

Jackie Garcia, twenty-four, was called a slut by black girls at her Queens public high school who were jealous that all the black guys liked her, a Latina. Even though she was not sexually active, girls broke into her gym locker and wrote "Jackie is a ho" on the cafeteria walls and in the girls' bathrooms. In response, Jackie stopped eating and lost twenty-five pounds. She explains that she was trying to reduce the size of her bust. (It didn't work.)

Julie dated guys who abused her emotionally and physically. "Like I was with one guy who used to hit me, and like I let him do it for a while. I was with him for four months. Eventually I was like, forget it. It wasn't fun always being on guard. I started to not see him as much, and then I just stopped. I always kind of assumed, 'I have this horrible reputation, I'm never going to get away from it, so I don't really have a choice about whether or not a guy treats me badly,'" she explains. Then she dated a guy who cheated on her. "I was definitely attracted to men who treated me badly, maybe because I thought I didn't deserve any better. Even in the relationship I'm in now, which is really good, there have been times where I've been like, 'Oh, I don't deserve you, you're too nice to me.'"

STRENGTH

While many girls crumble, some muster their strength to defy the slut label. Faced with rejection by their peers, they in turn reject the values of their peers. They come to believe that being known as a slut may not be so bad after all; it may even have liberating possibilities. These girls flaunt a proud, rebellious persona. Their attitude is: Why not flee the suffocation of conformity? Why not show everyone that being "good" is a farce? Why not be "bad"—and have fun with it?

"I'm a lot stronger now," says Paula Pinczewski, the young woman from Wisconsin who was called a "five-cent whore" in the eighth grade because of her breasts. "I can stand up for myself now where I couldn't before. If somebody stares at me, I think 'Go ahead, stare.' If somebody throws an insult my way, I'll throw one right back. I wear whatever I want to wear—clothes that are as baggy or as sexy as I want. I even dressed up as a Playboy bunny for Halloween last year, with the little tail."

Susan Houseman, thirty-one, reports that being known as a slut gave her the freedom to have a lesbian relationship during

overcoming the stigma *

her senior year of high school—something she never would have had the courage to do, at least at that age, had she stayed on course as a "good" girl. After graduation, instead of getting married right away as many of her classmates did, Susan traveled for a few years before going to college.

Because of her own reputation, Janet Jones, the cheerleader from South Carolina, decided to go to college four and a half hours away from home, to start fresh without any of her high school classmates. She was able to escape her small town, where "no one had any long-term goals. Everyone just wanted to stay there and do the same old thing. I felt like I grew up, but no one else did. So maybe the reputation stuff was a blessing in disguise."

None of the "sluts" I interviewed is a victim. Every one went through a painful experience, but each ultimately turned her experience into a positive thing. Having a "slut" reputation sharpened her thinking, gave her a sense of perspective about gender roles, and made her acutely aware of the small-mindedness of the sexual double standard.

As for myself, I attended Brown University in the late 1980s, where I learned about feminism. Many varieties of feminism proliferated at Brown, from "rape crisis" feminists to abortion-rights activists to English Department grad students exposing the works of unknown eighteenth-century female authors. I realized that out in the "real world" I would encounter "mommy tracks" and glass ceilings and contraceptives not reimbursed by health insurance. I thought about silicone balloon breasts and the demonization of child care centers and the immature way I instinctively glared when my roommate had yet another date with yet another hunky guy as I went off to the movies with a girlfriend. I understood that feminism—which writer Katha Pollitt describes as being "about justice, fairness, and access to the broad range of human experience"[28]—made sense: There simply is no legitimate reason why girls and women should be judged and treated differently than boys and men are. Armed with the feminist tool of critically assessing my present and future, and with the assistance of the AAUW poll of sexual harassment in schools, I was ready to revisit my past.

I gave away all my bulky clothes. I bought some belts. I bought jackets that nipped in at the waist instead of hanging boxlike over my torso. Everyone asked me if I'd recently lost weight, even though I hadn't shed an ounce. I allowed a Mary Kay saleswoman offering free makeovers to stop me on the street and put color on my face and lips. It seems silly, I know, but these superficial changes helped me revise the way I looked at my body—and, by extension, my sexuality. I still didn't wear a two-piece bathing suit without a sarong covering my hips, but from my point of view, walking on the beach in a two-piecer at all was progress enough. For the first time, I felt at home in my own skin. When I wore a big, baggy sweater and a natural face, it was for comfort and because I liked how I looked—not to hide.

To tell you the truth, I began this book embarrassed about my research into slut-bashing. Whenever someone asked me what I was working on, I mumbled something vague about "sexual harassment" or "teen sexuality" without offering any specifics. This was a deliberate tactic: if I volunteered that I was writing about slut-bashing, inevitably, I knew, I would be asked how I became interested in the subject, and eventually I would be cornered into admitting that, yes, I was a high school "slut." But I've become an eager, sometimes almost Oprah-esque, confessor. I have come to appreciate the experience I went through. I have learned that once a person is labeled anything, she becomes a caricature rather than a full-fledged human being with both talents and flaws. I have learned about the subtleties of emotional cruelty and the enormities of biological difference. And I discovered all this with the help of girls and women around the country who shared their own experiences with me. Their strength proved to me that it's those who use the insult "slut" who should be embarrassed, not us. Definitely not us.

CHAPTER 2

"THEN THERE WERE THE TRAMPS"

The "Slut" Label in the 1950s

When my reputation was at its height, classmates insult-ed me right to my face as I walked down the hall or even just sat silently at my desk. When a teacher called on me, boys snickered and girls rolled their eyes. My body and face burned. I felt mortified. I contemplated suicide.

These events occurred in the 1980s, not the 1950s—a time when assumptions about the merits of a virginal reputation were supposedly a quaint, vague part of cultural history. These events occurred after the sexual revolution and women's liberation movement, not during the sexually claustrophobic years of Eisenhower and McCarthy. These events occurred when Americans went to the movies to see *Fast Times at Ridgemont High* (1982), a sympathetic portrayal of a teenage girl who aggressively pursues boys, not *Where the Boys Are* (1960), in which a college student on spring break in Fort Lauderdale goes "all the way" with a guy she's just met, only to be punished later with a date rape.

In the 1980s girls were told that they could do anything boys could do. We competed with boys in sports, math classes, and Dungeons and Dragons. But <u>when it came to sexuality, it was as if we had entered a time warp</u>. The prevailing attitude about girls' sexuality wasn't much different from that of the 1950s era, in which the unwritten but self-evident rule was that "nice" girls did not put out, even though perfectly nice boys took what they could. "Nice" girls did not act or even look sexual; those who did were "tramps" without a prayer of "marrying well," the ambition of nearly every white middle-class girl. (I'd seen *Grease*: Even after Olivia Newton-John morphed from "good" girl in poodle skirts and saddle shoes to supposed "bad" girl in black satin pants and stilettos, I seriously doubted that she would ever let John Travolta feel her up at the drive-in.) My sexual habits were dissected and judged because I was a girl, while boys were congratulated with a hearty slap on the back when *they* fooled around. I was stunned that my classmates adhered to such an outdated moral code. It was so silly, so unoriginal.

You may very well believe that I deserved what I got—after all, I *did* make out with a guy on a first date. But the sexual rules for girls over the past twenty years have been confusing. There are competing pressures to be sexual and also to not be sexual. On the one hand, girls who have never kissed a boy are ridiculed as undesirable and unattractive, as "losers" or "schoolgirls" without a prayer of ever being asked out on a date. At the same time, AIDS is a constant reminder of the health dangers of sex; and girls who wear clingy, midriff-baring outfits (accented by loads of body piercing) are often made fun of for their overt and seemingly desperate sexuality. For teenage girls, being sexual—a term I use to include kissing, holding, and other nongenital forms of affection—is like drinking poisoned iced tea on a parched, hot day.

But conflicting sexual messages are not a new phenomenon. And the mixed messages were most unbearable in the 1950s. Twin beds for married couples in the movies aside, the postwar years were not a time of innocent asexuality. If anything, the postwar years stand out as a time of confusing sexual contradictions for white, unmarried, middle-class adolescent girls and young women.

The contradictory messages were everywhere, "not just in the movies or in magazines," points out media critic Susan Douglas. "We got them every time we turned on the radio, or our record players, or threw a quarter in the jukebox. We sang these mixed messages to ourselves day in and day out for years, branding ambivalence, defiance, and fear onto the innermost reaches of our psyches."[1] Former 1950s cheerleader Louise Bernikow, who wiggled her hips and wore a skimpy costume at basketball games but off the court always crossed her legs and pulled down her skirt, wonders, "What does it do to the mind of a sixteen-year-old girl to be Marilyn Monroe one moment and Little Goody Two-Shoes the next? I don't know, but it sure wasn't sane."[2]

Intercourse before marriage was taboo, but "necking" and "petting" were acceptable. Girls wore cone-shaped bras beneath tight sweaters, their sexuality practically bursting their seams, yet they also had to maintain an illusion of sexual innocence. The more dates they had lined up, the more evidence that they were popular; but the more dates they necked and petted with, the closer they came to being considered "tramps." "Nice" girls didn't have sex—but with sexual possibilities everywhere, the line between "nice girls" and "tramps" was becoming very fuzzy. Indeed, a girl could have vast sexual experience yet still be a "technical" virgin as long as her hymen remained unperforated. The necessary image of respectability was a false and hypocritical facade.

Teenage girls were not passive victims in the categorization process. They actively reinforced the sexual double standard by keeping an eye out for "bad girl" behavior and shaming the offenders, even though they may have gone just as far sexually themselves. Aware at some level that they were not treated as boys' equals, girls seized one area of power available to them—the power to destroy another girl's reputation—and utilized it at times to a tyrannical degree. In the end, teenage girls were complicit in their own sexual subordination.

If there have always been confusing sexual messages directed at teenage girls, then what has changed between then and now? I went straight to the source: I spoke with women who had had reputations in the postwar years. From their testimonies it's clear that, as far as the process of dividing girls into predetermined sexual categories goes, we've made little or no progress. The crucial difference is that then, in the absence of Pill prescriptions and legal abortions, the specter of pregnancy was a powerful prophylactic. Sexually active girls who did become pregnant were pressured into shotgun marriages or were shipped off to maternity homes. Today, if a sexually active girl is careful and responsible, she can minimize the risks of pregnancy, AIDS, or other sexually transmitted diseases. Besides, with pregnant homecoming queens and cheerleaders appearing on *The Montel Williams Show*, teen pregnancy has lost its shock value.

Despite having radically different backgrounds, the women I spoke with shared many of the same experiences. These women were conscientious students who relished the intellectual stimulation of schoolwork, but were anything but sexless "brains": They were openly sexually curious and wrestled with sexual expectations and desires. These women also felt a need to escape their households; sexual experimentation made them feel a sense of control at a time when they saw the struggles with their families as beyond their control.

PSYCHOLOGIST AND WOMEN'S STUDIES professor Phyllis Chesler—best known as the author of *Women and Madness* and *Mothers on Trial: The Battle for Children and Custody*—tells a typical story. When Phyllis was a teenager in the 1950s, her mother warned her that a girl could be "ruined" by sex. Phyllis knew that the warning was ridiculous because it was so unjust, but at the same time she knew that her mother was right: A girl who was called a whore was instantly branded.

Phyllis was lucky: she rebelled against the sexual rules (though, never having been taught about female sexuality, her rebellion could only go so far), but defiantly became neither unmarriageable nor a shotgunned housewife.

I was born in 1940 to an Orthodox Jewish family in Borough Park, Brooklyn. My father was a truck driver. My mother was mainly a housewife. They were poor and very authoritarian. My paternal grandmother had been killed by Cossacks in a tea shop; my paternal grandfather fled Russian-occupied Poland and sent for my father some years later. My father couldn't get through school beyond the tenth grade because he had to help support his stepmother when his father died. My mother was the only one in her family to be born in America.

Orthodox women don't wear makeup and they're not seductive. Their skirts are long and everything they wear is shapeless. I rebelled against that way of living from a very young age. I used to run around my block with a gang of boys because I wanted to play stickball. This was before I menstruated. And that was already a bad, odd, dangerous, crazy thing to do for which I had to take flak. But I was using my body, trying to get strength or pleasure or be part of the group where there was action.

Then, almost overnight, I had these breasts. I was about ten. And so of course the boys became interested in the breasts, not in my being a member of the stickball team. I was of two minds. I mean, I liked this attention. But I didn't know whether to think it was an insult or a compliment. I was confused. It was difficult developing breasts at a young age and having absolutely no older woman sit me down to talk with me about anything having to do with bodily changes or sex. I didn't have a clue.

I quit the stickball gang because I think they were more interested in feeling me up than in playing ball. And I was more interested in being felt up too! But I already had a sense that I was the one being humiliated and shamed by doing the very same thing that the boys were doing.

I think a lot of immigrant families, and even first-generation immigrant families, wanted the daughters to make out okay in America. And in order for that to happen, they had to suppress all natural wildness in those daughters—to make sure that we were marriageable, that we were virgins when we married, that we were not looking bad as Jews in the larger world, that we were not looking bad as poor kids in the larger world. I think it's very analogous to what some African-American mothers do with their sons, teaching them to be deferential. Because if they're not, they may be killed.

The authoritarian immigrant mother tells her daughter that the world is dangerous, and therefore the only protection that a girl has to keep a good reputation is never to go out, to basically veil herself in a sense. My mother taught me that girls were to be blamed for anything that happened to them. She believed that a girl could be "ruined" on just one date, her chance of a good marriage forever compromised. And to some extent she had a point. If you did anything that was slightly to the left or the right of the absolute path, you were called a whore. And that was like the worst thing—not that you were even clear about what it was. But it was like the worst thing. And you could be called a whore very quickly. My mother tried to make me wear a girdle because she said, "If you don't, you'll look like a tramp." The mothers and grandmothers at that time all wore girdles that were made of steel with laces and stays designed to keep flesh from jiggling—they were torture devices. I did agree to wear an elastic girdle for a few years.

On the other hand, my mother was also a very strong woman who arranged for me to take countless lessons in painting, music, dance, drama, as well as Hebrew. Both she and my father loved me and were very responsible and hard-working.

When you come from a fundamentalist family, you can drown in it or you can resist it. If you can stand up to that kind of pressure—if you survive the pressure to conform and the punishment when you don't—you can take on the world. I went to public school but also went to a Hebrew school in the afternoons.

I was the smartest "boy" in Hebrew school, but I couldn't have a bar mitzvah. So on my thirteenth birthday I had nonkosher food for the first time. I think I had ham.

My looks were often noted and always used against me, because I was regarded as beautiful and sexy. I remember when I went to Hebrew school, there were boys there who were paying attention to my breasts and not the Torah. Some of them now are very well known. I had big breasts, long hair, and a tiny waist—I was very curvaceous, very voluptuous. And that is something that young girls are made to feel ashamed of. Like it's your fault; you have to hide it. My mother, I think, sought to protect me by persuading me that I was ugly. So for a long time that's what I thought. I didn't understand that I really was attractive or beautiful until I was in college, and then it was so shocking, because I had not been allowed to really be aware of it.

In junior high school, P.S. 223, seventh grade, I started fooling around with boyfriends. I did a lot of necking, a lot of petting, far beyond what most of the girls who came from Orthodox families did—though it was not more than girls from working-class, nonreligious families or girls from non-Jewish families. I would say that for me being with boys was an escape from the ghetto and the family situation, whereas being with girls was more of the same: mother/female/dead-end/punishment/you-can't-do-it. Boys seemed to have an easier way of being in the world.

Looking back, I don't know what the hell I did sexually. At the time I thought I did a whole lot, that I did everything but go the whole way. But here's a telling anecdote: When I went to college, it was the first time I was able to use Tampax. I couldn't use it in high school because people thought it meant you were not a virgin, it meant you were a whore. It was like the Middle Ages. So I went into the bathroom with a bunch of other girls and said, "How do you do this?" They said, "You put it up there." I said, "Up where? Where do you put it up?" I also didn't know what an orgasm was until I was seventeen. I then discovered it because I was home with a bout of mononucleosis and I masturbated. So whatever my boyfriends and I were doing, it had nothing to do with female orgasm, about which most of us knew absolutely nothing. I did get pleasure: excitement, thrill, heat, passion, kissing, holding—all nice, but no orgasm. But then, the boys weren't always having orgasms either. So now I'm thinking, "What were we doing if I didn't have an orgasm? And if I didn't know where to put a Tampax in, how much did I know?"

I don't think that anyone in my circle, or in the entire borough of Brooklyn, for that matter, was better informed. Girls and boys did not talk to one another about sex. They didn't really talk to members of their own gender about sex. And they never talked to grown-ups—grown-ups never told us anything. Grown-ups just remained silent or said "you can't, you shouldn't." It took my generation an entire feminist movement to teach us about sex.

In the 1950s everyone knew that there were two kinds of women, good and bad, and that's it. You were one or the other, and there were no exceptions. The nice girls or the good girls—the white girls with cashmere sweaters and spotless reputations—never had any sex. And they didn't look trampy. They seemed to always do what their parents wanted. They seemed to have no problem with that. They also did whatever the teachers wanted them to do. They didn't challenge any of the material. They were popular, docile, obedient: they were centrists who never became obsessed with mathematics or poetry. I very much wanted the approval of some of these girls. But I was also very bored with them because they talked about superficial things and gossiped—and this was gossip that was meant to destroy another girl's reputation. If you didn't fit into the approved flavor or fashion of the month, whatever it was, then you were out. Anyone who couldn't fit into that imitation or version of assimilated middle-class Americana was considered dangerous or of no use or déclassé. These were not super-wealthy girls, but they knew enough to want to appear as if they were.

Another category of girls was the brains, who were usually "ugly" and "mousy." That doesn't mean they really were, but they thought they were and they were treated as if they were. And I was definitely a brain, but I wasn't mousy, although I think I was persuaded for a long time that I was ugly. I liked the girls who were brains, but I didn't think they had any guts. They didn't do anything colorful at the gut level and they didn't do anything colorful at the intellectual level. So they also bored me.

There were some very poor girls who weren't Jewish, some of whom were Italian. They were tough and dangerous and they became increasingly aggressive and engaged in physical fighting. You didn't want to get in their way and you didn't want to get too close to them.

Then there were the tramps. These were girls from very poor homes who dressed in a trashy way because that was what they could afford or that was their style. There were some tough, gum-snapping, stereotypic Italian girls from Bay Ridge who may have married as virgins, and certainly many of them dreamed of marrying as virgins, but to a religious Jewish family they looked cheap. They wore makeup and tight jeans. They were treated cheap because they were poor—or, because like me, they were as interested as boys were in experience, or in responding to some inner calls. But they hid their interest less, or they didn't know how to hide it. In this country when girls come from poor or middle-class or wannabe wealthy families, they don't have room to be sexual. There's too much symbolic weight attached.

I was the editor of the yearbook and the editor of the literary journal—in other words, I was a brain—but at the same time I also had a reputation as a tramp. We didn't have the word slut. The people who knew I was always reading and was pretty smart—who were themselves smart—had no way to factor in that I was also a tramp because it was so far away from who they were and how they behaved. And the guys who wanted to take advantage of me because I was designated as a tramp couldn't factor in how much books and ideas mattered to me. So it was almost like I was two people.

There were some older boys who, after I necked and petted with them, treated me like dirt. I remember them acting as if I could be had, or as if they didn't have to be careful about what would hurt my feelings. They didn't have respect for me because I acted on the same sexual urges that they had. I felt ashamed. If you were a very good girl, you knew that you always had to say no. But if you were not a very good girl, then you were set up: If he wanted sex, or some version of sex, then you went along with it. Because that proved that you were attractive, it proved you were powerful, it proved he loved you—in one's mind.

I have one memory of an older boy, he could have been in college. We sort of made out and petted a little bit. He wouldn't treat me fine or fancy or take me out on regular dates. He wouldn't integrate me into his real or regular life. It was something done on the side; there was something slightly mocking about it. There was a sense that he took advantage of me and got away with it, and I was conned or tricked. I was attracted to him, but I didn't understand that this manipulation would come inevitably along with the relationship. I was powerless over it, and I hated it, and was really confused.

My reputation was based on so little that it was really pathetic. The name-calling was largely whispered and not to my face. Some things were said to me, but they were so ugly that I instantly erased them from my memory, as if I had only imagined them and they weren't real. I remember boys treating me cheap and acting as if I were cheap. I remember looking at them very coolly, because even though I was implicated in the double standard and was almost skewered by it, I also didn't think that they were better than me.

The girls did it too. Girls never treat each other very well. Just because you are a member of a sorority—the tramps, the good girls, or the brains—doesn't mean you get treated well by the other members. It only means that you are potentially a member of a cult. If you follow the cult line, then you can remain in it. You may not be treated well, but at least you have a group identity.

I ended up having a serious Jewish boyfriend named Steven in my junior and senior years of high school. We necked and petted a lot. My reputation didn't bother Steven. He felt that he was so special that my being with him could redeem me totally. And I think he understood that it was based on so little. His father owned a candy store, and we would make out in the back of the store when he was on duty. He decided that we would not go all the way because we'd get married. So he respected me. We loved each other.

But I went to college and didn't look back. I got a full scholarship to Bard College, plus a Regents scholarship, which allowed me to leave Brooklyn. There was no way that I was going to marry a Brooklyn boy and stay in Brooklyn. It was out of the question. I had a huge sense of destiny and I was rushing to meet it. I felt a need to get out. Even a high school love that was dear and sweet could not fulfill it.

The first time I did go all the way was with a man whom I ultimately married, because I was a nice Jewish girl. He was a foreign student I met in college. But I was so unimpressed with what happened. We went to his dormitory, one thing led to another, and when I walked out on the way back to my dorm, I said, "Look, I'm not certain what happened. So let's do this again so I'll know for sure that we've done it."

I'm still not the good girl. I think if I had been prized within my family, and within whatever relationships I had in adolescence, I would have learned how to prize myself. And I would not have thrown myself away on worthless or dangerous adventures. This doesn't mean I wouldn't have taken risks, or that I wouldn't have done unusual things. My sexual bravado in adolescence was, I think, a typical sign of distress and of longing for love withheld and the desire to please, to be liked, to be loved, that I could barely understand at the time.

MIXED MESSAGES: THE HISTORICAL ROOTS

The slut-bashing that crescendoed in the postwar years didn't emerge out of whole cloth the moment the Japanese surrendered to the Allies. In fact young unmarried women had long been simultaneously sexualized and punished for expressing their sexuality. In eighteenth-century England women were widely thought to possess even more lustful appetites than men, and sexual permissiveness was an accepted ideal among the aristocracy. Dildos and condoms were available in London. Pornography was widespread. Among the upper classes, homosexuality was practiced openly, with homosexual clubs operating in London.[3] Yet only men were permitted to dip into the pool of sensual pleasure; only men were expected to gain sexual experience before marriage, and only men were allowed to commit adultery. Indeed, at that time the worst insult you could call a man was that he was a liar, but the worst insult you could call a woman was that she was unchaste. As one man in the 1730s observed, "He that doth get a wench with child and marries her afterward is as if a man should shit in his hat and then clap it on his head."[4] Upper-class women were punished for following their "physiological impulses," explains historian Lawrence Stone, because female chastity and monogamy constituted the bedrock for a propertied society in which there were to be no doubts about the legitimacy of heirs and titles.[5]

In comparison, young unmarried women in America were fortunate: They had a certain measure of sexual freedom. Eighteenth-century parents allowed their daughters to spend time with suitors unsupervised, and courting couples openly engaged in "bundling," the practice of sleeping together without undressing, in the girls' homes. (Theoretically, that is, they were sleeping together without undressing: in fact, premarital pregnancy boomed during the period of 1750 to 1780, when bundling was nearly universal.[6]) But by the turn of the nineteenth century, in a complete reversal of previous beliefs about women's sexuality, the idea took hold that only men were carnal creatures; women were thought to be passionless and therefore morally superior. Intercourse was now forbidden to everyone but married people; bundling disappeared. In its place young courting couples engaged in "petting"—which, interpreted broadly, meant that they could do anything sexual short of intercourse. Women were now held responsible for controlling men's beastly sexuality—halting them from simply plunging ahead—at the same time that they were expected to be sexually innocent: an impossible position.

Petting was a resolution of sorts. It was a means of upholding young women's virtue while still leaving some "room for erotic play," notes historian Ellen Rothman. There is, in fact, "ample evidence that women were often willing participants in the sexual play that was common in courting" throughout most of the 1800s.[7] Because they stopped at the threshold of intercourse, young women could uphold an image of being romantically affectionate rather than sexually passionate.

Their suitors, meanwhile, surreptitiously visited prostitutes, the "unskilled daughters of the unskilled classes,"[8] to relieve their sexual frustrations—without compromising their own honorable status. Sex for hire was widely available among all the classes, within a carefully delineated social hierarchy. "The New York sexual underground," for instance, "ranged from fashionable Fifth Avenue mansions, where wealthy men kept their mistresses, to Canal Street cigar stores catering to workingmen and sailors," according to historian Judith Walkowitz. The prostitution market was also racially segregated: In New Orleans, black brothels stood right next door to white ones, and Mexican, Japanese, and Chinese prostitutes were separated from their white colleagues within San Francisco brothels.[9]

Not everyone approved of the sexual status quo. In the late nineteenth century, social-purity workers (clergy, temperance workers, and suffragists) sought to regulate and streamline sexual behavior into a single cohesive standard for men and women alike. They worked to close brothels and raise the age at which women could legally consent to sexual relations. Their goal was to control male sexuality—but only a "good" woman, they believed, could exert the proper control. Even though men were the ones in need of salvation, women continued to be burdened as the enforcers of proper sexual behavior.

Luckily for sexually interested women and men alike, the social-purity movement fizzled. The face of America changed dramatically in the first decade of the twentieth century—with the influx of immigrants, increased urbanization, and expanded work opportunities for women—and a new spirit of sexual permissiveness flourished. Feminism, which was widely recognized as a distinct social movement by 1913, called for the sexual emancipation of women.[10] By the 1920s, premarital petting was as popular as ever. Dating couples petted in cars, theaters, and dance halls. Most petting occurred at "petting parties," which were common among high school students in the 1920s.[11]

But at the same time the notion that "good" women and girls were sexually restrained never lost momentum. The mixed messages of sexual freedom and sexual restraint reemerged, with all their guilt-inducing glory. What good was sexual freedom if those who were liberated were made to feel ashamed? In her book *The Body Project*, historian Joan Jacobs Brumberg quotes from the diary of Yvonne Blue, who at nineteen during the summer of 1930 spent the evening engaged in heavy necking and petting. She worried about her reputation, even though "I'm still technically a 'nice girl,'" she wrote. The belief that "nice" girls lack sexual desire was so ingrained that Yvonne felt guilty about enjoying herself. "Once in a while I feel slightly ashamed of myself for indulging in the greatest American sport but something must be the matter with me because while I *think* it's wrong I really, really can't *feel* that it is."[12] Despite women's supposed sexual freedom, premarital petting was a delicate sexual tightrope.

These sexual tensions were scrutinized by novelists and filmmakers some years later, in the 1950s and 1960s, who reminisced with marvel over the no-win choices they had faced in their youth. In her 1963 novel *The Group*, Mary McCarthy recalls that many Americans in the 1930s came to believe that sexual compatibility was crucial to the success of marriage; engaged couples began to feel not only entitled but impelled to consummate their sexual relationship before they married.[13] Dottie Renfrew, one of the eight Vassar '33 graduates whose postcollege lives are followed by McCarthy's wry gaze, had discussed premarital sex with her mother "and agreed that if you were in love and engaged to a nice young man you perhaps ought to have relations once to make sure of a happy adjustment. Mother, who was very youthful and modern, knew of some very sad cases within her own circle of friends where the man and the woman just didn't fit down there and ought never to have married."[14]

But Dottie takes Mother's modern outlook too far. Without the protection of an engagement ring, she initiates an affair in order to lose her virginity, even though what she secretly longs for is a love affair; she is devastated when her lover deserts her. Such a smart Vassar "girl" as Dottie, McCarthy seems to suggest, should have known that real sexual passion belonged only in the private marital bed—a point driven home by Hollywood in 1933 when the Production Code was drawn up, banishing from the screen all sexual tensions and innuendo between unmarrieds. Gone were the lusty Mae West, Greta Garbo, and Marlene Dietrich; now the movies showcased wholesome stars such as Rosalind Russell.[15]

On the other hand, Dottie's friend Norine, who was a "raw virgin" when she married, discovered that her husband Put was impotent:

> "After I'd read up on the subject, Put and I were able to talk. He'd had all his early sex experience with whores and factory girls in Pittsfield, it turned out. They'd pull up their skirts, in an alley

or a doorway, and he'd ejaculate, sometimes at the
first contact, before he got the penis all the way in.
He'd never made love to a good woman and never
seen a woman naked. I'm a good woman; that's
why he can't make it with me. He feels he's forni-
cating with his mother."[16]

The sexual double standard was oppressive not only to those
who defied it, like Dottie; it was a double-edged sword for
"good" women like Norine. Their "goodness" robbed them
of eroticism and the opportunity to discover until it was too
late that they'd been robbed. Perhaps they really *had* better
make sure to have intercourse before they set the wedding
date.

The 1961 film *Splendor in the Grass* likewise looks back at
these years between the wars to expose the pitfalls of abstinence in the name of being "good." Deanie (Natalie Wood)
and Bud (Warren Beatty) are beautiful, popular teens in love
in Kansas in 1928. They are consumed with sexual passion
for each other. Deanie's mother wants Deanie to date Bud,
since he's the son of an up-and-coming businessman, but she
also constantly warns her daughter that no boy would marry
a girl with whom he's "gone too far." When Deanie asks her
how she should deal with her sexual longings, her mother
replies that "nice girls" don't have sexual feelings: "A woman
doesn't enjoy those things the way a man does. She just lets
her husband come near her in order to have children."
Meanwhile Bud's father tells his son that if he gets Deanie
pregnant, he will have to marry her. Bud's father knows all
too well how a young woman's life can become ruined by an
unwed pregnancy: His own daughter, Virginia, has had an
abortion and is the "talk of the town" because she sleeps with
a variety of men, many of them married.

Deanie makes up her mind *not* to sleep with Bud. For his
part, Bud decides to stop dating his true love because if they

lose control and *do* go "all the way," he would forfeit his chance of attending Yale. But needing sexual release, he sleeps with Juanita, the well-known school tramp. When everyone finds out, they ridicule Deanie in that sly way that teenagers of all generations have mastered: They cast sideways glances at her and giggle knowingly when she walks by.

Deanie has an unsolvable problem. She can't go "all the way" with Bud because if she does, she'll become like Juanita or Virginia. But she also can't stand by as Bud finds sexual satisfaction with another girl: She's frustrated, unhappy, and, worst of all, a laughingstock. In the end, Deanie is driven to a nervous breakdown. (Bud, by the way, is just as torn by mixed messages: His father advises him not to sleep with the "nice" Deanie but with a Juanita, while his physician tacitly encourages him to remain abstinent for the sake of his love. By the end of the movie Bud is a poor farmer, married to an ever-pregnant, uneducated wife. At least Deanie can get on with her life once she's released from the mental institution.)

Marjorie Morningstar, Herman Wouk's beautiful New York Jewish heroine, is similarly fraught with contradictory messages about her virginal status. *Marjorie Morningstar* was first published in 1955; like *The Group* and *Splendor in the Grass*, it aspired to convey a slice of American social history. Coming of age in the 1930s, Marjorie is the only virgin among a crowd of would-be actors and all her theater friends look down on her as hopelessly middle class. Noel, her worldly, older boyfriend, sneers that Marjorie is nothing but a Shirley, his term for the stereotypical "good" girl who uses her virginity as an asset in acquiring a husband—and he would never, ever marry a Shirley. Gambling that having sex with Noel would prove to him once and for all that she's no Shirley, Marjorie finally gives in to his advances.

With one act of sexual intercourse, Marjorie Morningstar is transformed from prude to fallen woman overnight at the age of twenty-one. To Noel she's no longer a Shirley; she's *worse* than a Shirley; she's desperate and calculating. And to the man Marjorie ultimately marries, she is defective and impure. When she breaks the news to her fiancé, he "remained cordial, but quenched. She had never seen such a change in a man's face; he went in a few minutes from happiness to sullen melancholy." He considers her nonvirginal status a deformity. "For that was what it amounted to in his eyes and in hers—a deformity: a deformity that could no longer be helped, a permanent crippling, like a crooked arm."

In the end she has four children and completely and contentedly conforms to the suburban housewife role. The novel concludes with an old friend lamenting that Marjorie has become "just another suburban housewife gone to seed."[17] Talk about a double bind: Marjorie Morningstar loses whether she follows the chastity script or strays from it. There simply is no sure sexual path for her to follow.

SEXUAL CONTAINMENT

After surviving the Depression years and triumphing in World War II, Americans enjoyed great economic prosperity. Between 1945 and 1960 the gross national product jumped 250 percent and per capita income rose 35 percent.[18] But the fear of communism loomed, and communism was a symbol not only of Russian missiles. To white male America, "communism" became an excuse to express fear of anyone or anything considered "different" or deviant including blacks, homosexuals—and, yes, sexually active girls. Noting the association between anxiety over communism and anxiety over female sexuality, sociologist Wini Breines observes that there was a policy of containment in both spheres.[19] The 1950s' traditional domestic supermom helped to assuage nightmares over the atom bomb because she represented stability. And if stability were to continue, teenage girls had to be groomed to replace their mothers.

Girls themselves were also affected by bomb fears: "In those years there was a sense of cataclysm, of catastrophe," remembers Merle Hoffman, founder and president of a women's medical center. "I remember the Bay of Pigs invasion in 1962 and my friends and I talked about the world blowing up, and we really felt that it might—and that we had to get laid. I did not want to die a virgin." Girls may not have wanted to die as virgins if the world blew up, but their parents certainly would have preferred it that way. And so they tightened the reigns on girls' sexual freedom. "Controlling the body," remarks Breines, "was one way to contain postwar fears of sexual chaos and contamination."[20]

Control was at the heart of the public response to unwed pregnant girls and women. But because white and black females were thought to have entirely different kinds of inborn sexualities, they were controlled in different ways. Unwed white girls who became pregnant in the postwar years were considered psychologically disturbed but treatable, whereas their black counterparts were presumed to be biologically hypersexual and deviant. Historian Rickie Solinger demonstrates that in the 1950s an unwed white girl who became pregnant could go to a maternity home before her pregnancy showed, deliver the baby and give it up for adoption, and return home to her community with no one the wiser. (White parents concocted stories of their daughters being given the opportunity to study for a semester with relatives.) She could then resume the role of the "nice" girl.

Unwed pregnant black girls, on the other hand, were barred from maternity homes; they were threatened with jail or termination of welfare; and they were accused of using their sexuality in order to be eligible for larger welfare checks. Politicians regarded unwed pregnant black girls as a societal problem, declaring—as they continue to declare today— that they did not want taxpayers to support black illegitimate babies, and sought to control black female sexuality through sterilization legislation.[21] The virgin-whore sexual script, then, applied only to white girls because even though all unwed pregnant girls and women were considered sex offenders, whites alone were thought capable of avoiding sexual behavior.

More and more the distinction between virgin and whore was the only one between women that mattered. Esther Greenwood, the psychiatrically unbalanced protagonist of Sylvia Plath's novel *The Bell Jar,* sums up the way many in the 1950s saw the universe. "Instead of the world being divided up into Catholics and Protestants or Republicans and Democrats or white men and black men or even men and women, I saw the world divided into people who had slept with somebody and people who hadn't, and this seemed the only really significant difference between one person and another."[22]

Esther Greenwood may have been on the way to madness, but her assessment of the categories of women could not have been more astute. The virgin and the whore were the sole feminine archetypes portrayed in advertisements, television, and film in the 1950s. The Hollywood "tarts and tootsies" played by Marilyn Monroe and Jane Russell, shudders film critic Molly Haskell, "were incapable of an intelligent thought or a lapse of sexual appetite," while the "gamines, golightlys, and virgins" played by Audrey Hepburn, Grace Kelly, Doris Day, and Debbie Reynolds "were equally incapable of a base instinct or the hint of sexual appetite." (Katharine Hepburn was an exception: Her eccentricity amounted precisely to an exemption from the virgin-whore template.)[23] Along with their social studies and geometry lessons, teenage girls internalized the fact that not only parents but boys disapproved of girls who went "too far."

And yet the tidy division between virgins and whores belied a dirty secret: Most teenage girls hiding behind the cover of "nice" girl etiquette were in fact sexually active. The secret was out in 1953, when Alfred Kinsey's data on female sexuality were published. Americans were scandalized by Kinsey's report that half the women who married after World War I had lost their virginity before their wedding day (though most had had intercourse for the first time only after becoming engaged).[24] His finding that a quarter of all women had had extramarital sex was considered unpatriotic. With the publication of *Sexual Behavior of the Human Female* during the Korean War, members of Congress complained that the data would lower the morale of American soldiers.[25]

The most eye-opening revelation was that premarital petting was rampant and that adolescent girls had progressed far, far beyond deep kissing. Ninety-five percent of the women Kinsey surveyed had petted before the age of eighteen. Among the females in the sample "who had not yet had premarital coitus," Kinsey and his researchers noted, 72 percent had allowed their dates to touch their breasts, either covered or uncovered. Nearly a third had allowed their dates to touch their breasts with their mouths. Slightly more than a third had allowed their dates to touch their genitals. Twenty-four percent—and 40 percent of the youngest cohort—had touched the male genitalia. Some 17 percent had allowed "genital apposition," defined by Kinsey as the act in which "male genitalia had been placed directly against female genitalia during the petting relationship, without any attempt to penetrate the vagina." The coup de grâce was the finding that 45 percent of the younger generation of females had reached orgasm through petting.[26] To the horror of middle-class parents who liked to imagine that only "lower-class girls" were sexually promiscuous, Kinsey found no correlation between petting behavior and the occupations and social levels of the girls' parents.[27]

Kinsey disapproved of all this heavy petting, but not because he believed that it made girls "trampy." To the contrary, he regarded petting as necessary sexual education, but he scorned the artificial, illogical, and in his opinion dangerous line that divided every imaginable type of sexual contact, on the one side, from intercourse, on the other. Kinsey worried about all the teenagers who did not find sexual release. "Physiologic difficulties may develop if there is considerable arousal in the petting and the activity is not carried through to orgasm," he concluded. "In such a case, most males and some females find themselves nervously upset, disturbed in their thinking, incapable of concentrating on other matters, and [with] inefficient motor reactions."[28]

In recognizing that both girls and boys could benefit from petting, Kinsey was ahead of his time. Despite all the touching of breasts and groping of genitals in drive-in movies and lovers' lanes, however, the ironclad rule that girls stay sexually pure remained in force. A popular postwar sex education manual for adolescent boys—endorsed by no less than the American Social Hygiene Association, the American Library Association, the YMCA, *Parents' Magazine*, and the *American Journal of Public Health*—bluntly underscored the difference between a girl one pets with and a girl one hopes to marry: "The first girl a boy thinks of for a 'petting party' is not often the first one he thinks of for a wife. She may be all right for his 'good times,' but ordinarily he does not want 'second-hand goods,' or a woman who has been freely 'pawed over,' for sweetheart, wife, and mother of his children!"[29]

The mixed messages reached fever pitch with the emergence of the postwar, consumerist "girl" culture. Advertisers began to view teenage girls as independent consumers and marketed products directly to them—lipstick, deodorant, Breck shampoo—that were designed to make them attractive to boys. If a girl had the "right" look, she stood a decent chance of being popular, which meant she never had to spend a Saturday night alone (or, just as frightening, with the girls). When girls spent money on fashion and beauty products, they felt grown-up; they reveled in their new, adultlike status in American culture. But no matter how much mascara she wore, no teenage girl could bypass the sexual restrictions that kept her beyond the reach of true sexual equality with boys. (Only girls, after all, were targeted for products like douches, which equated being desirable with having clean genitals.)

As far as post–high school life was concerned, a similar push-pull dynamic was in force. New possibilities, previously undreamed of, were dangled before girls; but when they reached up to grab them, they found themselves stymied. "Like millions of girls of my generation," recalls media critic Susan Douglas, "I was told I was a member of a new, privileged generation whose destiny was more open and exciting than that of my parents. But at the exact same time, I was also told that I couldn't really expect much more than to end up like my mother."[30] Parents made sure their daughters received the same educational opportunities as their sons did, yet the daughters were also expected to "find a man" in college, get married young (20.1 was the median age at first marriage for women in 1956),[31] and become housewives. A sociological report on Vassar students in the mid-1950s, cited by Betty Friedan in *The Feminine Mystique*, stated that "Vassar girls, by and large, do not expect to achieve fame, make an enduring contribution to society, pioneer any frontiers, or otherwise create ripples in the placid order of things.... In short, [their] future identity is largely encompassed by the projected role of wife-mother."[32]

LOUISE DESALVO, BORN IN 1942, is the author of ten books including *Vertigo: A Memoir*; *Conceived with Malice: Literature as Revenge*; and *Virginia Woolf: The Impact of Childhood Sexual Abuse on Her Life and Work*. As a teen, she recognized that being sexual was acceptable within the confines of a relationship. But she didn't want to be confined: she wanted to be sexual without "going steady" or being "pinned" (when a boy gave his girlfriend a pin to wear on her sweater at all times). She paid the price.

I am, inescapably, an Italian-American woman with origins in the working class. I was born in Jersey City, New Jersey, and grew up in the Italian section of Hoboken until I was seven. Then we moved to Ridgefield, a suburb that for my parents was the

Promised Land. My father had served in the navy during the war, so moving to Ridgefield signified that the hell of the war years was finally behind us, that nothing could now tear this family apart, and that, suddenly, unexpectedly, inexplicably, we could be solidly, and respectably, middle class. There were only several Italian-American kids in Ridgefield. I don't think there was an African American or an Asian in sight. It was a community composed primarily of working-class, semiskilled, and skilled professionals.

My family life in Ridgefield settled into a pattern that made me want to escape it as often as I could. My younger sister gloomed around the house. She was severely depressed, but I didn't know it at the time. And my mother always preferred that I stay home to play with my sister. My mother was also very depressed much of the time.

I went to junior high in Ridgefield. I started wearing makeup in the ninth grade because all my friends wore makeup. My father disapproved. Too much makeup, he told me, made me look like a whore. Too much makeup would give the boys the wrong idea. But my friend Susan told me that my father was wrong—that too much makeup gives the boys the right idea: that I was a woman.

I was a very early developer. I'd say I began developing in the eighth grade. But I always had small breasts, the whole way. I was considered very good-looking, though I never considered myself good-looking. My parents never singled me out as pretty or said I was pretty. According to other people's reports, I was quite beautiful. My husband thought I looked just like Elizabeth Taylor. But this was an identity that was attached to me by my peers, not by me.

My first kiss was with Donny Lowell, who was in the eighth grade with me. He looked older than he was, and wore tight jeans. There were rumors that he screwed married women. On his birthday he gave himself a party and invited only girls, then suggested we play Spin the Bottle. When the bottle finally pointed to me, I stood up and kissed him for a long time. He told the other girls to leave, and we spent the next two hours kissing. I had learned that sexual excitement, when it occurs between equals, can be exhilarating. This was an important revelation because I had been sexually abused by my aunt when I was a little girl and had to spend summers with her.

In eighth and ninth grades I necked and petted with a lot of boys. My mother told me I was "boy crazy" and that it would "get me into trouble" if I didn't watch out. But I liked thinking about boys and kissing them. It kept my mind off my sister, who was always so unhappy and who I was supposed to take care of, and the fact that I was afraid of my father. I used sex to separate myself from my family and to establish my freedom. But that meant that girls didn't like me because they saw me as a threat— they saw me as a girl who, if given the chance, would go after their boyfriends. And they weren't wrong.

In tenth grade I went to Cliffside Park High School because Ridgefield didn't have a high school yet—they were in the process of building it. At Cliffside, there were a lot of what I would call greaser types or working-class girl and boy gangs— the kinds of gangs where kids wore satin jackets with their names on the back. Of course, not everyone fell into categorizable groups. There were lots of outsiders. I was always an outsider. I really wanted to be a cheerleader, more than anything else in the whole universe, but never made cheerleader squad. Instead I hung out with the more intellectual types in the drama club.

My first real relationship was with Carmine Carrero, who was a football player, wrestler, and bodybuilder. We met after school in the nonfiction section of the library, which was way in the back, to neck and pet. He broke up with me after I went on a class trip to Washington, D.C., without him and he found out that I had necked on the bus with Sam Lawler all the way there. After that I had a lot of free time and I became a voracious reader. When I was fifteen I began having sex with my first real lover, Roy. We had sex on and off throughout high school up until I was a junior in college, when I met my husband—a total of

ring
sweater

seven years. But at the same time I was with many other boys too. And he himself had a serious girlfriend, whom he ended up marrying years later.

Everyone in this town was very sexual. And so it wasn't really as if I was any different. The difference was that my relationship with Roy was clandestine. What distinguished the "sluts" from the rest of the girls was that we were not in monogamous sexual relationships. The other girls were with one guy at a time, wearing his sweater or his ring. The slut never wore a guy's sweater or ring. But all my friends, with only a few exceptions, were fucking people. One day, when I was a junior or senior, the police raided a local house and broke up a sex ring—it was a house where teens were having sex, and I remember that there was a grown man involved. It turned out that some of my girlfriends and ex-boyfriends were part of it. It was a very big story and the local papers ran pictures of soiled mattresses, girls' underpants and bras, sex magazines, and empty liquor bottles. So teens in the fifties really were having sex.

And then four of my girlfriends became pregnant when I was in high school. One of them had to drop out of school, another disappeared for a few months and gave up her baby for adoption before she returned, another filed a paternity suit against the father of her child and lost, and the other girl married her boyfriend while they were in their teens and they both gave up their dreams. Even though I didn't always use rubbers, I was lucky.

There were two of us—myself and another girl I'll call Liz— who were considered the real sluts of the high school. And the reason, from where I sit, was that we were having sexual relationships on our terms: We didn't want to be hooked up as part of a couple. I have a sense, looking back over my life, that the clandestine nature of my relationship with Roy, as I tried to describe in my book *Vertigo*, earned me a certain degree of autonomy. It was a choice. I mean, when I dated Roy, I chose him. And Liz did that too: She stole girls' boyfriends. So in one sense, the way I deconstruct this from this great distance is

that the two of us were a real threat to the prevailing idea of heterosexual monogamy. It wasn't that we were fucking when
nobody else was. It was the way we were fucking. We were
choosing not to be in relationships.

When I say "clandestine" I mean that people knew about me
and Roy, they knew that we were sexually involved, but nevertheless we weren't dating. I mean, we never showed up at parties together. Maybe Roy would leave a party with me. He would
not ring my doorbell to my house and say to my parents, "Hello,
I'm very happy to be here," and give me a corsage. I'd meet him
halfway down the hill. I think that maybe I was programmed to
have covert sex by the sexual abuse. So it was complicated. I
don't want to simply say that I was a sexual adventurer. And I
don't want to say that I didn't suffer, because I did.

On the other side, I do want to say that to this day, even
though I am married, I am not the kind of woman you can tie
down. I exist in a marriage in which the ground rule is: I get the
time and the space that I need, no questions asked. In high
school I was incredibly autonomous, and in a fiery kind of way.
Nobody could shit on me. No boy could be abusive to me. The
minute there was a hint of abuse, any kind of verbal crapping
around, I was out. I had no investment in being a martyr. And I
was really ferocious about it.

I was drinking at this point and I became a serious teenage
alcoholic. I wasn't drinking every day of the week, and I wasn't
hanging out on the street corner drinking, but I was a very heavy
social drinker. So every time there was a party, I would drink
until I was shit-faced. And I'd come home that way.

I first realized that people were talking about me as a flirt or
slut when my relationship with Roy threatened Roy's relationship with his girlfriend. One day when I was in Mrs. Purdy's
English class, we had to analyze Shakespeare's Sonnet 87.
Mrs. Purdy asked us what "Thyself thou gavest" and "Thus
have I had thee" means. I raised my hand and said that it was
about having sex, that Shakespeare was using the words
gavest and have to refer to the way you feel about someone

you've had sex with. Mrs. Purdy praised my answer, but the class snickered and cast knowing glances at one another. Most of the kids had heard the rumors about Roy and me. Even Mrs. Purdy looked at me with wonder about how I knew such things.

No one actually said the word slut out loud, but I felt humiliated. There was a kind of social exclusion, a kind of mockery of me. When it was announced that I was named Class Flirt I felt humiliated. It meant that everyone thought I was the most sexually active girl in my class, which wasn't true. "Class Flirt" was in the yearbook with my picture. I kind of went along with it—I had my picture taken for it—but I remember feeling humiliated. But at the same time I didn't stop my behavior or control it.

I knew that the guys talked about me in the locker rooms. There were a lot of snickers and glances. The trick of it was that I actually went out with all these guys, and of course they thought I was fast and loose, even when I wouldn't screw them. I think that my physics teacher knew about my reputation. He was the kind of teacher who walked the halls, who really saw what was going on, who connected with kids, in my judgment in a wonderful way. And maybe Mrs. Purdy knew about my reputation. But I think that none of the other teachers knew.

I mostly liked guys as friends. My best friend from ninth grade on was a boy. We were in the drama club together and he was a really wonderful guy. I found much more friendship with him than with girls. I was much more honest and open with him than I had been with any girls. And I think I loved him as a friend more. I wasn't big into female friendships.

I began to pour myself into my work. I had started out doing not too well in school but got better and smarter as time went on. By the time I was a senior, I was doing very well in English. I remember a term paper I did that was around forty-seven pages long—an incredible piece of work. Work became a kind of habit for me. I could always find pleasure—not solace, but pleasure—in doing my work, in keeping to my schedule, in making little study charts. These two seemingly opposite identities—slut and student—supposedly don't go together. But I don't know. I have always believed that the most interesting of us have been paradoxes. I'm sure there are millions of people like me out there, who combine in the same person rigorous interest in school and sexuality. I think the mythology that studiousness and sexuality don't go together is very controlling, and it's not necessarily true.

Somewhere on a deep level I knew that in the long run I was going to be way better off than these little compulsory heterosexual girls running around in these fraudulent relationships, who were doing essentially the same thing I was doing but in a socially acceptable manner. I mean, I knew that this town was a hotbed of sex. There was a hell of a lot of lying and fraudulence that went on in the gossip about who was doing it and who wasn't, all through the fifties. What I absolutely don't subscribe to is that we were all virginal and pure back then, and then suddenly there was the sexual revolution. That was not my experience at all.

THE SEX POLICE

In the public sphere the boys had the advantage—they were destined to embark on careers while girls prepared for marriage and motherhood—but among *themselves,* adolescent girls preserved a fearsome power: the authority to make or break reputations, to determine who was "nice" and who was a "tramp." The criteria for being considered "nice" or "trampy" hinged on very fine degrees of subtlety—how tightly a girl cinched her waist, on what number date she allowed her boyfriend to put his hand on her breasts, whether she used tampons or pads. Merle Hoffman recalls the gradations on the "nice"/"tramp" scale: "It was okay if a guy touched your breast through your clothes, but if he went inside your bra and felt your nipples, that was very bad, and also if you were too quick to have physical contact. If you touched a penis, forget it. If you did it with someone the first or second

*accept
a date on saturday
later than wed*

time you went out with him that was bad. And you definitely could not accept a date for Saturday night if it was later
than Wednesday."

And who was better equipped to consider judgments on
these grave matters and mete out the necessary punishments
than girls themselves? Girls gossiped about other girls. Any
girl who did not "fit in" with the sexual norms faced the
threat of social exclusion. But the popular "good" girls pos-
sessed more than the power to merely include and exclude.
They policed each other to enforce the sexual double standard, and those who were unlucky to be branded "tramps"
were ostracized with ferocious cruelty. Here was a space in
which at least some girls—those lucky enough to be deemed
"popular" or "semipopular"—could assert themselves and
feel a sense of mastery.

In labeling others, girls were tapping into the larger,
national impulse for containment and stability. In their
milieu, all the 1950s divisions between "us" and "them"—
whites and blacks, heterosexuals and homosexuals, capital-
ists and communists—were condensed into a single distinction: "nice" girl versus "tramp." All groups of people who
are under attack feel a need to defend their positions. Just as
their parents smugly scorned anyone who deviated from their
idea of "normal" in order to assuage their own anxieties
about the Cold War and racial integration, girls shamed anyone who seemed to trespass into "tramp" territory in order
to secure their own superior role as nice, good, and marriageable.

Nearly all girls tried to pass themselves off as "nice," of
course. But to be *really* respectable with no questions asked,
it helped to be "going steady" or to be "pinned." These conventions were crucial signals because they broadcast that a
girl was in a serious, monogamous relationship and therefore
deserving of a certain respect; she belonged to a boy and they
would date each other exclusively. Going steady had another
perk: As one social observer commented, it "allowed a

woman to be respectable and available at the same time."[33] Going steady was a legitimate excuse to engage in heavy petting without repercussions because it meant that the couple was "in love" or, at the very least, very emotionally involved, with the possibility of love to come. If the couple had been going steady for an extended time, and had earned the respect of their peers, they could even get away with having intercourse. Sex, you see, lost its tawdry quality if a girl felt deep affection for a boy. The whole arrangement smacked of hypocrisy: Unless one became engaged, going steady could only last so long; and many girls were pinned many times to many different boys.

In her novel *Class Reunion,* Rona Jaffe captures the mob mentality of those who punish a classmate who refuses serial monogamy. (Unlike today, when slut-bashing is generally confined to the adolescent years, in the 1950s even college-age women engaged in it.) Jaffe's best-selling novel begins at a Radcliffe twentieth reunion and flashes backward to the double-standard days of the fifties. Annabel Jones, Radcliffe '57,

> necked with every man she found attractive and sexy, and if she found him so on the first date, what was the point of waiting just to play games? She loved kissing. It was romantic and sensual; the closeness, the softness of being petted and stroked, the excitement of being held in the arms of a man who held the possibility of real love. And when he touched her in places that were supposed to be off limits, she let herself glide along with the tingling feelings and just never mentioned it to the other girls. She already knew what prudes they were, or at least pretended to be, and she was no fool.... Nobody knew she wasn't a virgin anymore; it was her secret.[34]

But before long everyone knows that Annabel Jones is the "Harvard whore," and they take pleasure in ostracizing her. They cease double-dating with her, speaking to her in the halls, and sitting next to her at meals. When she arrives fifteen minutes past the one A.M. curfew one Saturday night during her sophomore year, her punishment—decided by her dorm peers on the House Committee—is six weeks of eight P.M. curfew every night with no dates or callers. Such a curfew was unheard of: The norm was a few days or at most a week. "But I've got a date for the Yale game," Annabel protests. "You'll have to cancel it, won't you?" she is told by the four classmates, who appear pleased with their judgment. At Annabel's twentieth-year reunion, a former classmate, Barbara Forrester, comes up and starts yelling that Annabel had once dated someone who was Barbara's fiancé. "You bitch! You ruined my life. My husband left me, I had a hysterectomy, I went on welfare." Barbara then "tossed the contents of her paper cup of beer into Annabel's face and sprang on her, clawing for her hair."[35]

Annabel Jones's classmates had had the good grace to wait until they were engaged or, at the very least, involved in a serious relationship, before *they* had sex. Sociologist Ira Reiss has dubbed this exception to the rule that good girls can't have sex the "transitional double standard." But, he points out, "This is still the double standard, for men are allowed to engage in coitus for any reason—women only if in love or engaged."[36]

BORN IN 1932, ALICE DENHAM is the author of the novels *Amo* and *My Darling From the Lions* and the only *Playboy* centerfold model (July 1956) who has had a short story published in the same issue as her pinup. When she was in college in the early fifties, a "big man on campus," the president of a socially powerful fraternity, was stung when Alice rejected him; he then spread the word that Alice had participated in orgies. This event is also discussed in her new memoir, *Shabby Genteel: A Southern Girlhood.*

I was born in Jacksonville, Florida, and my family belonged to what we called the decadent southern aristocracy, which basically means people who had been rich with land and slaves. My family had sailed to Virginia in 1635 and then migrated to South Carolina, where they battled the Redcoats in the 1776 Revolution. When Florida opened up, they came in as new pioneers and formed plantations. My father's parents had been very rich, and so were my mother's. And they were all rather well educated. My grandparents on my father's side went to college—my grandfather to business school, Grandmother Denham to Mary Baldwin. Mother went to Saint Mary's in Raleigh and my father went to Yale.

I was born during the Depression. My grandfather founded a bank and my father was a stock broker and real estate speculator. But all my family's money was in my father's brokerage firm, and when the stock market crashed, all that money was gone. Then he started working for real estate companies as a manager. But the real estate market was going down, so we moved from Jacksonville to Miami to Tampa and then, after World War II, to Washington, D.C., where my father worked in the government. My parents were on a downward glide from rich to middle class.

We were never poor: my father was never without a job, and we always had a house with two to four bedrooms. But my mother felt we were terribly poor. Money didn't mean very much to her in terms of buying things. Money was important to her for status. Nevertheless I grew up feeling privileged because I was from the southern aristocracy. My family had been in Florida for a long time and there were always people my family knew wherever we went. In the South everybody knows who everybody's family is. Most people can do their genealogy all the way to when they came over from England or Scotland or Germany or France.

I went to a public high school in Washington that kids at the other schools called the country club on the Hill. This was the kind of school that the children of senators and congressmen and Supreme Court justices and generals and admirals went to. Nobody studied very hard, though I did. I was always a good student and got good grades, and I got teased for it a lot. Good grades meant you sucked up, even though I didn't. I always knew I was smart, and I thought I was smarter than the boys, which I often was.

In the Old South, the social scene was very important. We went to dancing school, where we wore white gloves and ruffly dresses. I thought it was very boring. The boys couldn't dance, so we girls taught each other how to dance. I was a real insider, someone who was very much accepted, from the seventh grade on. I was in a sorority every year beginning in seventh grade up through twelfth grade. We planned events and parties and held meetings.

I was an early developer: I think my nipples started popping out when I was eight and a half. I started menstruating when I was eleven. But you know, that happens earlier in the South—in the same way that plants grow faster and bigger—because of the warmth. By the time I entered high school, I had rather large breasts; I wore a C cup. I was popular with the boys, but I didn't understand why until a friend said to me, "It's because of your boobies, dummy." My brother teased me a lot about them. He would say things like "Some of Alice's best friends have never seen her face" or "You've got a bug on your shoe, but oh, I forgot, you can't see it." I got tapped for the best sorority. All the prep school boys came over to our school to see the girls, and we dated them. But I played second fiddle to my dearest friend, who was an Elizabeth Taylor–type beauty, so I was not considered beautiful. I was considered cute, and she was the beauty.

By nature I was a leader. I wouldn't take abuse from anybody. When we were being initiated into a sorority and they wanted to hit all of the pledges with a paddle, I got furious and refused.

"You hit me with that thing and I'll hit you," I said. I got around fifteen desirable pledges to quit the three major sororities and form our own, GDI—Gamma Delta Iota or God Damn Independents. We did not hit anybody.

My mother, having been a southern belle and engaged four times, wanted me to be popular. She nagged me, "Why don't the boys call you? They were always after me. You're not popular. You must have a lot of beautiful friends, more beautiful than you." She really treated me quite badly. She disapproved of everything I did. She couldn't leave my body alone. I was supposed to hide my breasts. She tried to get me to wear a girdle, because she said that nice girls wear girdles, but I refused. I knew that she was trying to break my will, and I wasn't going to let it happen.

I had begun dating in junior high, but that didn't really count because we always had adult chaperones taking us around. Starting in tenth grade I had a wonderful boyfriend, Luke, who I was very content with. But because my mother was always challenging me to be popular, I decided not to go steady with him. I decided to date other boys at the same time, even though he was the only one I cared about.

Everybody was a virgin; that was understood. You absolutely could not lose your virginity. And nobody talked about sex. You could not ask your parents anything. The word sex was never mentioned. You certainly couldn't use words like vagina or penis—oh, my dear, nobody said anything like that. Menstruation was "the curse." We didn't have birth control and knew nothing about it. I mean, diaphragms existed, but we didn't know what they were. And we were all deathly afraid of being pregnant. Because if you got pregnant, your life was destroyed. You were a fallen woman.

But I rather enjoyed being sexual. I thought it was great stuff. I liked all that breast kissing and feeling around and everything. What I learned to do was to jerk off Luke. I didn't mind doing it; I thought it was kind of amusing. I didn't tell anyone and I didn't worry about Luke telling anyone either, because I knew that he loved me. We would do it in Luke's car or in the woods. People spent a lot of time in the woods and they would come out with briars sticking to their clothes. Once I let Luke get it in about one inch, maybe less. He didn't get in far enough to break anything. I guess I just got nudged. I didn't know what had happened and I worried about getting pregnant, but of course he hadn't really done anything.

For my freshman year of college I went to a girls' school I hated, Mary Washington, which was the women's college of the University of Virginia. I had gotten a scholarship from Mrs. Alfred Du Pont, who was my grandmother's good friend. Sophomore year I went to the University of Tennessee, or as I like to call it, Redneck U., because academically it was a terrible school. That year I had sex really for the first time, with an all-American basketball player. I thought it felt like a finger without the nail. I was not too impressed. He was Catholic and confessed to his priest, who told him to avoid scenarios that might lead to sex, so we broke up.

In junior and senior years I went to the University of North Carolina at Chapel Hill. In those days girls could not get into Chapel Hill until they were juniors. The dorms were all single sex. The girls—the "coeds"—had lots of strict rules, but the boys didn't have any. In the whole girls' dorm, boys were only permitted in the formal salon. We girls had an eleven P.M. curfew. We couldn't drink on campus. We had to wear skirts outside the dorm.

When I got to Chapel Hill, I seemed to be considered wildly attractive and the big men on campus came after me like an express train, to my great surprise. I began to date Howard, who was the president of an important fraternity, Phi Gam, so he was a very powerful fellow. Since coeds weren't allowed to drink, I used to go down to the basement of the Phi Gam House with Howard and a couple of other guys to drink beer and sit around and talk. We would lock the door because any girl who might have seen me drinking would have turned me in. Howard and I never did anything sexually. I suppose I might have kissed him good night. But without even touching me, he managed to ruin my reputation.

I thought Howard was pompous. So when I met a guy who appealed to me, I dumped him. He was furious and told everyone that we had been having sex orgies down in the basement—me, him, and four of his fraternity friends. The reason he took revenge was so that he would look like a big man, as what I did made him look small. And the other guys who had been drinking with us never told the truth. They may have enjoyed having the story repeated because it made them look big too.

This kind of thing comes out very slowly. I didn't understand what was going on right away. But I knew there were stories about me by the time I went out for sorority rushing. I was rejected by all the major sororities because, as someone told me, I was a "Yankee Whoah." Since I had come down from Washington, they thought I was a Yankee, which was considered really bad. It wasn't that I especially wanted to be in a sorority; it was my ego that was hurt.

I thought the story was ridiculous and I couldn't believe that anybody would credit anything so stupid as that—that I had had an orgy with five Phi Gams. My God: ridiculous! I hardly knew what the word orgy meant! At first I laughed it off. But apparently everybody did believe it except for my boyfriend, who also thought it was ridiculous—I hadn't even slept with *him*—and the girls on my dorm floor, who were my friends.

People called me Sexpot, the Bod, Tiger, and Jugs. They started treating me differently. Some of the guys made cat calls. I felt intense pain. I was fine when I was in my dorm, but when I had to walk past everybody to get to class, I felt like a pariah. The way people looked at me, it was like they were lashing me, throwing darts at me. They looked at me like I was despicable. Nobody ever said anything directly to me, which made it impossible for me to defend myself. You can't go up to fifty different people on campus and say, "I don't know what you heard about me, but it's not true."

Chapel Hill was a fairly small school back then. There were

some people who weren't socially involved, so they didn't know who I was. A lot of these people were my friends—guys on the literary magazine and the newspaper. Either they didn't know or they didn't care. They were outsiders. But everybody else knew who I was and gossiped about me.

The thing that hurt me the most was the way the girls treated me. They were worse than the boys. A lot of the boys didn't seem to care or weren't paying attention. But the girls treated me like dirt. It was very hard for me to go up and talk to girls. Girls with reputations are often the ones who are the most outspoken, who have a smart mouth and say what they please. Girls are jealous of others who have good brains—and if you have a combination of big boobs and a good brain, as I did, then you get picked on. If there were sorority girls around when I came by, they would stop talking. I would try to make some bright remark, but they would just fade away. They would actually walk away. I stopped walking up to girls. Instead I walked up to boys. It probably seemed flirtatious, but I just wanted friends.

People shunned me the whole two years I was at Chapel Hill. I cried a lot because it was so unjust—I had done absolutely nothing to deserve it—but I didn't let anybody see me. The only girls I talked to were the girls from my floor. Once in a while I did laugh about it. My roommate senior year came back from a date once, hollering and roaring. She said, "Guess what, Alice? You've slept with everyone at the Phi Gam house except the pledges!" And I said, "What's wrong with the pledges?" I can't stand the idea of being cowed by something and letting it beat me. My father had always counseled independence to his daughters as well as to his son because he had lost his money, so he understood that you have to take care of yourself. I was always an independent thinker and a survivor.

Being called a Yankee Whoah was a valuable experience that shaped my adult life. It made me learn what it was like to be an outsider. Socially I had always had things easy before that. Learning to be an outsider is important, because an awful lot of people in the world are outsiders. If you don't know what that's like, then you don't know what a good part of human life is like. I learned to be alone. I learned to use my head in more complex ways than I would have been able to otherwise. And I learned about discrimination against women by both sexes, which I had never encountered before.

I didn't let my rep affect my sexuality. At first I wouldn't have intercourse with my boyfriend because I thought that by denying him I could somehow regain my reputation, but then I realized how absurd my thinking was. Soon the two of us were going to the woods to make love. It was scary because if we were caught, I would have been kicked out, though he wouldn't have been.

By senior year I decided that I was going to make Phi Beta Kappa. I stopped dating my boyfriend and cut my hair short and all I did was study. Senior year I took twice as many courses as required. I was extremely busy because at the same time I was working my way through school, since my parents couldn't afford the tuition. The head of the English Department called me into his office and suggested that I go to graduate school at the University of Rochester, even though there were six guys who wanted the same scholarship. I said, "Well, if you can help me at the University of Rochester, then why not help me get into the doctoral program here?" And the professor said, "Because this college discriminates against women." Another revelation! They didn't encourage women to go into doctoral programs and there were no female professors. That's when I realized that the women who had taught freshman English part-time—they were lecturers, not professors—couldn't get promoted if they tried. I did end up getting the scholarship to the University of Rochester, where I got a master's in English.

I moved to New York in 1953, determined to be a writer, but as a woman I couldn't get a job in publishing or advertising—I couldn't even get interviewed. The discrimination was terrible. So to make money, I decided to model, working mainly as a pinup and figure model. I walked into ad agencies as a model and was interviewed by guys who'd gone to Chapel Hill with me

who had been English majors with C averages and only had a
B.A., and here I had made Phi Beta Kappa and had a graduate
degree, but I couldn't get a job. I did do interesting work,
though, in general-product modeling. I did Clairol ads and record
album covers—everything but fashion, because I'm too short
for fashion. I once worked as Miss Minute Maid for a year. In my
little orange costume I posed with the president of the stock
exchange when Minute Maid went on the Big Board. I posed
inside a refrigerator to show how roomy it was. At the opening
of a circus I posed on top of an elephant wearing a black
bathing suit and a million dollars' worth of Harry Winston jew-
els. Modeling paid a lot of money for only a few hours of work,
which enabled me to write. It brought me attention, as had the
bad rep. I rather liked to *épater le bourgeois.* The bad rep taught
me to conquer shame, the first commandment for a writer.

THE SEXUAL REVOLUTION

And then came the sixties and seventies—the sexual revolution. Momentous changes occurred in the American sexual
landscape during these years, and teens were influenced by the
sexual habits of the adults around them. As a result you might
guess that slut-bashing ebbed across the nation's high schools,
at least until the 1980s, when President Reagan and AIDS
revitalized sexual conservatism. But you'd be wrong. Yes, the
sixties ushered in a period of sexual freedom—a time when
young, unmarried women were encouraged to achieve "that
perfect combination of a lady in the living room and a mar-
velous bitch in bed"[37]—but the transitional sexual double
standard never went out of fashion. When Benjamin Morse
participated in a sorority discussion group in researching his
1963 book *Sexual Behavior of the American College Girl,* he
"continually noted references which gave the distinct impression that there were two types of premarital coital behavior,
one to be viewed tolerantly and the other to be rejected as dis-
tinctly improper." The essential ingredient for tolerance of a

girl's premarital intercourse, he was told, was "the attitude of the girl, her emotional feeling for the boy she's with and her feelings about sex as an expression of love."[38]

After 1960, when the FDA approved the Pill for contraceptive use, women could enjoy sex without the fear of pregnancy. Unlike barrier methods of contraception, the Pill was ingested, so it was easy to forget that sex had anything to do with reproduction. It was only a matter of time before the taboo against premarital sex faded away. In 1969, 68 percent of those surveyed in a Gallup poll believed that premarital sex was wrong, but by 1973 only 48 percent agreed.[39] In the mid-1970s nine out of ten *Redbook* readers reported having had premarital sex.[40]

Monogamy was the next sexual norm to go. Helen Gurley Brown—soon to become founder and editor-in-chief of *Cosmopolitan*—convinced young, single women to actively pursue as many men as possible (even married ones, as long as marrying them was not the goal) because "During your best years you don't need a husband" and men are "a lot more fun by the dozen."[41] Psychiatrist Mary Jane Sherfey wrote an influential article concluding that neither men nor women, but especially not women, were designed for monogamy. Women's natural hypersexuality ("Theoretically, a woman could go on having orgasms indefinitely if physical exhaustion did not intervene") was suppressed, she argued, because it interfered with maternal responsibilities and the paternal certainty required in a propertied culture. But there was no biological reason why monogamy should prevail.[42]

Sherfey's statement was shocking in light of the Western medical tradition's long-standing denial of women's sexual satisfaction. In her fascinating history of the vibrator, *The Technology of Orgasm,* Rachel Maines demonstrates that for millennia Western physicians had advanced the idea that women who did not find satisfaction through sexual intercourse were pathological: They suffered from "hysteria," a disease characterized by symptoms such as fainting, nervousness, insomnia, appetite loss, and a tendency to "cause trouble for others."[43] Unwilling to encourage masturbation because they were suspicious of the pleasure it yielded women, physicians from the age of Hippocrates until the 1920s commonly prescribed genital massage for "hysterical" women to relieve (at least temporarily) their symptoms. These physicians denied that the clitoral orgasm was a normal part of female sexuality; instead, it was considered to be the "crisis" of an illness, the "hysterical paroxysm."[44]

In the early twentieth century Freud shattered this illusion: he correctly identified the clitoral orgasm as a function of female sexuality. But he didn't exactly help women when he distinguished between two types of orgasm, vaginal and clitoral. Freud misled generations of women with his statement that vaginal orgasms were normal and mature, as opposed to clitoral orgasms, which were abnormal and immature.

With the women's liberation movement swelling at the same time that the sexual revolution was under way, masses of women began to feel entitled to demand sexual enjoyment. They heeded the call of feminist writer Barbara Seaman, whose 1972 book *Free and Female* exhorted women to "respect and enjoy" their bodies and to come "out of the artificialities of our recent past and into a world that is more natural and more human."[45]

Armed with information about clitoral orgasms provided by William Masters and Virginia Johnson, they railed against, in the words of feminist Anne Koedt, "the myth of the vaginal orgasm." Koedt argued that since most women do not have orgasms through intercourse—clitoral stimulation being a necessary ingredient for orgasm—they should "create new guidelines which take into account mutual sexual enjoyment."[46] Indeed, Shere Hite revealed in her Hite Report on female sexuality that women had orgasms more frequently through oral sex (42 percent of the time) than through intercourse (30 percent of the time).[47]

But for heterosexual women, guidelines for "mutual sexual

enjoyment" were successful only if men were willing to accept their partners' new sexual agency without treating them like prostitutes. Yet many men felt threatened by women who had as much sexual experience as they did. In the 1971 film *Carnal Knowledge,* Jack Nicholson plays Jonathan, a man who seeks out sexually autonomous women but has zero respect for them. The film concludes with Jonathan having sex with the only woman he can feel comfortable with—a prostitute. So what good was it to be a sexually liberated woman if men regarded you with nothing more than a mingling of lust and contempt? And insult of insults, the film seems sympathetic to Nicholson's character, whose descriptions of women range from "cunt" and "slob" to "ballbuster" and "Jap in the sack." It was fine for him to be a voracious playboy, but disgusting if his girlfriends behaved the same way.

The female alter ego to Jack Nicholson's character is Isadora Wing, the protagonist of Erica Jong's staggeringly popular 1973 novel *Fear of Flying.*[48] Isadora is on a quest for the "zipless fuck"—passionate sex with an anonymous man. At first she is ambivalent about her desire because she's married, and she was raised "not to desire any other men after marriage. And you expected your husband not to desire any other women. Then the desires came and you were thrown into a panic of self-hatred. What an evil woman you were! How could you keep being infatuated with strange men? How could you study their bulging trousers like that?"[49]

Isadora overcomes her trepidations. She abandons her husband and goes off on a passionate summer romp through Europe with British psychiatrist Adrian Goodlove. But along the way she discovers that there's more to life than sex, no matter how good it is:

Men complained that women were cold, unresponsive, frigid.... They wanted their women wanton. They wanted their women wild. Now women were finally learning to be wanton and wild—and what happened? The men wilted. It was hopeless. I had desired Adrian as I had never desired anyone before in my life, and the very intensity of my need canceled out his. The more I showed my passion, the cooler he became. The more I risked to be with him, the less he was willing to risk to be with me. Was it really that simple? Did it all come down to what my mother had told me years ago about "playing hard to get"?[50]

It turns out that Adrian, himself married, had planned all along to end the summer with a vacation with his wife and kids. Isadora may be sexually free, but she's not equal. Adrian is the one who calls the shots. What Isadora really wants, she finally realizes, is passionate sex together with commitment. She does not want to compartmentalize her personality—one part her "real" self, the other part her sexual self. She wants to integrate her sexuality with the rest of her passions. But while she has progressed beyond the old idea that one can't be a sexually active "good" girl, Adrian has not. He wants only her sexual self, her "bad" self. He can get everything else from his wife back at home. Isadora is left disjointed.

Teens picked up on the contradictions of the sexual revolution. They knew that they were coming of age during a time that was supposedly the heyday of sexual equality for women, yet they also knew that females were still characterized as "good" or "bad." Barbara Eastman, a communications analyst in New York, confirms that among teens, slut-bashing and the sexual double standard remained alive and well. In 1967 Eastman was fourteen and a new student in her Silver Spring, Maryland, junior high school. Her best friend had developed a "slut" reputation because she had "gone all the way." To diffuse it, the friend spread false rumors about Eastman's sexuality. Soon everyone in school was talking about Eastman, not her friend; they said that she was a "wild nymphomaniac" and that she was going to "keep fucking until she got pregnant." Girls insulted her looks. Boys grabbed her breasts. One boy hit her head against a locker so hard that she bled. A group of five boys broke into her house and nearly gang-raped her.

Eastman transferred to a different school, and a year later her family moved away. But when she returned four years later, Eastman discovered to her horror that her reputation had actually been embellished in her absence. "My sister went back to school and she told me that the brothers and sisters of my former classmates were still talking about me," recalls Eastman. "Except the stories had become so mythological and legendary that I don't think a human being could possibly perform the things they were saying. They had me pulling trains of twenty guys. They were even saying that when I had been a student there, I had run a prostitution ring."

By the 1980s many Americans began to rethink the wisdom of one-night stands for women. In their book *Remaking Love,* Barbara Ehrenreich, Elizabeth Hess, and Gloria Jacobs note that at the beginning of the decade, women's magazines published survey after survey demonstrating that women were delighted with their new sexual freedom. Yet at the same time, polls about men exposed their anxieties about women who had premarital sex or extramarital affairs. This gender dissonance had its price. "Where women had once participated wholeheartedly, some were now having second thoughts when confronted with male ambivalence—and sexism," write Ehrenreich, Hess, and Jacobs. "Despite all the talk of the sensitive, feminist 'new man,' too many women claimed to be meeting men who simply could not let them participate with equal control in a sexual relationship."[51]

At the same time a mood of sexual conservatism replaced the old ideal of sexual libertarianism. The mainstream media increasingly emphasized traditional sex roles (men as sexual aggressors and breadwinners, women as sexual subordinates and full-time mothers) and presented women who "were fed up with casual sex."[52] Sociologist Lillian Rubin confirms that most Americans began to believe that sex was not worthwhile without at least some emotional connection, even a temporary one.[53] Meanwhile, antiabortion activists bombed hundreds of clinics around the country, sending the message to women that the only worthwhile sex is marital and procreative.

The nail in the coffin of women's sexual liberation came with news coverage of the "G spot" in the early 1980s. According to gynecologist Ernst Grafenberg and his defenders, women could achieve vaginal orgasms superior to clitoral ones through stimulation of the G spot, located on the anterior wall of the vagina. In other words, women needed male-centered intercourse—and only male-centered intercourse. Never mind that most women never found their own G spot, and that there was no scientific evidence for any of Grafenberg's claims.[54] No wonder that even today the word *sex* is commonly used to refer to vaginal intercourse rather than the broad range of sexual acts, many of which better serve women's needs.

Even before AIDS erupted, therefore, teenagers witnessed a backlash against women's autonomous sexuality. In turn they emulated the sexually conservative attitudes of their parents and strengthened the sexual double standard among themselves. If slut-bashing among teens in the 1960s and 1970s was bruising, in the 1980s and 1990s it would become crippling.

CHAPTER 3

"SHE'S SO LOOSE"

The Sexual Girl

When news broke that Monica Lewinsky had allegedly had consensual sexual relations with President Clinton, I was astounded by the torrent of nasty remarks, headlines, and public opinion polls picking apart her body, hair, psychological state, and sexuality. *New York* magazine reported that as an adolescent, Lewinsky had spent two summers at weight-loss camp, and that she had "paid particular attention to the guys."[1] Jokes about Lewinsky's "big hair," and how she was sent home from the White House because she dressed too provocatively, became instant clichés. When *Vanity Fair* published photos of Lewinsky in glamorous poses, a female acquaintance of mine scrutinized the layout and decreed that the only reason Lewinsky looked so attractive was that the magazine gave her a great makeup job and airbrushed the photos. Clinton himself referred to Lewinsky as "that woman" ("I never had sexual relations with that woman"); with those two words alone he managed to portray her as a classic "slut," a woman he clearly did not want to humanize by invoking her name.

A concerted effort to smear Lewinsky as an oversexed, hyperaggressive woman was under way. Speculation abounded that Lewinsky had invented the whole affair in a girlish fantasy; Representative Charles Rangel of New York said, "That poor child has serious emotional problems. She's fantasizing. And I haven't heard that she played with a full deck in her other experiences."² In an editorial, *The Wall Street Journal* called her a "little tart."³ After being portrayed as a stalker who "used emotional blackmail to trap" a married lover by the *New York Post* and a "manipulative, sex-obsessed woman" by the *Daily News,* Fox News released a poll investigating whether the public thought she was an "average girl" or a "young tramp looking for thrills." Fifty-four percent rated her a tramp.⁴ Later it was revealed that President Clinton had referred to Lewinsky as a "stalker" with his staff.⁵ And all this was months *before* Independent Whitewater Counsel Kenneth Starr served up his own salacious report depicting Lewinsky as an exhibitionistic, sex-obsessed provocateur.

Personally I think Lewinsky is a good-looking woman who happens to have a voluptuous figure. Starstruck, she participated in an act that was reckless, and sad, because she believed that having a sexual relationship with a powerful man was the only way she could have a sense of control over her own life, and foolish, but hardly worthy of such national attention. Originally she did not want to publicly advertise the affair (as Gennifer Flowers did in 1992 about her own extramarital relationship with the president); indeed, by lying about it initially in an affidavit, she demonstrated respectful discretion. Her March 1999 interview with Barbara Walters and cooperation with the author of *Monica's Story* were part of a defensive measure to try to counter her image as a tramp. All in all, I believe, Lewinsky does not deserve to be written off as a *Melrose Place* bimbo.

But even as her name fades from late-night punch lines, there is no doubt that Lewinsky will spend the rest of her life in the shadow of her tarnished reputation. Obviously Clinton's own reputation has also suffered, but most Americans have been disappointed that he lied about the liaison for seven months, not because of the liaison itself.[6] And even those who do find the liaison disturbing tend to describe Clinton as someone who has a "problem" or "disease," suggesting that his sexuality lies beyond his control. Meanwhile many Americans believe that an unmarried woman who capitalizes on her sexuality—to feel good about herself, to capture the attention of powerful men, for recreation—is debased. But why should sex and femininity necessarily be at odds? Of course, sex is often used in ways that degrade women (rape, sexual harassment, forcible prostitution), and too many women mistakenly perceive that their sexuality is their only source of power. But sex is not always and inherently sexist, nor should it transform women into dirty tramps. When Clinton and Lewinsky participated in their liaison, the only people who got hurt, as I see it, were Hillary and Chelsea Clinton—and that's for them to decide.

Meanwhile, in the women's locker room at my local Y, semi- and fully naked women walk from their lockers to the showers and then back again every day. But when a repairman recently entered one circumscribed corner of the locker room for less than five minutes (all the while monitored by a female staffer), all hell broke loose. I had to pass that corner to get to the shower, and I didn't feel like waiting. I was wearing one of those gym towels that were clearly not intended for women, since they cover either the breasts or the hips, but not both. But what did I care? In the three years I've belonged to the Y, hundreds of different women had already seen me naked; why was I to be intimidated by the fact that one busy male might catch a quick glimpse of my flesh? Yet two clothed women "tsk-tsked" me as I padded by the repairman in my towel, telling me with the shake of their heads that I had committed some grave lapse in judgment. (He didn't even seem to notice.)

double
Standard

This is the sexual double standard: the idea that women are disgraced by sex outside of marriage, that sex transforms them into "sluts." The 1997 movie *Chasing Amy* illustrates how the sexual double standard effectively sidesteps men's concern about their own sexual abilities. In describing the film, reviewers said it was about the sorrows of a postcollege man who has the misfortune to fall in love with a young, cute lesbian. In fact, the movie says less about lesbianism than it does about the fear of "sluts." Holden is attracted to Alyssa, who is, it is true, a lesbian. When she falls for him too, he assumes he's the first man she's ever slept with. But Alyssa wasn't always a lesbian. It turns out that when she was in high school, Alyssa had considerable sexual experience with boys—including, once, a *ménage à trois* with two male classmates. Holden, who was infatuated with Alyssa when he knew that she had had sex with many women, is now disgusted. Having slept with men transforms Alyssa; it makes her a "slut" rather than a chic lesbian. And so Holden treats her like a "slut" by asking her to participate in a *ménage* with his best male friend. Deep down, he admits, he is intimidated by and fears her sexual experience with men. He feels inadequate and wants to even the score. Alyssa, who feels cheapened by the proposal, leaves him.

Likewise, in the 1986 Spike Lee movie *She's Gotta Have It,* Mars Blackman says, "Look, all men want freaks. We just don't want 'em for a wife." Blackman, played by Lee, is frustrated that his girlfriend, Nola, is sexually involved with two other men as well. All three men want Nola, but do they respect her? No. Boyfriend No. 2 sneers, "A nice lady doesn't go humping from bed to bed." Boyfriend No. 3 snickers, "Once a freak, always a freak." Then he rapes her. But it doesn't matter to Nola whether or not these men respect her: she respects herself. "I am not a one-man woman," she says with defiance.

You, too, might think that Alyssa's and Nola's casual attitude about sex is inappropriate, disgusting, or just wrong.

You might be opposed to casual sex in principle, believing instead that sex should be reserved for a meaningful, romantic relationship. That's fine—but beside the point. There should be one sexual standard for both genders—and that applies to older teenagers and to adults over the age of twenty-one. If you think that sixteen-year-olds should not be having intercourse, that includes boys as well as girls. If you think that some sixteen-year-olds are mature enough to express their sexual longings, that includes girls as well as boys. Though sexually active girls alone carry the burden of potential pregnancy, both genders must be treated as equals since they share equally in the heterosexual act.

Holden's low opinion of Alyssa, and Mars's contempt for Nola, is indicative of the continued widespread prominence of the sexual double standard. Three quarters of young men and nearly 90 percent of young women surveyed by the Janus Report agreed that the sexual double standard prevails.[7] Roughly half of American teenagers are sexually active—in 1997, 49 percent of boys aged fifteen to nineteen reported ever having had sexual intercourse, compared with 48 percent of girls[8]—but when it comes to moralizing about the excesses of teenage sexuality, girls alone are ridiculed and made to feel cheap. As Steven, a Rhode Island high school junior, comments, his male friends always hang out with the freshman girls known as "sluts," not because they like those girls but because they can "get some." And like in the 1950s, it's usually girls, not boys, who are on the front lines of making fun of others as "sluts."

"In the eighth grade, I had a boyfriend and we sort of explored things sexually, though we never had intercourse," recalls Hannah Wallace, twenty-five, a magazine editor in New York. "I was quite honest with my best friend, Stacia, and told her about it. Her reaction was that she was disappointed in me. She and another friend got together and wrote me a letter that really upset me. It wasn't that they were worried about me, because everything I did with my boyfriend was consensual. They were chastising me for my behavior, which they thought was disgusting. They were moralizing. I felt: Did I have to hide my sexual relationship from my friends?"

Hannah's friend, Stacia Eyerly, vividly remembers the incident. "We did write her a note," she told me. "We were concerned about whether she was doing the right thing. A little of it was envy, but mostly it was the feeling that she shouldn't have done what she did, that it was inappropriate. But this feeling only applied to girls. It was definitely because she was a girl that I had a problem with it."

I learned a great deal from the sexually active young women called sluts who tell their stories here. Before I met them, I assumed that they would be defeated by their experience. I imagined that they might have chosen abstinence. (Such is the goal of the Christian "secondary virginity" movement, for which hundreds of thousands of teens have signed chastity pledges.) But in fact these women are fiercely protective of their right to be treated with dignity and respect without surrendering to the sexual double standard.

Despite humiliating encounters like Hannah's, sexually active "sluts" have an advantage over "good" girls. Once they are singled out for derision, they realize they have little to lose by living up to their reputations. And in defying the "good girl" rules, they develop a necessary critical perspective about love and sex. Unlike most girls, self-aware "sluts" perceive the unfairness of the sexual double standard. They know they are in a double bind: That boys like girls who are a little bit "slutty" but also look down on them as cheap and inferior. They are aware that girls as well as boys experience sexual pleasure; they know that if they are responsible, they can minimize their risk of disease, pregnancy, and emotional distress. And they recognize that most girls take adolescent romance much more seriously than boys do—too seriously. Sexually active "sluts" think of themselves as independent sexual agents and are less inclined to use sex as a bargaining chip for love and affection. As a result, I would argue, they, and not the "good" girls who call them insulting names, are more likely to have a healthy attitude about themselves and their futures.

PAMELA SPRING, TWENTY-FOUR, was known as one of the "smart girls" in the advanced classes at her Massachusetts middle school. Yet in high school she cultivated a reputation for being promiscuous: in part she was reacting against her reputation as smart, but she also was living the lessons she had learned when she was sexually abused at a young age. Now she works for Planned Parenthood, where she tries to get more schools to support reproductive rights, sex education, and family planning for teens and families.

When I was a senior in high school, in 1990, I was called out of class and told to go to the principal's office. He walked me out to the back of the school, where it was spray-painted *Pam Is A Slut.* I was the only Pam in the school. It was on the whole back of the school building, in huge letters, facing the soccer field and the football field.

He asked me, "Do you know who would do this?" There was no preparation. There was no concern, no compassion for me. No "How are you?" Just: "Do you know who would do this?" I didn't know it was there until he showed it to me. It was awful. He was very accusatory about it, like, "What did you do wrong that would make somebody do this?" I remember thinking, "I don't know who would do this; why are you asking me?" I just walked away. I remember crying in the bathroom and crying to a few girls. I felt that I was being branded for something that had happened to me, as if I were responsible. The writing had to be sandblasted off.

This incident happened four years after I began to be thought of as a slut, in ninth grade. Part of me wondered, "Why didn't anyone do this sooner?"

I grew up in a small town in Massachusetts. It's a very rural area, with farms and apple orchards. A lot of the parents of my classmates were involved in farming and hunting. Even the boys in the smarter classes wouldn't come to school during the whole first week of hunting season. There were girls who belonged to 4-H and Girl Scouts. I think my parents didn't really fit in and I never really felt that I fit in. I always felt like an outsider.

I was with the same classmates all the way through school until twelfth grade. I was one of the smartest kids in class. I remember in kindergarten the teacher asked me to read to the class when she stepped out of the room or had to go to the back to clean or something. That year a couple of kids ruined an art project of mine. I remember being teased in third grade because I was chosen to stay inside and help the teacher with a project. Things like that traumatized me. I would always try to get out of things like that. That year I became afraid to go to school. I had a lot of nervousness about wanting to do well in school, but I also felt that I couldn't or shouldn't.

In the area where I grew up, academic and cultural excellence were not important. Everything was about sports. In middle school I took advanced classes, where I made a lot of good friends. By the time I got to high school, there were between twenty and thirty kids in the advanced classes, so we had our own group of people. I was one of the few girls in the advanced classes. There were more advanced girls as I got older, but as far as girls who were at the top of the class in math, there weren't many of us. I felt ashamed of my academic achievements as I got older, so I tried to hide them, and I did things to compensate for them because I didn't want to be thought of in those terms. I started to express myself in a kind of aggressive way. Around fifth grade I started to realize that I definitely did not want the teachers to like me, because I didn't like the repercussions with my classmates. And then I started not liking the teachers, because I felt that they weren't very smart. I also became very argumentative in my classes.

good vs bad

I had a lot of visibility, in terms of activities. I played sports and I was in the band. I was editor of the school paper. I was captain of the soccer team. But I ended up graduating number three instead of number one because of the things that I started to do. I was late for school all the time, I was doing drugs, I was fooling around—a lot of bad things that detracted from my intellectual focus.

The cliques were divided into "good girls" and "bad girls." The "good girls" were smart. They were nice and plain. They were kind of preppy—they wore turtlenecks and "boat shoes." Most of their mothers were pretty domestic. These were the 4-H girls. They never got into trouble with teachers. When I was in elementary school, I fit into that group. But I never felt like one of them. And that's why I think I became someone who wasn't part of that group. My sister, who is two years older, was sort of a "good girl." I felt like I couldn't be like her.

The "bad girls" came mostly from broken homes. Their parents were divorced. They didn't do well in school. They smoked and did drugs at a young age, which I started when I was a little older. They were more sexually active than the "good girls," definitely. But some of them were considered "bad" just because they hung out with the "bad girls," and got labeled "bad" even though they weren't having sex. They wore jeans and more black than the "good girls" did. They went out more, drove around in cars more.

So how did I become promiscuous? There were several sexual incidents. The first one happened between the ages of seven and eleven. Because I was the youngest in my family and my parents worked and my siblings were never home, I would go to different baby-sitters' houses every afternoon after school.

There was one baby-sitter who was about ten years older than me. The sexual abuse lasted three to four years. By the time I got to about eleven, my parents felt that I didn't really need a baby-sitter anymore. I didn't tell my mother about the abuse until I was in college. It sounds crazy, but I didn't know it was wrong. A couple of times I got upset about going over there, but I didn't express it. This was also at the same time that I started refusing to go to school. It was ironic, because I was comfortable being away from school, yet the baby-sitter was also the source of sexual abuse. It was like there was no place for me to go that was safe. But I preferred being out of school. Maybe I didn't see that the abuse was as much of a threat as the teasing in school.

After that I started to become promiscuous, though it wasn't conscious or deliberate. It was something I did because I felt I was supposed to. It happened in part as a result of the abuse, but obviously I didn't realize it at the time. There was also my rebellion against being perceived as an intellectual student and my desire to escape that identity. It's as if I said to myself, "I'd rather be 'bad,' because that's what I really am."

I started kissing neighborhood boys in fourth grade. At this point I was still a "good girl." By sixth grade it got more into fooling around. And then by eighth grade it was everything but intercourse. I definitely enjoyed it. I had physical pleasure. But at the same time I felt that it was wrong, and that there was something wrong with me. Not that what I was doing was wrong, or that there was something wrong with the guys, but that I was wrong.

The first time I realized that other people thought I was a "slut" was when I made my confirmation in the eighth grade, when I was thirteen. Before you make your confirmation, you meet with your priest and say a long confession. The whole class is sitting out in the pews, waiting for you as you're in there making the confession. Girls went together, then guys went together. I remember specifically being teased because I took the longest amount of time. I came out and everyone said, "You were in there for half an hour! We were only in there for two minutes!" I felt that either they lied or they hadn't done anything interesting yet.

By eighth and ninth grades I was considered attractive to the older boys. It was like, "Wow, look at her younger sister," that kind of thing—especially since my sister was kind of a "good girl." And I derived good feelings, both physically and emotionally, from all this, and so I became kind of vain. Even though I was still involved in sports, boys became a top priority for me. I was boy-crazy.

The first time I almost had intercourse was the summer before ninth grade. It was with Andy, my friend's brother. He was two years older, in the same class with my sister. It was kind of a predatory experience. It was at his house. He never actually penetrated me, although he tried. Then there was John, during the first month of ninth grade. John was a twelfth-grader. It was the night of my sister's Sweet Sixteen birthday party. I remember exactly what I was wearing: white pants and a black and white shirt. I remember feeling flattered that he liked me, that he thought I was pretty. I thought he would be my boyfriend. But it was just for sex and that was it. It was in his car. I remember going to the bathroom later and looking in the mirror and thinking, "Wow, this is it." I had bled on my white pants. After one more similar incident, he never talked to me ever again.

I did not enjoy these two times. I felt manipulated. I felt that it had gone too far, and I didn't like that. Both boys were older, and both cajoled me when I wasn't entirely ready. I had no voice whatsoever. No words came out of my mouth at all. I don't think that either boy was taught that he should be held responsible for his sexual actions.

The Monday following the Sweet Sixteen party and the incident with John, I walked into the school cafeteria. One girl, who I knew from sports and was a few years older, called me over to her lunch table, which was packed. This girl intimidated me and she was part of a larger group that intimidated me. She said, while everyone was listening, "Pam, did you fuck Andy and John?" And I said, "No, of course not." Then I walked away. Everyone was cracking up, laughing. John must have told people. I was really caught by surprise. Later I cried in the bathroom. For the next few months there was a lot of whispering and talking. I would go out on weekends to different clubs and parties, and the reputation was ever-present.

My attitude became rebellious: "Well, if you're going to talk about me, you're going to embarrass me, then I'm going to have sex and not care what you say." I became more stuck up about it. "This is who I am and what I do. If you have a problem with it, that's your problem." I would say that from ninth through twelfth grades I had sex with about ten guys, mostly from other schools, because I didn't care if girls from the other schools hated me since I didn't have to see them every day. With each guy I would hook up a few times. They weren't generally one-night stands. This whole time I craved a boyfriend, a long-term relationship, which I never had. It hurt inside.

A few of the coaches and teachers knew, and they would look at me funny, or they would say things. There were a few young male teachers who would hit on a lot of the girls. There was definitely a culture of sexual harassment. I remember the football coach stopping me one day and saying, "I heard you were drinking at parties"—because I was on the soccer team and wasn't allowed to drink. The irony is that at that time I wasn't drinking. Whenever I got in trouble for something, I had never done what they accused me of. But if the football coach knew things about me, then I'm sure other teachers did too.

Another big thing is that I didn't get into the Honor Society. The guidance counselor told my parents that the reason I didn't get in was that I did not fulfill the character requirement. Plus I was drinking and smoking pot. I did it a lot, but mostly on weekends, and only sometimes on weeknights. It was never during the school day. I had to be either drunk or high to have sex with the guys. I thought it made me like it better, but now I realize that it was because I really didn't want to do what I was doing.

The summer before tenth grade there was another incident that was huge in my life and in our community in general. My sister's best friend had a party. But the only girls who were there were me, my sister, and her friend. It was a spaghetti dinner for four football players.

My sister went home early. So it was down to four guys and me and my sister's friend. I was flirting and drinking and having a good time. I went upstairs and fooled around with one of the guys for a little while. Then I came downstairs and discovered that my sister's friend was upstairs having sex with one of the guys. She was making a lot of noise. She was drunk—she had had something like a gallon of wine.

The next thing I knew she was in the bathroom. I was downstairs. There were two or three of the guys with her in the shower. They had put her in the shower and were taking pictures of her without her clothes on. I don't think she was capable of saying no because of her drunken state. They were touching her and were tape-recording the noises she was making; she was babbling incoherently. The guy I was with was laughing; he didn't care. And I didn't even know that what they had done was wrong. That's how screwed up my values were. I remember going and getting a blanket off of her mother's bed, and I wrapped it around her.

But I was mad at her. She was wasted. She was sixteen and I was fourteen. I had trusted her because she was older and I figured she knew what she was doing. I held her responsible and I didn't want to be responsible for her. I don't remember feeling mad at the guys.

It gets much worse. They circulated the pictures and tape around the entire county. They passed around the pictures at football games and played the tape at every party. And the person who started circulating the photos and playing the tape for everyone was actually the guy that I had fooled around with that night.

My sister and I both felt that her friend should have done something to prevent it, that she shouldn't have gotten drunk. My loyalty was not with my sister's friend, where it should have been. It didn't occur to me at the time that the guys might have hurt me, too. I didn't regard it as a coercive sexual encounter until years later, when I was in college.

It was horrible for her. She couldn't go out. She couldn't go anywhere. Her life was totally ruined by it. It was the end for her. And at this time her parents were getting divorced. It was a hor-

abortion

rible, horrible time for her. For years she was known as the "slut" of the county.

Senior year in high school I had an abortion. I had to quit soccer as a result of it because I had to get it the day we had scrimmage, and I couldn't go to the game. The next week my coach wouldn't start me in the game because I had missed the scrimmage—even though I was a senior. I remember thinking, "I shouldn't be punished for this." So I walked off the field and quit, something I never would have dreamed I'd do or want to do, especially with the influence of my overachieving parents and siblings. The guy who impregnated me was a football player, and I couldn't help but wonder whether or not he was starting in his game that Saturday. A lot of girls in my school got pregnant and had abortions. Which is ironic—I was the "slut" but I knew at least ten girls who had gotten abortions, or who had had babies by their senior year. A couple of the girls who had babies were part of the group of girls who said I was a slut. I think that they probably thought of me as worse because I had had an abortion.

 I definitely think that my "slut" reputation is part of the sexual double standard. Men are not held responsible for their actions the way that women are. I think it's up to adults to let young men know that they need to be responsible. When we talk about sex in our culture, it's all about how women are to blame, women "get" pregnant, it's all women's fault, women are bad. We're supposed to be sexual beings who satisfy the needs of others, but we're not supposed to enjoy or want sex.

Today I'm a writer and returning to school for a graduate degree focusing on education and English. To me education about sexuality is the one thing I needed the most when I was in high school, and it's the one thing I never had. I lacked sex education in school, parental knowledge about sexuality, and honest communication or support. Instead I had to deal with the negative attitudes of teachers, male chauvinism, and a culture of sexual harassment. So it might surprise you that I'm actually looking ahead to my ten-year high school reunion. But I want to tell everyone from high school that the negative experiences did not ruin me; in fact they made me stronger and more aware. It's because of those experiences that I'm now working with schools through Planned Parenthood and teaching teenagers today about their sexuality, so that they can be informed and empowered to make wise decisions.

WHO IS A "SLUT"?

The *Jenny Jones* talk show is obsessed with makeovers for teenage girls considered trampy-looking. In a typical episode a mother complains to Jones about the provocative way her teenage daughter dresses. The assumption is that anyone who wears tight miniskirts and cropped tops must be sexually promiscuous—even though, as one thirteen-year-old wearing a bathing suit and short shorts protested, "I ain't sexually active." The daughter defends her skimpy style ("You guys are just jealous") while the audience publicly shames her ("I have a seventeen-year-old daughter. If I ever catch her at seventeen with an outfit like that on, trust me, you'll read about it").

This ritual is the talk-show equivalent of what happens to girls in school every day. The *Jenny Jones* guest is presented as a cautionary tale for all the girls out there at home who may be flirting with spandex—just as the ostracized school "slut" is a case study for all the other girls considering hooking up with a guy on Friday night. Slut-bashing "is about keeping sexuality under control," explains Deborah Tolman, a developmental psychologist at the Wellesley College Center for Research on Women, "and an efficient way to do that is to deal with one person at a time as a kind of a scapegoat. It's a message to everybody. It's not just a message to that one girl, though she is clearly sacrificed in the process. The message is: if you step out of line, this will happen to you, too." Because "good" girls can become "bad" girls in an instant, slut-bashing controls all girls. And it does not discriminate based on race: *Jenny Jones* showcases girls of all races, and girls of all

un ap
d'
punk?

races report that they are singled out as "sluts" if they are perceived to have a casual attitude about their sexuality.

There is one important difference between the slut-bashing on the *Jenny Jones* show and the slut-bashing of everyday life. On the show the "slut" is defined by what she wears—and therefore she can be easily redeemed. During a commercial break the daughter is transformed, via a conservative outfit, new hairdo, and toned-down makeup application, into a respectable-looking young woman. The mother, Jones, and the audience express their approval; more often than not, the daughter appears miserable ("I hate these clothes").[9] The show ends with an upbeat, Horatio Alger–like message: *It's easy to shed a trashy reputation! Anyone can do it!* But in real life, once a girl is branded a "slut," it is enormously difficult to counter the charge.

It's hard to contest something that is so amorphous. Today there is no general consensus about what qualifies a girl as a "slut." Instead there are multiple, shifting distinctions between "good" and "slutty." In the 1950s, the bottom-line definition, everyone agreed, was a girl who had premarital intercourse (though, to be sure, there were subtle nuances to the categorization process). Today, when having intercourse with a steady boyfriend does not raise an eyebrow, the definition has broadened; it changes from community to community and from school to school. To some it's a girl who has intercourse with many different boys. To others it's a girl who "fools around" with different boys even without having intercourse. To some it's a girl who has intercourse with one boy too soon. To others it's a girl who "messes around" with one boy too soon. But who is to judge how many boys are "too many"? Or what it means to fool around with someone "too soon"? Everything is subjective and open to interpretation. In today's climate "slut" refers to any girl who appears open and carefree about her sexuality.

Sometimes a girl can be called a slut simply because of the way she looks: Her clothing or makeup make her *seem* like a "slut." One fifteen-year-old girl, Theresa from Fall River, Massachusetts, reported to me that "some girls get reps by wearing short stuff. Sometimes girls look at a girl and are like, 'Oh, she's a slut,' if she's all dressed up in something tight and short." In some schools the word is applied to any girl who is simply preoccupied with thoughts of boys and sex, according to sociologist Donna Eder. In one midwestern middle school where Eder observed students aged ten to fourteen for three years, girls who expressed an interest in more than one boy were derided as "sluts."[10]

Meanwhile, in other schools, having a serious, monogamous relationship is not necessarily insurance against a bad reputation. In an upper-middle-class community near a major city on the East Coast, pseudonymously called Sheepshead by sociologist Joyce Canaan, the "whore of Sheepshead High" earned her reputation for supposedly engaging in kinky sex with her longtime boyfriend. The legendary tale about the girl, Debbie, was that her boyfriend had bought several packages of French fries at Burger King, went back to his house with Debbie, and proceeded to dip them in her vagina and eat them. Another oft-told story was that Debbie had been gang-raped by six local boys; it was said that after protesting at first, Debbie relaxed and enjoyed it.[11] The subtext of these rumors couldn't have been clearer: First, "kinky" sex isn't normal, and therefore "good" girls don't engage in it. Second, anyone who does engage in "kinky" sex deserves to be punished—but since "sluts" are unrapable, being raped isn't really punishment. Canaan told me that there was so much pleasure in relating these stories that even her doctoral supervisor joked, when Canaan invited her to a party, that she would bring the French fries.

Theresa from Fall River is an unrepentant slut-basher who happily divulges the logic behind her actions. The daughter of Portuguese immigrants, Theresa has long dark hair, olive skin, and dark eyes. When I first meet her, she is wearing a tight minidress and clunky black shoes with high platform heels, an outfit that shows off her very shapely bust and legs. She knows she has the body of an adult woman, and makes sure that everyone else knows it too. Despite her curves, she's hard-looking. You don't want to mess with her. "There's one particular girl that I don't like because she messed around with my ex-boyfriend while I was dating him. When she walks near me, I say, 'slut.' If she walks on the stairs and looks at me, I'll look down and say 'slut.' I'll say 'bitch.' I'll say whatever the hell I feel like saying. And then she doesn't turn around. Everybody else called her a slut too, because she messes around with everybody's boyfriends. But she doesn't say anything. She just keeps walking, because she knows it's true. She cries all the time. But nobody feels sorry for her because she brings it on herself, you know?"

Theresa is proud that she's a virgin. But what would happen if she lost her virginity? Would having intercourse turn her into one of the "sluts" she mercilessly picks on? She contemplates this hypothetical with the utmost seriousness. "If I met a kid today and slept with him next week, of course I'd be called a slut. Because one week—what the hell is that? But if I was with a kid for four or five months and then I wanted to sleep with him, I wouldn't be called a slut.... I don't think." Theresa's voice betrays a sliver of doubt: maybe even she would be called a slut, too.

GOOD GIRLS HAVE NO DESIRE

Pamela Spring was sexually curious at a young age. She started kissing boys in the fourth grade and fooling around with them in the sixth grade. By eighth grade she was doing everything short of intercourse; by ninth grade she was no longer a virgin. So didn't Pamela deserve to be known as a "bad girl"? Weren't her classmates justified in spray-painting "Pam Is A Slut"? The question, in other words, is: Isn't it abnormal or unusual for girls so young to be engaged in sexual play?

In fact her behavior was entirely normal, given biological

circumstances. Girls today are beginning puberty at a remarkably young age—possibly because of improved living conditions or environmental factors (chemicals and hormones used in dairy and meat production are believed to trigger early sexual development). A recent study involving more than seventeen thousand young girls confirms that American girls are developing sexually years before their mothers did and doctors expect—beginning around nine years old. The mean age of onset of breast development for black and white girls is 8.87 years and 9.96 years respectively; for pubic hair development, the mean age is 8.78 years and 10.51 years respectively.[12] The researcher who led the study, Marcia Herman-Giddens, emphasized that we need to pay attention to the psychological effects of early puberty. "What you often find after a workup on these girls is that everything's normal except the emotional part. A lot of girls who mature early are treated like freaks and are teased by boys."[13] Young girls with big breasts are nearly always ridiculed; according to sociologist Barrie Thorne, even teachers gossip about them.[14]

In her autobiographical film *Slums of Beverly Hills*, writer-director Tamara Jenkins presents the character of Vivian Abramowitz, a fourteen-year-old girl who develops C-cup breasts practically overnight. Vivian's breasts are the focus of conversation and stares among everyone in her world—her father, brothers, next-door neighbor, aunt. Her breasts make her seem sophisticated, even though she hasn't even entered high school; her breasts disqualify her from girlhood even though she's not ready for adulthood. No wonder that Vivian feels "deformed" and almost undergoes breast-reduction surgery.

Along with the early development of physical sexual characteristics comes early development of sexual attraction. Researchers have discovered that at age ten, years before gonadarche—the hormonal event signaling the final maturation of the testes or ovaries, which typically occurs at age twelve for girls and fourteen for boys—there is another sig-

family

nificant hormonal event called adrenarche, the maturation of the adrenal glands. Age ten is the mean age of first sexual attraction for both boys and girls, regardless of sexual orientation, according to three different recent studies.[15] Gail Sheehy, author of *New Passages: Mapping Your Life Across Time,* noted to me that "Girls' bodies are developing at an accelerated pace, but emotionally their development may be delayed. With girls developing breasts at nine and erotic sensations at ten, you've got a recipe for unpreparedness."

Girls need to have someone with whom they can discuss their first stirrings of sexual desire. They need someone to reassure them that their feelings are normal and that they aren't "bad" for having them. Yet girls enter the years of sexual development alone, without guidance from their families. They learn at an early age not to discuss with family members anything related to sexuality. As Pamela recalls, she had "normal sexual feelings that were never discussed, in school or elsewhere. I was sexually curious but had no outlet or validation for it."

Because teenage girls are so reluctant to introduce sexual topics in conversations with their parents, parents should go out of their way to provide an open atmosphere for frank talk. But that rarely occurs: Many parents are worried about initiating a chain of events culminating in their daughter being known as a slut (if they talk about sex with her, she will in turn go out and have sex, which would lead to her developing a reputation). And if their daughter is a "slut," then the entire family loses its good standing in the community.

In a recent study on family communication about sex, it was revealed that significantly higher proportions of mothers and adolescents discuss AIDS and other sexualy transmitted deseases than issues surrounding sexual behavior, contraceptive use, and physical development, including masturbation. (Mothers, not fathers, are the primary parental communicators about sex.)[16] Of the 770 adolescent girls surveyed by Shere Hite for her 1994 book *The Hite Report on the Family,* over three quarters said their parents "seem to more or less pretend that dating and sexual feelings aren't happening."[17] Many fathers are openly antagonistic about their daughters' sexual development. Forty-six percent of the girls surveyed by Hite reported that their fathers "exhibited hostile attitudes to their dating" and 21 percent had to hide their dating from their fathers. One girl told Hite, "When we were growing up and my younger brother stayed out all night with a girl, my father couldn't wipe the smile off his face for a month. When I came in late—and hadn't done *anything*—he yelled at me, and I quote, 'Do you spread your legs for everyone?' Unquote."[18]

On the other hand, total openness is not necessarily desirable either. I remember that the summer I got my period (one month to the day after my twelfth birthday), I was away at camp. I wrote an urgent letter to my mother, marked PRIVATE on the envelope, informing her of the big event and asking her to send me menstrual pads. (I didn't know enough about my body even to consider using tampons; I'm not sure I could have figured out how to use them even with all the hand mirrors in the world.) Imagine my horror to discover, when I returned home at the end of the summer, that my letter was fastened to our refrigerator with some kitschy magnet, on display for all my parents' and brothers' friends refilling their iced tea to see. You can be sure I was in no hurry to ask my parents about masturbation or orgasms or oral sex, lest my inquiries become cocktail-party anecdotes for their friends. (This was before the Internet; if I were a teenager today, I'd worry that my sexual coming-of-age might be documented in a news group.)

Sexual development is inherently awkward; teens of both genders are inevitably embarrassed by it. There may be no panacea for parents who want to initiate sexual discussions with their children. Nevertheless parents should strive for some conversational middle ground. They should introduce the concept of sexual desire to their daughters as well as to their sons; but at the same time they must respect their children's privacy. They must have adequate knowledge themselves and be able to listen, to answer questions, and to understand the emotions lurking behind their children's questions. If parents can achieve this delicate balance, their daughters and sons will turn to them with sexual questions and will be at an advantage when they are ready to engage in sexual activity.

Beyond the family, silence about girls' sexual desire is pervasive. Rarely is there acknowledgment in movies or TV that sex is pleasurable for girls, just as it is for boys, and that girls have desire, just as boys do. Sex for boys is blissful, according to popular culture, whereas for girls it has repercussions. "In the media, sex is always up to the boy," complains fourteen-year-old Lauren Davi of Atlanta. "He pressures her to have sex. Either she gives in or he breaks up with her." Davi cites the example of David on *Beverly Hills 90210,* who broke up with Donna when she wouldn't sleep with him (she wanted to maintain her virginity until marriage). "It's a very rare occasion on TV when there's a boy who does not want to have sex. You also don't see a girl who wants sex as much as the boy does."

It's the same in sex education. After combing through sex education literature and researching public school curricula, psychologist Michelle Fine found that young women are rarely depicted as autonomous sexual beings. They are portrayed, rather, as wanting sex only for the emotional intimacy and as utterly lacking in sex drive. The point conveyed is that "good" girls do not have sexual desires. If a girl does have sex, it's because she is pressured or coerced—or else she's a "slut." The few times that sexual pleasure for girls is mentioned in sex ed, points out Fine, "it is tagged with reminders of 'consequences'—emotional, physical, moral, reproductive, and/or financial."[19]

Journalists reporting on sexual issues also ignore girls' sexual desires. An alarmist *New York Times* article about the rise of oral sex among teens, who believe it is safer than intercourse, cites psychologists, school nurses, and health educators who worry that teens are not learning about "responsible sexual decision-making" because they are not using condoms or dental dams.[20] Not a single person sought out by the reporter mentions the obvious benefit of oral sex for girls, most of whom do not have orgasms through intercourse.

SASHA ROTHMAN, A TWENTY-FOUR-YEAR-OLD documentarian, remembers in the sixth grade trying to talk to her mother about sex; the only information her mother provided was that she was to make sure boys didn't have the opportunity to touch her sexually. Her father never told her anything about sex but did once call her mother a slut in front of Sasha when she was in the sixth or seventh grade. At the same time, Sasha herself was being called a slut by her classmates.

Sasha has never had an orgasm and says she feels disgust whenever she experiences sexual pleasure. She knows intellectually that women have the right to be aggressive about their sexual desires, just as men are; yet she finds herself unable to practice this theory by applying it to herself. She was never taught that pleasure was natural, or that she was entitled to it, in the first place.

I grew up in Boston. My father is a lawyer and my mother is a travel agent. They separated when I was nine and I moved from house to house. At first it was on a weekly basis, and then mostly it was on a monthly basis. I had stuff in each house, but I basically packed every month. They lived very close to each other and I stayed in the same school. I have an older sister, who's two years older, and a younger sister, who's three years younger.

I went to a posh private school that I'll call Maplewood, which prides itself on its diversity and multiculturalism. There are a lot of children of successful people. I started at Maplewood in

kindergarten. But then my parents took me out when they separated, in the middle of fourth grade. I had to go to public
school for two years. They were fighting over who would pay the
tuition.

The public school I went to is about 80 percent black. I was-
n't treated very well because I was seen as the rich white girl,
since I'd gone to Maplewood. I had two really good girlfriends,
both named Susan, and we hung out with this kid named Josh,
who was in the sixth grade. He supposedly had had sex already;
I'm sure that was a lie. During the first week of school Josh
asked me out and I said yes. But I didn't "do" anything with him,
so everybody started calling me a prude.

When someone calls you a prude you start wondering about
the other side: "What would I have to do to not be called a
prude?" Josh wanted to kiss me and make out with me, but
that scared me. I was always like, "I'm not a prude, I'm not a
prude," and everyone would be like, "Well, prove it." So I
responded by becoming a huge flirt.

At the end of fifth grade I finally let Josh kiss me. But I would-
n't let him kiss my mouth. We were lying on the couch and he
was grinding up against me. He was kissing all over my neck and
I was like, basically wanting to throw up and get out of there. I
was completely passive. During the whole thing I felt so incredibly guilty, because I knew you were bad if you let boys kiss you.
You were bad if you were grinding with a boy on a couch. I felt so
disgusted with myself.

In sixth grade Josh left the public school, and some new students came in from another school in the system. The new girls
said all these things about me, including "Oh, she's been with
lots of guys." They also called me a slut. These girls were white
and came from blue-collar families. They told me I "switched my
ass"—that I moved my butt when I walked. Some people called
me a tease or a dicktease.

I think that the girls were jealous because I was considered
attractive. Men had been looking at me since I was ten. I started to become conscious of it, especially in sixth grade, because

I had done some modeling. One day, I don't know what provoked it, a group of girls circled me and threatened me. I sat there crying on the steps right outside the front door of school. They were like, "Oh yeah? You're a model? What are you a model for? Oatmeal? You're shit. You look like shit." It sounds kind of funny now, but it was very hurtful at the time. And then all of a sudden I felt something on my head. This one girl, Joanna, had thrown a lougie—you know, spit—on my head. It was really awful.

The girls hated me and were just jealous in general. My girl-friends, the two Susans, were also very jealous of me. It was something that I was unaware of until one summer they both dissed me and had a discussion about how awful I was, and then later they apologized to me. I think girls are set up to be cruel to each other. They are catty. Our greatest goal is to get the guys. And there are only so many guys that we want to get. And when there's a shortage of resources at the top, it becomes a competition, like anything else.

I went back to Maplewood in seventh grade. I was really psyched to go back. But to the kids at Maplewood I was a fast girl because I had gone for two years to a public school and had these friends who were a little bit faster than the private-school kids—you know, we drank beer and went out with each other. And probably they also heard things about me and guys. Immediately I was called a slut and a tease. The name-calling was not done to my face as much as it was said under people's breaths. It made me incredibly upset.

My old friend, Gloria, turned weird on me when I got back. She started wearing tons of layers of clothes to hide her body. She was becoming a woman and couldn't deal with it. At that time she was having a real hard time with her sexuality. But I was really boy-crazy. I loved having male attention. So I became friends with three other girls, and together we had a reputation as the "fast girls." Then we joined up with another group of girls, and people thought of us as the "popular" girls.

I counted once how many guys I fooled around with in seventh and eighth grades. Probably fifteen to twenty. Hand jobs galore. But then I really stopped doing any of that stuff for a while. My attitude was: I will hook up with as many people as I want, but only sleep with someone I love. By eighth grade my friend Claudia had blown eight guys, and even I was calling her a slut. Being "slutty" was something that we knew about ourselves.

My little sister also had a reputation. She had the label more than I ever did. And because she was a "slut," boys thought they could do things to her. She told me that she once invited over a boy she liked, and he invited his friends and they were hanging out. And then she went into the back and gave him a hand job. And then he was like, "Well, Bill wants one too" and she didn't want to, but she ended up giving five guys hand jobs because she felt pressured.

I did want to fool around with guys because I was guy-crazy and curious and sexual and all that. And there were some parts of fooling around that I loved. But I think that I always felt really disgusted with myself if it went too far, and it made me feel disgusted even if it didn't go all that far. I remember in ninth grade this guy I'd been dating on and off went down on me. I remember going back to the car and all I wanted to do was get away from him and I just felt like throwing up. I thought it was disgusting. I think it felt good physically, but all I felt was guilty and horrible about myself.

The big question of my life is: Where do these feelings of disgust and guilt stem from? I think some of it was from my mom. I remember trying to talk to her about sex in sixth grade and she was like, "You know, you shouldn't let guys touch you in certain places." My dad was a very closed person sexually. He always hid himself and I never saw him naked. It should be a natural thing and not a big deal. I also remember once, around sixth or seventh grade, my father found out that this guy across the street was living with my mother, and he hated him. He went into a rage and called my mom a slut.

The first time I had intercourse was when I was a junior in high school. It was my boyfriend who I was going out with for about three years, John. I wanted to have sex because we were so totally enmeshed with each other that I wanted to be as close to him as I could. I also wanted to do it because I was curious. I genuinely wanted to try it and I wanted it to feel good. But then it just didn't feel good.

I definitely felt pleasure, but not the Big O. I've never had the Big O—ever. I do reach a peak, but I don't think it's what other people call an orgasm because it's not a feeling of total joy and then great relief. It feels really good, and then boom, I stop having pleasure, it's over. I always feel that I've missed something.

John knew that I wasn't having orgasms. He wanted me to in the beginning, but he was also never a very sensitive person in that way. I don't think I was ever very open about trying to work on it with him. After a certain point in the relationship I knew there was no way I was going to have an orgasm with him.

You know how you're supposed to "hold out for the right guy"? Well, I changed that to, "I'm holding out my orgasm." I figured out that I could keep myself a "forever virgin" by not having an orgasm. I don't want to orgasm with just anyone. I know sometimes when I'm with guys, when I feel pleasure it just cuts off because I don't want to do that in front of them. I don't want to lose control. Guys have always wanted to make me come. But my feeling has been, "I don't want you to make me come."

I've thought a lot about having sex with women. I figured that since men don't do it for me, maybe it's that I'm gay. Maybe that's it. But it just doesn't work for me. I've made an effort to get interested. I've kissed a lot of women, but it hasn't gotten much farther than that. My feeling is that if I met the right woman, absolutely, I would love to. But it would have to be because it's the right person, not because I'm trying to be with a woman.

The sexual double standard definitely exists for me. I know that women are allowed to be the aggressors. And I am the aggressor. But something is lost in the translation from "women" to "me." I know I have the right, but at the same time

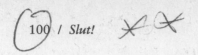

I don't have the right. I would love to be able to sleep with five men five nights a week and have fun with it. But I also know that I couldn't live with myself.

In college the whole point of your weekend is to hook up with someone else, especially in your senior year. My best friend is sleeping with a different man every weekend. I think that's very normal behavior for men, but not for women. If a guy sleeps with a different woman every weekend, I don't want to be with him—not because he's a "slut" but because I recognize that I won't be special to him. But I don't think that a man ever worries that a woman who sleeps around won't care about him, since he's not looking for affection from her.

I think sexuality is messed up for our society in general. We are built on this puritanical society that has to hide and repress everything. Women are taught that their goal is to find the right guy but that they shouldn't give in sexually too soon. Guys are applauded for their sexual performance. I just don't think that's the way sexuality should be. I think women should be able to walk around topless. I think having one partner for life is not natural. I just think we need to be more open in general. I think that puritanism works against both sexes, in terms of repressing sexual freedom, but it works much more strongly against women.

THE ROMANCE MYTH

Teenagers take sexual cues from the adults around them. As notions of sexual conservatism spread among adults in the years following the sexual revolution, so too did it escalate among teens. Many adolescent girls have been taught that sex is acceptable only if a girl is in love with a boy and involved in a serious, romantic, monogamous relationship with him. Many boys, however, don't consider romance an essential ingredient in a sexual relationship. Because of this dissonance, the romance-sex connection often backfires against girls.

Having a boyfriend can confirm a girl's value to herself: as *Seventeen, YM,* and *Teen* magazines teach her, getting a boyfriend is the most important thing in life. If she doesn't have a boyfriend, she comes to believe, she must be fat and ugly; she is worthless; she has no identity. But boys don't feel the same way because they've been taught all along that they have intrinsic value *as boys*. Having a boyfriend also enhances a girl's value in the eyes of her classmates (and her value skyrockets if he's well liked or good-looking): the relationship is her ticket to popularity. A boy, however, may be rewarded by his peers for sleeping with different girls. (Even some boys who are respected by their peers for maintaining adult-style monogamous relationships hope to score action on the side from other girls.) Girls are left to bargain for love—using the one thing they have that boys are dying for: their sexuality. So boys generally have the upper hand in their relationships with girls and often take advantage of their power by cajoling their girlfriends to have intercourse, even when their girlfriends have told them they'd prefer to do other sexual acts instead, or to avoid sex altogether.

The message that love with a boy is the end-all and be-all of a girl's existence is transmitted not only by teen magazines but also by teen romance novels. According to the Book Industry Study Group, romance novels are the third most widely read books by preteens and teenagers, after adventure novels and mysteries; one series alone, "Sweet Valley," has more than 30 million books in print, with a first printing of 350,000 books for each monthly volume.[21] Linda Christian-Smith, a professor of education at the University of Wisconsin, has traced the development and mechanics of the genre. When market research revealed in 1980 that teenagers were reading adult romance fiction series such as Harlequin and Silhouette novels, Scholastic adapted the genre for preteens and teens with the creation of the "Wildfire" series.[22] Many others soon followed, with series names such as "Sweet Dreams," "Love Stories," and "Sunset."

According to the romance-novel formula, the boy controls the romance by choosing the heroine, and it is only when the boy commits to the heroine—and she becomes "his girl"—that she sees herself as special and worthy. Nearly all romance-novel heroines are, to be fair, sassy and smart; many are quite daring and adventurous. But when it comes to romance, the typical heroine inevitably waits for the boy to make the first move. And when it comes to sexual desire, she generally has none until she becomes involved in the romance. Once her sexuality is awakened, it is expressed only in relation to the boy's desires and requests. She is not an autonomous sexual being with independent sexual feelings and behaviors. Moreover the sexual language of adolescent romance novels is maddeningly vague, even though the protagonists generally do little more than kiss. The morals conveyed could be described as: Sex is valid only if accompanied by love and commitment; intercourse and even "petting" are out of the question for teens; and boys are the only ones allowed to make sexual overtures.[23]

When Christian-Smith investigated who reads these novels, she discovered that they are heavily promoted in school book clubs, are included in classroom libraries, and even make their way into reading classes. The heaviest romance-fiction readers she encountered when she did fieldwork in three midwestern schools were all identified by teachers as "reluctant" or "slow" readers who had been tracked into remedial or low-ability reading classes. These girls read an average of six romances a month at home and school. While some of their teachers objected to the girls' reading material, others were gratified that they were reading at all.[24] With little interest in school or ambitions beyond school, the girls most influenced by romance novels are also the ones most likely to find solace in the message that they can and should depend on a man.

This point is driven home by other media. In films, television (including commercials and music videos), and in magazines for teenagers, women are seen as more preoccupied with romance and personal appearance than with going to school or working at jobs, according to a 1997 study released by Children Now, a children's advocacy group. In both television and films, women were more likely than men to talk about romantic relationships.[25] And since young people are heavily influenced by the adults they know and see, girls are much more likely than boys to emphasize the importance of romance and to see themselves as involved in romance. In a Roper Starch survey of five hundred teenagers in 1994, 71 percent of the girls said they had been in love with their last sexual partner, while only 45 percent of the boys said they felt that way.[26]

Perhaps many of the girls needed to convince themselves they were in love in order to avoid being thought of (or perhaps more importantly, to avoid thinking of themselves) as sluts. If they have had intercourse within the context of a romantic relationship, they rationalize, then they are not really lustful or bad or dirty. In their minds romance can cleanse sex. It's those *other* girls—the ones who sleep around with just *anyone*—who are "sluts."

Teenage girls who may not feel comfortable talking about sex can talk about romance. Being in a meaningful, romantic relationship today is comparable to going steady in the 1950s: It legitimates sex. However, going steady back then was a public affair—a girl wore a boy's pin or ring or ID bracelet—whereas romantic relationships today are often private and may not be exclusive.[27] In some communities teens tend to group-date: They go out with a group, and date within that group, never officially pairing up (an ideal setup for insecure boys who don't want to face the pressure of asking out a particular girl). In other communities boys and girls do maintain exclusive relationships, but only for short periods of time—sometimes as short as one month—and as a result don't bother to publicly announce their dating status. Many younger boys are unsure what precisely "going out" means, and therefore are reluctant to acknowledge that they are "going out" with a particular girl (even though she may long for such recognition). And of course there are always boys who would like a serious relationship but fear being made fun of as "pussy-whipped" girly-men.

One seventeen-year-old girl, Kim Klouda, told *The New York Times* that she had been exclusively seeing one boy for several weeks but wasn't sure if he was exclusively seeing her. One night she asked him about the status of their relationship, but he acted as if he didn't understand what she was talking about. (This boyfriend sounds like Bill Clinton denying to the world that he was sexually involved with Monica Lewinsky. Clinton, however, had a good reason for his cover-up: he was engaged in adultery with an employee.) Another boy, eighteen-year-old Grant Hilton, reported that when his girlfriend asked him what to tell people when they asked what was going on between them, he told her to "just tell them that we're dating."[28] For girls who fantasize about marrying their high school boyfriends, this secretiveness is troubling and scary: A boy who hides his romantic relationship from his best friends is hardly eager to plan a wedding. Desperate to shore up the romantic relationship's tenuous, elusive nature, many teenage girls have intercourse in exchange for the promise of love and commitment. Many end up heartbroken, sometimes pregnant, often feeling so needy that once one relationship ends, they rush right into another.

Sharon Thompson, author of *Going All The Way*, interviewed four hundred teenage girls from all social classes, races, and geographic regions of the country. She relates how most adolescent girls spend "thousands of hours planning for the first sex" and then, ironically, forget to use contraception. (They told her, inexplicably, that when it finally happened, sex was "spontaneous.")[29] They echoed the words of one sixteen-year-old girl, Teresa Moore of Milwaukee, who explained to *The New York Times* that she knows girls "who won't take birth control because it means they're planning to have sex. Then, if it happens—sex—you have the excuse that you weren't planning to do it, you just got overwhelmed by the moment. That way, it's less of a guilt trip if you get pregnant."[30]

Thompson's girls derived little, if any, physical pleasure from intercourse—orgasms were rare—but did not engage in other forms of sexual activity. When the relationships failed, they were distraught—"weeping and obsessing and looking backward, daydreaming about the day their real prince would come, setting themselves up for another devastating round."[31] These girls' unrealistic expectations of fusing love and sex led directly to profound unhappiness. Those who became pregnant, and whose boyfriends walked out on them, were often put in dire circumstances; those "lucky" to marry or at least move in with their boyfriends reported that their partners made it difficult for them to continue school or use contraception consistently.[32] "A change in strategy could have broken the deadlock: Girls could have chosen to condition consent on pleasure and desire, for example, rather than on love," observes Thompson.[33] But "good" girls do not admit to wanting pleasure or having desire. Nor, as we have seen, are they even taught that such things exist for girls.

EQUALITY "SLUTS"

Unlike these "true-love narrators," a small number of girls interviewed by Thompson kept romance and sex in healthy perspective. These girls, whom she calls "equality narrators," sought sexual pleasure *as well* as romance while maintaining an independent sense of themselves. They took responsibility by using contraception. And these girls had a good time. When relationships failed, they maintained their sense of humor and the outlook that there were always other guys. "Because they weren't bargaining for love," Thompson explains, "they had plenty of leverage in structuring intercourse according to their own desires."[34]

Sexual girls labeled sluts are similarly open-eyed about the pitfalls of romance and the realities of sexual desire. Some sexual "sluts" are, to be sure, far from balanced or content. But all are unafraid to snub the "good girl" rules. All gradually reconciled themselves with their feelings of sexual curiosity. Barbara Seaman has noted the connection, discovered by Kinsey in the postwar years, between female sexuality and intellectual or creative development. Kinsey revealed that the most accomplished women—intellectually, academically, or professionally—had had their first orgasms at an age earlier than the norm. Former Kinsey Institute researcher William Simon told Seaman, "Most girls are raised to believe that they have a time-bomb between their legs. They are encouraged to devote much of their creative energy toward preventing this time-bomb from going off. The women who manage to escape devoting their energies to repression seem to be the ones who have the most energy left for mental activities, and who also enjoy the most active sex lives."[35]

Sexual rules lead to sexual repression. Girls and women who shoehorn sex within the confines of adolescent romance describe their sexuality in shades of dull gray. Those who are sexually active yet refuse to commit to one boy, portray their sexuality—and, indeed, their entire lives—in vibrant color.

Given that many girls' first sexual experiences are coercive, those who fall into this group need all the education they can get about sexual pleasure. Girls who have been sexually abused are more likely than others to report also having had consensual intercourse before the age of fifteen—as well as having more than one sexual partner and not using contraception[36]—so they need guidance more than anyone. But every girl is hurt by the widespread silence about female desire. A girl needs to learn that sexuality can be consensual and pleasurable. She needs to feel in control of her body and that she is capable of entering into sexual relationships as an equal partner. The last thing she needs to learn is that enjoying sex makes her a "slut."

BORN IN 1978, ROSALINA LOPEZ grew up in a tough, inner-city neighborhood. She was always very open about sex and gave away condoms as part of a volunteer position at her local community health education center. When she was in the eighth grade, she and a friend were gang-raped; the rapists' girlfriends then started calling her a slut and beating her up. But her reputation did not prompt Rosalina to meekly hide her interest in sexuality. Instead she became more involved in sex education and more open about her own sexuality— which fueled the reputation even more.

Given her environment of male sexual domination and female sexual subordination, I find it amazing that Rosalina had the strength to insist on her right to an independent sex life. This stubbornness, I am certain, serves her well. Now a student at the University of California at Berkeley, she has left her old loveless environment, and she carries with her an important lesson: to be open about her sexuality yet responsible in her actions. Unlike Isadora Wing of *Fear of Flying,* Rosalina does not compartmentalize her sexuality; it's an essential part of her, like her skin and pores.

I grew up in a really rough neighborhood in the inner city of Oakland, California. There were always problems and fights in school. I happened to hang around the wrong group of girls, who were really hard-core into the gang scene.

My parents were born in Peru. My mom came when she was nineteen and my dad came when he was twenty. They met here. They own a small business. I was born in California, along with my brother, who's one year younger. We were raised Catholic, but we don't practice anymore.

I went to a big junior high school called Calvin Simmons Junior High. There were about a thousand kids in seventh, eighth, and ninth grades. About 70 or 80 percent are Latino. It's a very poor neighborhood. The school has no money and sometimes we didn't even have a substitute teacher and it was all chaotic. So you had to learn how to be very street-smart at a very young age. And you had to learn how to survive. If you were hungry and you didn't get lunch money, you had to learn how to get food, you know? So you became really smart. There were times when my dad gave me a dollar for lunch. I was never greedy with my money, but a dollar wasn't enough. So I would steal candy bars and other little things. Or I would flirt with guys to get free stuff.

When I was in eighth grade, I talked about sex a lot. My dad is an art lover, and in our house we have all these nice pictures of nude women. He would always tell me how fascinating the human body is. He's a really open guy. So I would be very open about sex too. And the people at school would look at me like, "What?!" Also that year my mom wanted me to do volunteer work, so she sent me to a local clinic, where I worked for the community health education center. I did outreach and gave out condoms to kids on the street and to prostitutes. So I always carried a pack of condoms to school and talked to people about safer sex, and the school invited me to do a lot of presentations. A lot of people thought I was a weirdo.

I always hung around guys and was a real tomboy. I got a lot of attention. But actually I was fooling around with girls. But I didn't really know what the term lesbian was, so I didn't count what I did with girls as sex. They talked about it at the community health center, but nobody ever got graphic with me. I thought that since there was no penetration, it wasn't sex. I didn't really know what it was. We would lie naked next to each other and touch each other. I would have orgasms, but I didn't know what they were. I always found the right girls, you know? We would go to the bathtub and play. We would act out romance novels and stuff. But the girls I fooled around with never told anyone, so no one really knew about it. Otherwise they would have called me a dyke. The guys didn't know, but maybe they sensed it. So maybe for them I was almost like a challenge. It was like I was something they couldn't have.

One day in the middle of eighth grade, my friend Shawna and I went to Kentucky Fried Chicken and there was a gang of like fourteen guys in there. I knew them from school; they were eighth and ninth graders. I was thirteen and Shawna was fourteen. One of the guys said, "I want to have sex with you." I said no, because I was still a virgin. And he said, "Well, if I can't fuck you, then we're all gonna fuck you." He was serious and I got really scared. Me and Shawna looked at each other and were like, "Let's get out of here." Then the guy said, "Hey! Get them! Get them!" So we started running. We went to an abandoned lot behind Kentucky Fried Chicken, which is where we always used to hang out, and hid inside one of those big long round pipes, like a sewer pipe. And that day me and my friend got raped. I know there were at least eleven men inside of her. She's very cute and has big boobs, so I know they all messed with her. I remember that they took my clothes off and were all violent. At least two guys—maybe up to seven guys—raped me. I was really angry that it was happening. Then I passed out, and Shawna was the one who woke me up.

I didn't understand the concept of rape at all until later. I never told anyone until I was sixteen years old. At first I wondered if I shouldn't have been cutting school. I shouldn't have been hanging around. But later I knew it was their fault. They were the assholes. But I didn't see myself as having the ability to get them back—sending somebody to beat them up, you know?

Being street-smart helped me deal with the rape. It didn't knock me down. I'm not saying that it didn't hurt—it actually hurt a lot to be silent about it—but it didn't destroy my life. I became immune to it. Life becomes so difficult that you just say, "I have to get over this." I was used to getting into a lot of fights and always getting harassed by the police. So the rape was just like another aspect of life.

When Shawna told her father about the rape, her father beat the shit out of her and told her that it was because she was dressing like a slut. This guy is just crazy. He's kind of an abusive father, you know? So she didn't come back to school for a month. But I went back to school three days later. My parents really wanted me to go to school every day. When I got back, the whole school knew. They said to me, "You slut." "You ho." "You whore." "Why you be sleeping with everybody's boyfriend?" They said it right to my face. The girls would come up to me and say, "You're a fucking slut." To them I represented something awful. They feared me. I represented something that they could not understand.

The girls started fights with me. They would either come to my house or get me on the street. It was always more than five or six girls. I remember getting my ass kicked at least five times in eighth and ninth grades. They'd go, "Hey, bitch. Why are you sleeping with my boyfriend?" But I never fought back really hard. I knew I could never win, so I would just fall on the ground and go limp until they stopped. Shawna would yell and fight back. They'd be pulling her hair and she would be yelling, "Bitch! Bitch!" They would beat her up forever. But after I went limp, they would just leave me alone.

The teachers seemed oblivious to the whole thing. They acted like they didn't care. Look, the school district in Oakland has a lot of problems. Teachers are always going on strike because they're underpaid. The teachers did not at all seem sensitive to the needs of young women, much less a group of young women of color. A lot of them are white. I had very few role models in terms of teachers. I think they thought they were doing us a favor by teaching us, since we were an inner-city school. They did not have the least idea of what was going on in the families. A lot of them would leave in their fancy cars and they would leave the neighborhood for the day and go to their comfortable houses. So they had no idea, especially because a lot of the parents didn't speak English. Now my parents speak English, but back then they didn't talk to anybody. So there was no bond between my parents and my teachers.

But I always did well in school and I never lost interest in it. My mom always said, "The only thing I can leave with you is your education. That's the only way you're going to survive, because who knows if you're going to get married." So it was never an option for me to not do well. But unfortunately the school became very segregated when we were at an early age because of racism within the school. All the black kids would play basketball together, and the teachers never made an effort to integrate the playground. They never encouraged the Mexicans, who would go outside of the fence, to come back in. They never made an effort to encourage the girls to play basketball. Everything was just a given.

In the classroom the tracking system lasted all the way through high school. The Asian kids were in the good classes. The troublemakers, who were predominantly blacks and Latinos, were in the lower-track classes. Sometimes I was in those classes, but usually I was in the highest track, where I was with Asians and poor white kids. The teachers would patronize me. It always bothered me when a teacher would say to me, "I'm glad *you're* doing well."

The mean girls were the most popular. In the type of environment I was in, the one who can survive the most is the one you're supposed to learn from. The girl gangs were the scariest gangs. I never officially got initiated into a gang, because to get initiated they all kick your ass at the same time. But Shawna and I would hang out with a gang called Da Crew. They wanted me to go wherever they went. They would say, "Oh, look at that girl. Let's go fuck with her and steal her stuff." But Shawna eventually got kicked out because supposedly she had slept with all their boyfriends, even though they had raped her. She is considered the whore of the city. Everyone knows about her. And I was her best friend, so I was like the number-two "slut."

I didn't analyze this too much back then, but I was really happy that Shawna and I couldn't go to any of the parties. We couldn't go anywhere without being mouthed off to. They would tell us, "Get out of here or we'll kick your ass." So the two of us just did our own thing. We would go places together and she would always tell me that I'm beautiful and I would always get a

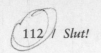

lot of compliments from her. She really made me feel that I was beautiful.

The whole thing made me feel very free. I felt that nobody could touch me: I was an untouchable. The more they called us names, the more we separated ourselves from the group. If it hadn't been for the name-calling, I think we would have fallen into the pattern of being followers, like following the girl who's the prettiest. I remember that we were the first ones who started wearing dresses to school. I always liked being different. So it was liberating in a way. We didn't have to fit in.

Being called a slut makes you more daring to experiment. It opens up a lot of doors. There are all these connotations that go along with being a "slut." People assume you're having sex. They assume that you're scandalous—that you're very sexual. I was not that way before, but now it was an option for me. Whereas if people thought of me as a virgin, it would have been hard for me to experiment. So I became a very sexual person with guys. I would sleep with three or four guys in one year. I'd have a relationship with them for a little while. All the guys wanted a piece of me and Shawna. The two of us would just laugh at them. But I knew that I would never get raped again because if anyone else tried, I would kill him. When I started sleeping with guys, I did not see sex as an emotional attachment. That ideal had disappeared a long time ago. I was more concerned about myself and my own sexuality.

They called me a slut because I slept with guys who weren't my boyfriend. This was coupled with the fact that I was doing sex education. The two things together were like a lethal combination. But I really think the reason they called me a slut is because I was a woman doing things that they considered deviant behavior. When they see someone else doing things they consider deviant, it symbolizes something very bad and out of place. "Slut" is the name for a woman whose sexuality can't be understood. In the girls' view, either you wait for the guy you marry or you're with your boyfriend and you have sex with him. And if you deviate from that, you're a "slut" and a "whore."

People are not given the verbal framework to express how people can be different. And they can't express sexual desires. Even when they do talk about it, it's a very limited language—words like fuck. So when they talked about me, they couldn't describe me as a "sexually active young woman." For them I was a "slut" because that's the only word they knew.

The girls were so bad to me. It was all Latinas. The Asian community was mostly recent immigrants, so I didn't have very much to do with them. I didn't really have problems with the black girls or the white girls. The Latinas gave me trouble because they lived in my neighborhood and were in my gang and their parents knew my parents. I saw in their eyes that they did not understand me. There was a lot of anger and resentment in their eyes because I did things that I know they wanted to do.

Girls are so encouraged to not talk about sex. Nobody talks about sexual pleasure at all, even though sexuality is such a big part of who you are. When people talk about sex, it's always attached to a stigma, like homosexuality or disease or rape. So when we do see a woman who is sexually active, she is a threat.

They knew I was free and they were jealous. They didn't understand the concept of freedom, but they knew that something was different about me. It's not that I was more sexual than they were. It was my attitude. Like I remember one day I had sex with this guy, and then I wanted to go home and do my work. And he said, "No, hang out with me." And I said, "No, I have to go home." And I walked home because he wouldn't give me a ride. I think he was so mad that I didn't stay with him. And people knew that I was like that. I was independent.

I really think that being called a slut empowered me. The more people are marginalized, the more they see things in a critical way. You start to have almost a double consciousness: You see the role you're supposed to be in, but you also see that you're not in it. I'm really critical about the fact that women are not encouraged to talk about sex and that they don't even know words like penis. They say "that thing down there." I'm critical of the fact that women are always supposed to be passive. I think men and women see sex differently, and that's really glossed over in sex education classes. I think men are more encouraged to experiment and women are more encouraged to not pursue it and not talk about it. What woman has not heard her mother say, "Look at that prostitute. Look at that whore"?

CHAPTER 4

"SHE ASKED FOR IT"

The Raped Girl

Like many women, I routinely receive unwanted sexual attention. It happens when a stranger on a Manhattan street looks directly at my chest and makes a sexual comment—something along the lines of "Nice tits" or "Hey baby" or "You've got big ones" (I always feel like responding, "Thanks for letting me know")—occasionally accompanied by kissing noises. Men in suits with briefcases, men on a break from their construction job, men in baggy jeans and backward baseball caps—I've gotten comments from them all. Some of them clearly want to intimidate me; some no doubt like to imagine themselves as gentlemen paying a lady a compliment. But all, I think, believe that the act of bellowing "Nice tits" and making kissing noises is a self-defining act—one that contributes to their own sense of their male identities. It's an easy way to reassure themselves of their masculinity. (Personally I wish they'd just go home and watch a football game instead.)

Now, there are many instances when I desire to be desired, when I want to be sexually admired. But generally I don't want to be sexualized in asexual contexts, such as a New York City sidewalk when I'm on my way to an office or an appointment. For many men, *woman* equals *sexual being*, and *sexual being* means *sexually available all the time*. But I don't want my femininity confused with my sexuality. This confusion flattens me into a nonthreatening, cartoon figure: My sexual identity becomes my *only* identity, my every other characteristic wiped out. When I receive sexual comments on the street, I feel the old, irrational wave of self-doubt that is the residue of my high school experience: *I am a bad girl*. I worry that my sweater is too tight, my suit too form-fitting, my body too...much. I just can't loosen up and accept the comments as compliments—as many men, and even some women, have advised me to do—because even when "Nice tits" is intended as a compliment of sorts, it tugs something private from my grasp. When a stranger on the street makes a sexual comment, he is making a private assessment of me public. And though I've never been seriously worried that I would be attacked, it does make me feel unguarded, unprotected.

Regardless of his motive, the stranger on the street makes an assumption based on my physique: He presumes I might be receptive to his unpoetic, unsolicited comments. (Would he allow a friend to say "Nice tits" to his mother? His sister? His daughter?) And although I should know better, I, too, equate my body with my soul and the result, at least sometimes, is a deep shame of both.

Rape is a thousand times worse: The ultimate theft of self-control, it often leads to a breakdown in the victim's sense of self-worth. Girls who are molested, for instance, often go on to engage in risky behavior—having intercourse at an early age, not using contraception, smoking, drinking, and doing drugs.[1] This behavior, it seems to me, is at least in part because their self-perception as autonomous, worthy human beings in control of their environment has been taken from them.

If rape is defined as full penetration occurring against a person's will with the use or threat of force, then one in eight American women is raped during her lifetime, according to the most cautious, government-financed, independent survey.[2] One fifth of American women have been forced to do something sexually at some point in their lives, according to two separate studies.[3] Girls are disproportionately raped: girls under eighteen were the victims of over 60 percent of all reported rapes in 1990.[4] Eight percent of high school age girls said yes when asked if "a boyfriend or date has ever forced sex against your will" in a representative national survey conducted by Louis Harris & Associates in 1997.[5] These statistics themselves, while troubling, are perhaps not as disarming as the way rape victims feel about the crime and about themselves: More than 70 percent say they are worried about their families discovering they were raped. Two thirds worry they might be blamed for it.[6]

Rape victims have every reason to be worried. Unlike the victims of other crimes, girls and women who have been raped are automatically assumed to have initiated the act in some way: wearing tight clothes, entering a date's apartment, having a drink, smoking marijuana. Simply being physically attractive can be used against them (though, in a paradigmatic example of the proverbial double standard, being handsome helps the rapist, who presumably doesn't need to force anyone to have sex with him).

A high school rape victim has a uniquely difficult dilemma. The rape itself transforms her, in the eyes of her classmates, into a "slut." Of course, calling a rape victim a slut makes no sense: it's like accusing the pedestrian victim of a hit-and-run driver of being reckless. So why do teenagers (and adults) do it? Boys no doubt fear sexual rejection and therefore don't want to consider that a girl might say no and mean it. Girls need to find a reason for rape and to separate themselves from the raped classmate because they worry that they could easily be the next victim. For both boys and girls, calling the rape victim a slut surrounds the source of their anxiety—the raped girl—with a sense of order and reason.

I spoke with several young women who had been raped in high school—two by guys they knew, one by a stranger. All of the women, quite interestingly, were athletes. Even though being involved in sports made them physically strong and therefore at an advantage when fending off an attacker, it also put them in proximity to male athletes in team sports, who comprise a disproportionately high percentage of rapists. (Researchers have found that males in team sports, like rapists in general, tend to use force and to value aggressiveness. Male team sports are also segregated from women's sports, leading some male athletes to shun anything considered feminine.[7]) Other similarities: Two of the women were disbelieved when they told their classmates they had been raped; the third didn't even bother informing anyone because she was smart enough to know her story would be dismissed. All were laughed at and looked down on as cheap and easy (being raped motivated the third woman to become very sexually active on her own terms). All believed, at least for a while, that they had done something wrong to deserve being raped, though even when wracked with self-doubt none felt she deserved being known as a slut.

KIMBERLY CHRISTIANSEN, twenty, was a popular athlete in her Illinois high school. With long brown hair, brown eyes, and a muscular build, she is striking-looking and is used to being the center of attention. In her junior year Kimberly was raped by a former boyfriend, a burly football player. From that point on, Kimberly's days as a popular girl were numbered.

I grew up in a very small city in Illinois, and I've lived here since I was two. My mom's a teacher and my dad owns a store. I don't have any brothers or sisters. I was happy in ninth grade and had a lot of friends. I was very involved in athletics and played four sports: softball, volleyball, basketball, and track. I would say that I was part of the popular crowd. How would I describe it? Gosh, I don't know, because I was in it, so I never had to look on. The kids in my crowd were good-looking; they came from good families. Most of the crowd were either in sports or they were cheerleaders or they were active in school.

In my sophomore year I dated this guy, John, who was a year older and played football. It wasn't that serious. We just dated and it was mutual when we broke up. Then he switched to the Catholic school right across the street from the public school so that he could get more playing time on the field. In my junior year I started dating Jason, one of John's best friends. That was a little more serious. Both John and Jason were popular and good-looking. They both had really good bodies and other girls would sort of fawn over them. Jason was like the star athlete at the public school and John was the star athlete at the Catholic school.

Like John, I switched schools in January of my junior year to the Catholic school, in order to get more playing time pitching softball. My parents thought that if I could play more, I would get more recognition, and then I would get a college scholarship. It didn't end up working out at the end, but at the time I didn't know that. Athletics are really important to everyone in my neighborhood. People get very involved and go to all the games, and all the parents are really into it. My dad played football, basketball, track, and baseball when he was in high school, and played tennis in college. My mom didn't play sports but she likes to watch and be involved.

I went from a class of four hundred to a class of thirty. There were sixteen girls in my class, and when I got there, there were these three girls who were just like *the* girls of that class. It was John's girlfriend, Teresa, and two other girls, Sarah and Jenny. They were the popular girls and the ones everybody thought were so cool. They became three of my good friends, so I fit right in with them, and then it became the four of us. By this point Jason had gone away to college, so I had stopped dating him.

In August before senior year, right before John was going off to college, he called to invite me to a going-away party at the cabin of our friend Colin. I wanted to go. I figured it would be fine to go out there with him; it wasn't a date or anything. So he picked me up and said, "They're going to meet us out there and we're supposed to go out there and open up the cabin and get it ready for everybody else." I said, "Okay, that's fine."

We got to the cabin and we were sitting and talking, and John said, "You want to watch TV?" The TV was in the bedroom, so we went in there. But when we got in the bedroom he locked the door. I thought that was kind of weird but I really didn't think anything serious would happen. We sat down and started talking. He started asking me if I ever wanted to take a risk. I said, "What are you talking about?" He said, "Don't worry, Teresa would never find out." And then he kissed me. I said, "What are you doing? Teresa is one of my good friends." So he said, "Oh, she'll never know." So then I said, "No, stop." And he just wouldn't. And it just went from there. He held me down and penetrated me. He's really strong and muscular. There's no way I could have gotten out from underneath him.

He didn't threaten me, but I was terrified. I really didn't know what to think. I guess I didn't really know quite what was happening. I think I was in shock. I don't know how long it lasted because time kind of stopped for me. I had never had intercourse before and it hurt a lot. There wasn't anybody around who could have heard me. We were totally alone. I kept telling him to leave me alone and get off, that I wanted to go home.

I finally pushed him off. Then he walked out of the room. By that time Colin and his friends had arrived, and they were hanging around outside the cabin. I went outside to talk to them and said, "Will somebody please take me home?" They were like, "What's wrong?" I said, "Nothing, I just want somebody to take me home." None of them would take me home. So I said to

John, "Please take me home," and he said yes. I didn't look at him or talk to him or anything on the way home.

I knew John had been interested in me, but I had never taken it very seriously because he was kind of a womanizer. You never knew when he was being serious and when he wasn't. He was very cocky. He knew he was good-looking and he knew he was good at sports and that girls liked him. But it had never bothered me. I thought he was my friend.

I told one good friend, Katie, from my old public school, right away. She was the only one I felt comfortable talking to about it. John came up to her the next day and she said to him, "Don't talk to me." He was like, "What's your problem?" And she was like, "Does the name Kimberly mean anything to you?" He said yes, so she said, "Then don't talk to me." So he knew that she knew something.

He came to where I was working—a department store at the mall. He walked in and my eyes just filled up with tears. He asked me what was wrong, and I was like, "John, think about what you did." He said he didn't know what I was talking about. I was like, "Just leave me alone." I started crying and walked away, and he left. He never apologized.

I was scared to go back to school because I didn't know who knew or what people thought or how I was supposed to act. I was afraid that John would tell his friends that he had had sex with me. He wasn't going to be there because he had graduated, but Teresa was going to be there, and I would have to look at her every day and wonder if I should tell her.

Things were basically fine on the outside. Nobody really knew anything had happened at that point. John might have told a couple of his friends, but they had all gone to college. But I became really depressed. I was crying all the time at home and I never wanted to go to school and I didn't want to go out or anything. I just didn't eat. I lost about fifteen pounds in two months. I did a pretty good job of hiding my depression when I went out. But my friends wondered why I didn't do as much with them. I spent more time with my old public school friends because they

didn't remind me of John. I was able to forget about it for a little while and have fun. My mom knew that something was wrong but she didn't know what it was. So I told her what had happened. That was when I realized that I had been raped.

I felt like I did something wrong that led him on or that led him to think that what he was doing was okay. I felt it was my fault because I gave him the opportunity: I was there and I went there alone with him and I let him go into the bedroom to watch TV. But when I talked to my mom, she was like, "Kimberly, it wasn't your fault."

In December of my senior year everything kind of blew up. I had noticed that my friend Jenny had been acting kind of strange toward me. We had been inseparable before. So I called her up one day right before Christmas break and asked her what was wrong. And she said, "You know." I said that I didn't know. So she said, "I think you need to talk to Teresa. I'll let you two handle it yourselves." So I went over to Teresa's house and pretty much told her the whole story. I made it clear that he had forced me. I thought she deserved to know what John was like. She said, "Oh, he would never do that." But she also said, "You and Sarah and Jenny are my only friends at school and I would never do anything to you." She made it sound like she believed me, and that she was going to confront John.

But he must have turned the story around to her. He must have said that I wanted it. And she believed him. Teresa didn't want to believe that John would rape anyone. She turned it all around into how I wanted to have sex with him, and how could I do that to her. How could I sleep with John, knowing that he was going out with her, and I was this big slut.

When I came back to school after Christmas break, the school was getting ready for homecoming, which is in January during basketball season. Jenny, Sarah, Teresa, and I were the candidates for homecoming queen. I had been nominated before the whole thing started. So when we got back to school, we had to do stuff together to get ready for homecoming. And during that whole time they were pretty nice to me, so I thought things were going to be fine. I figured that everything would work out.

But after homecoming was over—Sarah was elected queen and I think she and the other candidates told everyone not to vote for me—they didn't want to have anything to do with me. They didn't want to talk to me and they wouldn't look at me. They would say things behind my back so that I could hear them. Things like "She's such a bitch" and "She's a slut." I would go to school and I wouldn't say a word to anyone all day. One day at the end of January at lunch I sat down at this table with Teresa, Sarah, and Jenny, plus some of the popular girls who were sophomores and juniors. And they all got up and left, so I was left sitting there all by myself. I didn't want to get up, because I didn't want to give them the satisfaction that it got to me. So I just sat there. One of my guy friends came over and sat with me. He said, "I'm not going to let you look like a fool. I'm going to talk to you."

Not one girl in my class would have anything to do with me. Only girls were mean to me. Even the less popular girls were mean because they looked up to Teresa and that crowd so much that whatever they said went. If they said, "Don't talk to Kimberly," then they wouldn't talk to me. The guys didn't really care too much for the most part. I think that made the three girls even more mad because I had guy friends now, and it made me look even worse. It sort of confirmed for them that I was a "slut." They were like, "Look at her—she's with all the guys all the time." But all I had was guy friends. They were the only people who would talk to me. It wasn't by choice. I tried to tell Jenny that John had raped me. I was like, "I don't know what you've heard, but this is what happened." She was like, "Yeah, whatever." She didn't believe me.

I tried not to cry in school. I tried to hold it all in. There was one time when I went to the bathroom and cried, but usually I just tried to avoid the girls as much as possible. I'd go straight to school and come straight home. I ended up quitting basketball in the middle of the season because I couldn't handle going to practices and being totally ignored. They would never pass me the ball or anything. I told my coach that I was just going to focus on softball. Track was okay because we did it combined with another small school, so I had some friends there. My mom made me go see a counselor. I started taking Prozac, which I still take now. This was the first time in my life I'd been depressed.

The name-calling continued for the whole rest of the year. It wasn't every single day, but I got ignored every single day. It was like I wasn't even there. For everything we did I would sit by myself. If we had assemblies, I would sit by myself. My senior year we could go home for lunch, so after that day they all got up and left, I never went back to lunch ever again. Teresa and Jenny keyed my car—they scratched it with their keys. It looked like they started to write something but someone came and they couldn't finish. It was bad enough that my insurance gave me money to repaint it. One day toward the end of the year I had on a dress and I remember walking by Teresa and a friend of ours, Tom, and she said something like, "Oh my God, look at her in that dress. She looks like such a whore." And Tom said, "Well, your boyfriend slept with her, so she must not be all that bad." I didn't date anybody for the rest of the year. I wasn't invited to any of the graduation parties. At graduation some of the guys came over to me and said, "We'll miss you" and hugged me, but none of the girls said anything to me.

I chose a college that is six and a half hours away from home; I figured I would be away from everybody and that things would get better. One day a few months ago our college was playing in a basketball tournament, so I went to the gym to watch. The school we were playing against, which was from Chicago, sounded very familiar. I knew that someone I knew went there, but I couldn't remember who. I looked out and John was on the team. It was really strange to see him there. So I went back to my room. I didn't tell anyone why I was leaving; I just told my friends I was tired.

I guess after the game John was asking around about me,

because he knew that's where I went to school. And someone told him which dorm I lived in. He called my dorm and asked if I wanted to stop by the hotel where he was staying. I was like, "Don't call back here" and I hung up.

Then I just lost it. I thought I was away from him. My roommate wanted to know what was wrong but I said I was fine. I went into one of my really good friends' room and I was like, "Angie, I can't take this anymore." I just spilled everything to her. I was feeling suicidal. She took me to the hospital and they made me stay overnight. I was so upset, they were afraid to leave me by myself. The next morning I had to talk to a psychiatrist and go through an evaluation. He suggested that I take a week off from school and go home, so that's what I did. I've been taking my medication so I haven't been depressed.

It took a long time for me to want to even hold a guy's hand. It was hard for me to go out on a date. I was scared and I didn't know what people would think. I was real paranoid, thinking that guys would ask me out just because they thought they could get something.

I am dating someone now. He really cares about what I think and what I feel. He always wants to make sure that I'm happy. We can talk about everything and I can be totally open with him. And he'll listen to me. Some guys will change the subject but he'll just sit there and listen to me for however long I want to talk. I've had sex once since the rape and it was really hard for me to do emotionally even though I enjoyed it physically. It was something I wanted to do to get the memories of John out of my system—so that when I thought of sex, I wouldn't think of him. I think it worked a little bit. I mean, nothing will ever totally get rid of it.

BAD VICTIMS

Alice Vachss, former prosecutor in charge of sex-crime cases in Queens, New York, has pointed out that rape victims of all ages are pigeonholed into one of two categories: Good

Victims or Bad Victims. "In New York City," she observes, "Good Victims have jobs (like stockbroker or accountant) or impeccable status (like a policeman's wife); are well-educated and articulate, and are, above all, presentable to a jury; attractive—but not too attractive; demure—but not pushovers. They should be upset—but in good taste—not so upset that they become hysterical."[8] Even if a woman is lucky enough to be a Good Victim, and can prove that she fought the act of intercourse (even though submitting might have been the smartest way to survive), she still must deal with the judges and lawyers. Vachss relates that they routinely degrade women in cross-examinations with the "She's loose, so this was consent, not rape" approach, or the crowd-pleasing "It was consent, with rough sex" line.

Bad Victims are the ones most susceptible to being portrayed as untrustworthy, and whom a jury would be inclined to disbelieve. One Bad Victim represented by Vachss was an unattractive and unpopular teenager who had a crush on a handsome classmate, an athlete. When he asked her out, she was thrilled. He then forced her to have sex with him and his friend. The girl's family didn't care. "Her brothers yelled at her for getting raped. Her mother wouldn't interrupt her bowling night to take the girl to the police precinct." The jury didn't like her either, since she was sullen and unresponsive in cross-examination. Jurors want victims to cry, Vachss explains.[9]

Until 1974 a victim in New York State could be cross-examined about her sexual history and was required to provide corroborating evidence of the rape. Until 1983 a victim had to prove that she'd fought the attack with "utmost resistance."[10] Despite reforms, the instinct to doubt women who say they've been raped prevails. After one woman was raped from behind, Vachss reports, a judge ruled that because she hadn't actually seen the rape, she couldn't really be sure there was penetration. He wanted graphic descriptions of what she had felt during the act.[11]

Crime journalists mimic the courts in determining who is innocent and who is guilty. When you're reporting on deadline, you latch onto the first conceptual framework that pops into your head. Journalism professor Helen Benedict, author of *Virgin or Vamp: How the Press Covers Sex Crimes,* finds, like Vachss, that sex-crime victims are judged good or bad, trustworthy or untrustworthy—and that among news media professionals, "good" is associated with virginal and "bad" means slutty. The victim "tends to be squeezed into one of two images—she is either pure and innocent, a true victim attacked by monsters—the 'virgin' of my title—or she is a wanton female who provoked the assailant with her sexuality—the vamp." Eight factors tilt a woman toward the "vamp" identity: If she knows her assailant; if no weapon is used; if she is of the same race, class, or ethnic group as the assailant; if she is young; if she is considered pretty; and if she in any way deviates from the traditional housewife-mother role.[12]

The widely reported 1989 Central Park jogger "wilding" event, Benedict points out, was reported within the framework of a virgin narrative. The six youths who raped the jogger also beat her unconscious with a lead pipe and rock, smashed her eye socket, and left her for dead in a freezing puddle. The victim held a majority of the virginizing factors in her favor (she didn't know her assailants; she was brutally beaten up; and she was of the dominant race and class); white journalists painted her attackers as inhuman beasts. The fact that they were black was lead material. The victim was proclaimed "innocent."[13]

The victim of the 1983 "Big Dan's" gang rape, on the other hand—assaulted by six men on a pool table at Big Dan's Tavern while others in the room cheered them on—was vilified by her Portuguese New Bedford, Massachusetts, community. (The case was later popularized in the movie *The Accused.*) Initial press coverage focused on the defendants' ethnicity, as if that had something to do with the rapes. In their anger at this prejudice, neighbors made the victim a scapegoat and began to portray her as a prostitute, a charge that journalists eagerly repeated, unverified. Numerous news stories reported that she had left her children in bed, unattended, while she went out to the bar—a complete fabrication. Her boyfriend, in reality, was at home with them (a fact mentioned only in one story in one paper).[14]

The jury ultimately believed the victim, but the community did not. After the guilty verdicts were decided, community members told reporters (who quoted them without providing any context) that "If she had been home with her children, this would not have happened" (*Providence Journal*); "She is the one who deserves this sentence" (*Boston Globe*); and "I'm also a woman, but you don't see me getting raped" (*Standard-Times*).[15] They held street demonstrations and threatened to bomb the victims' house. Forced out of town, she soon committed suicide. Benedict remarks that the woman had had every one of the eight biasing ingredients against her.[16]

In another, well-publicized Bad Victim story, when Patricia Bowman accused William Kennedy Smith of tackling her, tearing off her dress, and raping her at the Palm Beach Kennedy estate, she was slandered by reporters. Even though the first detective to see her after she reported the rape observed that Bowman was "hysterical," bruised, and "roughed up," the fact that she had accepted Smith's offer to walk along the beach on his family's estate was widely regarded as evidence that she had consented to have sex with him. NBC News and *The New York Times* revealed her name despite their usual policy of not naming the complainant in rape cases. NBC featured a picture of Bowman.[17]

The *Times* also ran a lengthy and accusatory profile of Bowman. It noted that she "was born into a modest working-class family...but moved sharply up the economic ladder 10 years ago after her divorced mother married a wealthy industrialist"—the implication being that Bowman and her mother were gold-digging opportunists and that Bowman was so dazzled by Smith's wealth and fame that she initiated sex with him. The *Times* profile continued that Bowman "held jobs sporadically, took college classes occasionally, had a child and moved into a house near Palm Beach that was bought for her by her stepfather....She was popular socially and 'had a little wild streak,' said a woman who knew her at the time. That meant she and her friends liked to drive fast cars, go to parties, and skip classes." Readers also learned that Bowman had received seventeen tickets for speeding, careless driving, or being involved in an accident and that once, while on an impromptu dinner date, she struck up a conversation with other men.[18] (The nerve!)

The *Times* coverage dovetailed with the widespread assumption among Americans that Bowman was a "slutty" type who either deserved to be raped or wasn't raped at all. A majority of Americans over the age of fifty, and nearly a third of those ages thirty-five to forty-nine, believe that a woman is to be partly blamed for her rape if she dresses provocatively or agrees to go to the man's room or home, according to a 1991 *Time* magazine survey.[19] And the *Times* in the spring of 1991 suggested that William Kennedy Smith was innocent, even though the case had not yet gone to trial. Three weeks after the Bowman profile, the *Times* published a glowing profile of Smith that quoted friends describing him as "a man of gentleness and humor" and "a good listener and a thoughtful conversationalist who seldom had more than a glass of wine or a mug of beer."[20] Meanwhile three women came forward claiming that Smith had raped or assaulted them in recent years.

During the trial Smith's defense lawyers argued that Bowman suffered from a "psychological disorder" that caused her to invent the rape charges. They questioned her about her bar visits and passed around to the jurors her panties and bra. The prosecutor, however, was not allowed to disclose evidence about the other women who alleged they were assaulted by Smith. William Kennedy Smith was acquitted.[21]

oglus

THE CULTURE OF SEXUAL ENTITLEMENT

In many schools there is a culture of girls' sexualization and boys' sexual entitlement. In this atmosphere sexual harassment is seen as normal behavior. Nearly every coed school has a group of popular boys, often well-built and attractive, usually jocks, who are boisterously sexually aggressive toward girls. In many cases these boys are liked by teachers and administrators: Even though the boys' grades may not be high, they bring honor to the school through their self-assured presence in extracurricular activities and their prowess in athletics. This situation puts girls in an impossible position. Those who seek these boys' attention are at risk of being called sluts, since girls are not expected to want sex the way boys do. Those who complain about the harassment are often not taken seriously, since masculine toughness is not considered worthy of criticism; alternatively they may be considered sluts for somehow having "invited" the boys to call them sexual names or grab their bodies.

Many boys equate masculinity with aggression against girls and women, or against anything they associate as feminine (such as homosexuality). Being callous and dominating toward females is, in their view, proof that they are "real men" and that they fit in with the other boys. This "masculine mystique," as philosopher Myriam Miedzian calls it,[22] suggests that if girls and women are equal to boys and men, then boys and men cannot be sufficiently masculine. The masculine mystique masks a sense of vulnerability: Masculinity must continually be proven lest the "truth"—that a boy is not genuinely masculine—be revealed. As the rock group Sublime sings, "If it wasn't for date rape I'd never get laid." Beneath the rapist's frightening alacrity for violence lies an astonishingly honest expression of insecurity—the anxiety that he could never successfully attract a woman. Date rape, this song's character suggests, is a brutal but sometimes necessary act of last resort—if one is to remain a "real man."

The masculine mystique leads many boys to feel entitled to treat girls like bodies that can be used to satisfy sexual needs. Many jocks in particular share the macho belief that nothing matters more than scoring, on the playing field and in the bedroom. These boys may use the word "bitch" as a synonym for "girl"; their idea of summer fun may be to "whirlpool"— to go to a public pool, lock arms and shoulders with their male friends, surround any girl unlucky to be in their path, and rip off her bathing suit. Ten years down the road, some of these boys no doubt will be sexually harassing their female colleagues.

Sometimes, obviously, sexual teasing is playful, not malicious, and it's unfair and ridiculous to presume that all boys are sexually exploitative and that their every sexual initiative is an act of harassment. Many teenage boys treat girls with respect. They may urgently want a sexual relationship with a girl, and may make sexual banter with her but would never dream of physically or emotionally pressuring her. Besides, many teenage girls not only enjoy the attention of boys who eye them up and down, they return the once-over themselves. The point is that adolescent sexual expression, like all sexual expression, can be welcome or unwelcome, respectful or bullying. A key in determining which is which is the balance of power. If the girl is treated as an equal, if she is in control, and if she feels free to reciprocate, then let's chalk up a point for women's rights.

But sexual equality is a rare find in high schools. The fact is that you would be hard-pressed to distinguish some schools from Tailhook conventions. Indeed, two thirds of girls in grades eight through eleven reported in a 1993 survey conducted by Louis Harris & Associates that they had been touched, grabbed, or pinched in a sexual way. As a result of this sexual attention, a third of the girls reported that they did not want to go to school or talk in class, and 17 percent said that they thought about changing schools.[23] Nan Stein, director of the Sexual Harassment in Schools Project at

Wellesley College's Center for Research on Women, keeps an eye on the routine acts of sexual harassment that occur in elementary and high schools around the country: boys groping at girls' bodies, pulling down their gym shorts, and flipping up their skirts. They do it brazenly, beneath the bright glare of fluorescent lights, in full view of students and teachers. Stein cites other everyday examples of school sexual harassment: circulating "summa cum slutty" or "piece of ass of the week" lists; designating special weeks for "grabbing the private parts of girls"; and sexualized jokes and skits mocking girls' bodies performed at school assemblies or half-time performances.[24]

Sexual harassment is part of the culture even at the tony Saint Paul's boarding school in Concord, New Hampshire, according to Maya, a recent graduate. At this "WASP white male bastion," she reveals, "the boys would call the most attractive girls 'beavers' or 'tunas,' and soon the girls started calling themselves 'beaves.' For instance, the girls called other girls from New York 'cosmo beaves.' There was also this cat-calling thing that the boys did to the girls. They would make this noise that sounds like 'fwop' and they would call you a fwop. Basically it was the sound of a vaginal fart. The word took on the meaning of a girl who is pretty and desirable. And then the girls started to call each other fwops too—like, 'Oh my God, that's so fwoppish.' The boys instigated it and the girls took it on in order to fit in. It was a way for girls to make themselves more powerful by making others less powerful and putting them in their place. Looking back, I'm most horrified by the fact that the administration never did anything. They never said a word that it wasn't okay, that this was not the way to treat girls."

By equating desirable girls with their genitalia, the boys at Saint Paul's were saying that the only enticing thing about femininity is the possibility of sex—denying the fact that girls also possess humor, skills, and personalities. But why did the girls themselves take on the words beave and fwop? Perhaps seizing ownership of the words was their way of fighting back. If they used these words casually, jokingly, then the words' insulting tenor could be transformed into ironic self-awareness of their subordinate position—much in the way that many gays like to call themselves "queer" and blacks "nigger." On the other hand, by going along with the insults, the girls also yielded to the prevalent idea that it's normal for boys to reduce females to their sexual parts, and that "good" girls remain loyal to boys. Girls, too, can be seduced by the masculine mystique. In many schools, jocks are a source of immense pride, and no one wants to dampen school spirit, much less hurt the reputation of the community. In the case of Saint Paul's, for instance, formerly an all-boys school, the male students represent the school's prestigious legacy and ensure that its burnished image will continue to glow—and what girl would want to be responsible for tarnishing that image?

In any event, protesting to school authorities often doesn't get results. Many girls recognize that somehow the blame will fall on them, not on their harassers. In an all-too-typical case, a fifteen-year-old girl reported that she repeatedly had her buttocks grabbed and objects thrown down her shirt by a group of six or more boys. During each incident she told the boys to stop and that their behavior upset her. The girl complained to the teachers (who had observed the boys' behavior without intervening), but they did nothing to stop the incident. Then the girl reported the situation to the vice principal, who told her to handle it herself. Finally the girl returned to the vice principal a second time, who did nothing more than tell her to stay out of class that day if she was upset. Ashamed, the girl confided in her sister that the teachers and vice principal made her feel "like a 'slut.'"[25]

Some boys feel entitled to grope, grab, and have sex with "easy" or "slutty" girls—and they may see all girls as sexual objects who are "easy" or "slutty." Consider members of Lakewood, California's, Spur Posse, who in 1992 and 1993 competed with each other to score "points" for sexual conquests. The higher the number of girls a Spur Posse member had intercourse with, the higher his point tally. (Fifty or a hundred acts of intercourse with the same girl didn't count: one girl was equivalent to one point, no matter how many times a Spur had intercourse with her.) Seven members of the Spur Posse—named for the San Antonio Spurs basketball team—were arrested in March 1993 for allegedly molesting or raping a number of Lakewood girls. Charges were dropped in all but one case—involving a ten-year-old—because it turned out that the girls had consented in at least some of the cases, and in the others the D.A. was unable to prove that nonconsensual sex had occurred. Many classmates complained that the charges were unfair because, they said, the girls had been willing partners; Joey Soelter, a female Spur Posse defender, said that the girls involved deliberately sought out sex with members to improve their popularity ratings.[26]

Regardless of whether or not some or none of the cases fit the legal definition of rape, everyone who witnessed the Spur Posse members in action described their sexual behavior in predatory terms. One girl revealed that when teachers weren't around, the Spurs would corner her in the halls and solicit sex, that they said to her, "Hey slut, why don't you come over and do me, bitch?" and that they would hit her in the buttocks and pinch her.[27] Several others told investigators that they submitted to sexual acts because they were afraid of the boys.[28] One student said that the boys "take advantage of girls and treat them like crap in the morning."[29]

Even Soelter admitted of her friends that "If one guy gets it from one girl, then the other Spur Posse members think it's their right to get that point from the same girl." In one such incident, when the girl refused, the Spur allegedly took her clothes and refused to return them; he only relented when she screamed for help.[30] The Spurs' sense of entitlement apparently extended beyond the sexual sphere: At the time of the arrests Spur Posse founder Dana Belman was awaiting trial

for charges of stealing guns, credit cards, and jewelry and trying to run over several girls with a pickup truck (charges that
The New York Times described as "unrelated" to the rape
charges).[31]

But guess who was villainized? That's right: the girls. Most
Lakewood students rallied behind the Spurs, defending them
as "red-blooded American boys" and denouncing the girls as
"sluts."[32] Don Belman, father of founder Dana as well as
Kristopher, an arrested Spur, bragged that his sons' behavior
was normal and healthy and that the real culprit was the girls,
who "are promiscuous. We live in a promiscuous society. I
can tell you these girls around my son are giving it away. It's
frightening."[33] Even if we imagine that every single sexual
encounter had been consensual, is that a legitimate reason to
insult the girls as "promiscuous" and "sluts"? Meanwhile the
Spurs were treated like celebrities as they toured the talk-
show circuit, making appearances on *Maury Povich, Phil
Donahue, Montel Williams, Jenny Jones, Jane Whitney,
20/20,* and the *Home Show.* Some of them earned as much as
$2,500 for an appearance. One Spur, Chris Albert, revealed
that producers from one show took them out to "the greatest
restaurants in New York.... We felt like movie stars or something."[34]

We may never know the extent to which the Spurs coerced,
conned, or simply cajoled their sexual partners into having
intercourse. What we do know is that they regarded girls as
"slutty" sexual objects rather than as equals, and that the
boys, girls, and adults of Lakewood largely accepted this attitude. Indeed, girls can be so in need of social approval that
they confuse harassment for acceptance—thinking that any
attention is better than none. Since many girls as well as boys
buy the idea that sexual aggression and exploitation is normal
masculine behavior, it may not even occur to them to demand
to be treated as equals.

ANDREA BAUMGARDNER, THIRTY, grew up in a small town in the Midwest wanting everybody to like her. In high school she strived to become very popular and regularly went to parties with older boys. She admits that to be respected by the popular kids at school, she "would do anything." One night at a party she drank so much she became semiconscious—in that state she was incapable of consenting to sex—and was raped by her boyfriend's best friend. Word got out around school that Andrea had had willing sex with her boyfriend's friend, and she experienced all the usual forms of slut-bashing. But three years later Andrea ended up dating the boy who had raped her. "I was kind of excited that I was getting all this attention from him," she concedes, though she's also fully aware that "in light of everything, it was sort of perverse."

My mother is a teacher by trade, but basically she raised us. My father paid back his medical-school tuition through the army, so until I was about eight we moved around a lot. Then we settled in a very parochial, small town in the Midwest. By the time we got there, I was shy and well behaved. I tested well and I was sensitive. I tried to do things to keep everyone around me happy.

One day, several years after we had moved, we spontaneously moved again to the other side of town, which was older and more established, because my mother had found an old house that she fell in love with. I was going into eighth grade when it happened and I had to switch junior high schools. At the time the move seemed like a really huge thing, and for me it was traumatic. I resented my mom for making the decision and I felt that my parents didn't understand that it was so hard for me.

I had already gotten my period but I wasn't developed. I was tall and gangly. I thought I was fat, but when I look at pictures, I see that I was very normal, even on the thin side.

I remember my first day of school very vividly. It was a cliquish school because the kids had been going to school together since they were six and their families seemed almost related. I remember getting out of the car and walking up to the door and weaving through these little groups and I didn't know anybody. I didn't have the aplomb to introduce myself; I just stood there, terrified that I wouldn't live through it.

But in a sense it was a chance to remake myself. I propelled myself to try out for basketball, which I had never played in my life. My dad was a big athlete and really busy and I think I gravitated toward the sports that he played so that we could play them together. I rode my bike to the first basketball practice and got hit by a car and was scraped up. The police came and offered to take me home, but I felt compelled to go to practice because I thought that if I didn't make it I couldn't be on the team. So I just went to practice all bleeding and dirty, and after that I became known, strangely enough, for being tough. After that incident I had some piece of notoriety.

I started smoking cigarettes and tried drinking a few times. I did it after practice in the afternoons or in between classes out by the gas station, which was a block and a half away. I was pretty lame at it, but in order to get respect I would do anything.

I definitely wanted everybody to like me, regardless of who they were. It didn't matter if they were popular or not. It was especially good if the popular people liked me, of course, because life became easier, but I generally just wanted to be everyone's friend. There were about 250 people in my grade and I think that pretty much everyone knew who I was. I started telling jokes and became sarcastic. I was "on" all day, but then I came home and just fell to pieces because it really wasn't me. Of course at the time I had no sense that that was what was happening. When I was at home, I would yell at my mother and stomp around and cause problems with everyone in my family because I was enraged and frustrated.

In late fall I went to a party with mostly people my age, ninth-graders and a couple of tenth-graders. I had kind of broken up with this guy Jeff the week before, but we were supposedly getting back together that night. I sort of felt like, "Okay, I have Jeff in the palm of my hand. I just have to play tonight right." I drank too much in the beginning, trying to whoop it up with people and create a sense of camaraderie, without realizing that I was propelled by nervousness. I was smoking and being sort of outrageous. At one point I realized that I was really drunk; my head was spinning. So I went to lie down in one of the rooms and fell asleep.

Jeff's best friend, Tommy, came in when I was sleeping and started kissing me. Basically he took off enough of my clothing so that he could have sex with me. I wasn't knocked out so much that I was unconscious. I was out of it, but I wasn't dead asleep. I had this feeling that something really awful was happening. He penetrated me, and it was the first time for me. I just lay there. For some reason I didn't feel the strength to change anything or to get up or to scream or to act. I think that part of that was that I really wanted to be accepted by all these people and be cool—yet at the same time I think I knew that they wouldn't accept me once they found out what was happening, that everything would be over.

In the true sense of the word I was raped because it wasn't consensual and I wasn't truly awake. I had gone into this room because I knew I was passing out, not with the intention of having sex. But I didn't classify it as rape until years later. I was home from college and I was talking with my sister about it when it dawned on us at the same time that it was rape. I had always felt that I had done something really wrong, that I had allowed it to happen, that I had allowed someone to take advantage of me, that I had allowed myself to be cheapened. Sometimes I wonder now why I didn't stop it. It amazes me to think of the powerful and double-edged fear of not being accepted or of being a prude or of being a "slut." Not too long ago I told my therapist about it and I said, "You know, I feel this overriding guilt because I wasn't tied down, so there's no concrete, easy explanation for why I couldn't move."

I don't know if Jeff knew that Tommy had come in. They were

such immature boys that who knows. Afterward I got up and out of there and was really upset. I was crying. I ended up going home and I felt very weird, like I was in some sort of limbo. The party was on Saturday night, and the next day I still felt strange and weird about the whole thing but didn't really know how to move forward. Then Jeff called me that day and said, "I will never talk to you again. You are such a fucking bitch, you're such a slut"—all the blanket reprisals a person can say. He had learned about it through Tommy.

By Monday most of the people I'd ever seen at school knew that I had sluttily gone into some room with Tommy when Jeff liked me. Tommy had told everybody. I don't know what things he said exactly, but by the time I heard them, they were crazy. I heard stories about how I was at another party and fucked two guys, even though I had really been at home with my parents. From that point none of the girls who had been at the party would talk to me and no one at school would talk to me. I think there were two people out of 250 at school who would talk to me. Even my best friends, later, asked me, "Why are you sleeping around?"

The really bad stuff lasted for several months. It was so hard for me to get through a day in school. For a long time I pretended to have the flu. And I didn't go anywhere; all of a sudden no one was calling me. I had no friends left. I wonder if the teachers knew that something bad was going on. No one ever protected me, that's for sure. I was still a really good student, just because the school wasn't that hard. The teachers probably figured, "Oh, she's not a problem, so why worry about her."

I felt that I had done something really wrong. The only time I felt righteous in fighting back was when they started writing in pen on my locker at school. Things like "You big fucking fat whore," "You take two guys at the same time." Stupid junk that was so crushing. I told my mom, "These people who were my friends are writing on the locker." And she said, "You tell them that we will press charges for libel and slander. You pass that around and it will stop." And it worked; it scared the hell out of them.

It did definitely get better and then I did have some friends, different friends. I was on a quest to reinstate myself as a popular person. I tried very hard to be everything to everybody. I helped people with homework and became involved again in sports. I played tennis and went to basketball games and football games and hockey games. I just sort of insinuated myself in the action all the time. It worked in a certain sense, since I became socially involved again, but I never felt comfortable. I always felt like I was sort of hanging on. I met two people—one girl and one boy—during that time who became really good friends and never believed the hype. The boy had his locker next to mine and he won my mother's heart forever because he erased the graffiti on my locker before I got there.

I started dating some older guys, juniors and seniors, because of course after the stories circulated about me, they were fairly interested in me. There were some awful experiences, but nothing unusual—just the general stuff that happens to everyone on high school dates—when someone tries to take advantage of you or do things you don't want and it's not comfortable or good but not something I would characterize as criminal. I remember people who supposedly were dating friends of mine would basically maul me at parties. They came up to me and tried to make out with me or stick their hands up my shirt. It must have been related to the fact that they thought I was easy. Why else would they do that? On the other hand, even though I had the reputation, I didn't really put out. I dated only about three people.

In high school I got what I felt I needed to get, which was a ridiculous goal of popularity. I was up for homecoming queen and I spoke at graduation. Just stupid stuff. I continued going to parties every weekend night and I still smoked and drank occasionally. But at the same time my self-esteem was shattered. I felt very helpless and worthless.

I dated Tommy as a senior, which is sort of a weird twist. He was funny and charismatic and kind of cute and popular. It started because he came to my tennis games in the summer before senior year. He would show up and he ingratiated himself with my parents. If nothing had happened previously, you could say that he was acting in a gallant way. But in light of everything, it was sort of perverse. I was kind of excited that I was getting all this attention from him. We went out on and off during senior year. It was not a healthy relationship.

I was really squeamish about sex. For the rest of high school I was able to handle sex only as long as I wasn't involved with the person and didn't really care about them. I don't remember ever feeling excited about sex with Tommy. It was just like—whatever. "This is what we're going to do right now, but I'm not involved in it. You can't get to me." There was such a separation for me in order to get through certain parts of my life that I was never really tuned in. I didn't feel involved until I was twenty years old. Even though the mechanics of sex didn't scare me, the idea of being intimate with someone did.

When we graduated, I was at the point where I was really angry and I confronted him about what he did to me freshman year. I said, "You don't even realize that you fucked a whole year at least of my life." He intimated to the younger sister of a friend of mine that he had taken advantage of me when we were younger, and he cautioned her against guys like him.

I haven't dated a "guys' guy" in a long time—someone who watches football. Those were the kind of guys I had tried to date in high school. But since college, the men I end up getting close to are supersensitive. I don't identify these men as foreign and scary. I like people who are in touch with their emotions and I especially like men who have a lot of other women friends in their lives and can deal with women really well.

Being raped and having the reputation made me realize that I could trust nobody. I think I've had a very cynical view of people ever since and I have a hard time trusting people with anything that is very important to me. For the past few years I've developed a few very close friends and I've certainly lost interest in being

Glen Ridge

popular, that's for sure. I've become more insular. The experience made me angry and I didn't deal with the anger until much later. Even now sometimes I wish that I could write an open letter to my old community because I know it happens again every year. It's such a common experience. "For the girl you take out to the back-seat of your car, this is what she's going to think about for the next six years, and she's going to spend this much money in therapy dealing with it."

I'm sometimes now amazed that at the time I didn't break. I think if I had been in tune with myself, I would have fallen apart. But something made me go on. I ultimately know that I am strong, even if I do get depressed. I know that I can withstand anything, and I think it's from that experience.

A RITE OF PASSAGE

Like the Spur Posse, the jocks from Glen Ridge, New Jersey, looked at their female classmates as nothing more than sexual servicers. And, like the girls who "dated" Spurs, the jocks' sexual partners were degraded in the process. In March 1989, four popular, beefy Glen Ridge athletes—all seniors—lured a severely retarded seventeen-year-old girl to one of their homes. Once there, they rammed a broomstick, baseball bat, and another stick into the girl's vagina while nine others pulled up folding chairs to witness the action as if they were watching a movie. They cheered on the participants and yelled, "Put it in farther" and "Do it more." Six of the watching and cheering boys eventually left the basement, but not one tried to stop the rape or intervene in any way. The next day a group of thirty boys tried to convince the girl to return to the basement for a repeat performance, but she refused. The girl, who had no friends, attended a special school for retarded children, and had long been the target of jokes and pranks, did not actively resist the boys and was reluctant to report the assault because she regarded them as her friends and desperately sought their approval.

The four rapists—twins Kevin and Kyle Scherzer, Christopher Archer, and Bryant Grober—were the town's star athletes in football, baseball, and wrestling. When charges were brought against them in the spring of 1989, prompting national media scrutiny, people around the country were incredulous at the callous brutality of the boys, particularly since they came from such a "good," prosperous suburb, the very embodiment of the American Dream. But—once again—most of the residents of Glen Ridge rallied around the athletes, not the victim. They called her a flirt, a tease, a slut. They said that she had not been raped, that she had participated in, and even encouraged, an act of consensual sex. It's true that she never said no. But on the other hand, was she capable of saying yes? This is a girl who had the IQ of an eight-year-old. She thought that there were five states in the United States and that the country's two political parties were called "public" and "private."[35]

When investigative journalist Bernard Lefkowitz attended the boys' graduation reception, one parent standing near him said with a sigh, "It's such a tragedy." It took Lefkowitz a moment to realize that the man was not talking about the victim but about the boys who had raped her. "They're such beautiful boys and this will scar them forever."[36] During the five-month trial, neighbors donated over thirty thousand dollars to the families of the defendants to defray their legal bills. Rather than exploring the incident with students, the faculty and Glen Ridge High urged them "not to be judgmental"; the female superintendent of schools asked them to "stand by our boys."

In his masterful account of the Glen Ridge gang rape and the environment that bred it, *Our Guys,* Lefkowitz exposes the jocks' contemptuous treatment of girls throughout childhood and adolescence. He demonstrates that what happened to the victim could easily have happened to any other girl, retarded or not, and that in many respects her experience is very similar to that of rape victims everywhere. He notes how

categories.
submissive

in high school the jocks divided girls into two categories, both of them characterized by their submissiveness. The first comprised cheerleaders, who baked the jocks cakes and decorated their lockers; in return they got invited to the jocks' parties and were considered "popular." The only other girls the jocks paid any attention to were those regarded as sexual objects. But "[f]ace-to-face intercourse, sharing pleasure equally, was rare. Sex was something that was done to them, not something they actively participated in. Hand jobs and blow jobs—*jobs* that girls performed at their bidding."[37] The jocks bragged to one another about their sexual conquests and enjoyed degrading their sex partners, calling them "animals." "For a lot of boys," says Lefkowitz, "acting abusively toward women is regarded as a rite of passage. It's woven into our culture."[38]

On the other hand, it would be patronizing to assume that all of the girls were victimized. Surely some engaged in these sexual encounters willingly, enjoyed themselves, and remained in full control, perhaps unaware that behind their backs they were called animals. But let's face it, even these girls were exploited. From the way residents of Glen Ridge described the jocks' sexual behaviors to Lefkowitz, it sounds like the last thing on the jocks' minds was giving pleasure to the girls. The jocks certainly did not want sexual relationships based on mutuality.

If a Glen Ridge girl gave the jocks oral sex they said she was "Hoovering"—a reference to vacuum cleaners. One of their favorite practices was what they termed voyeuring: As one boy engaged in a sexual encounter at a party, his friends, tipped off in advance, would watch from inside the closet. They would then ask the girl if she could do it to them too. In school on Monday morning they would tell everyone about the girls they'd "voyeured." One teacher told Lefkowitz, "You hear the asides, but, as a teacher, what do you do?"[39]

The principal and vice principal, both former coaches, never reprimanded the jocks. On the contrary, they identified themselves as jocks as well and proudly displayed the boys' trophies in glass cases. When the jocks' grade-point averages sank below the required minimum to stay on a team, they succeeded in convincing the school to let them remain anyway. Lefkowitz points out that during these kids' middle and high school years there were no females in high-level positions in the school administration.

One of the boys who would later participate in the rape, Kevin Scherzer, habitually exposed his penis and masturbated in the middle of class (he wore sweatpants for easy access), tapping the shoulders of girls sitting nearby to make sure he had their attention. His teachers saw the behavior but did nothing about it. As they swaggered through the school's halls, Kevin and the other jocks would grind their bodies against girls in mock copulation and would pin them to their lockers.

Yet when Kevin Scherzer and his jock buddies were charged with rape, all of a sudden it was the rape victim who couldn't control *her* sexual impulses. Years' worth of sexually hostile acts forced upon female classmates went unmentioned because that's how normal, healthy, red-blooded teenage boys behave, right? When the rape case came to trial in 1992–93, the defense attorneys called the victim a promiscuous "Lolita," repeatedly characterizing her as a sexual aggressor who had consented to everything that occurred in the basement. They dismissed the idea that she didn't understand that she had been insidiously manipulated. Outside the courtroom one of the defense attorneys, Michael Querques, said, "This girl is a pig.... She's just a plain pig. If she wasn't retarded, everybody'd say, She's a pig. She's somebody I'd keep my kids away from. I'd make sure I protected them from *her*."[40] He was referring to a girl who had the mental capacity of a second-grader and who, right before she testified in court, clung to a doll she had kept since she was two years old.

Ultimately the jury arrived at a guilty verdict for first-double standard

degree rape for three of the jocks, but the judge let them go free until after their appeals were decided. Eight years after the rape, two of them were sentenced to maximum terms of fifteen years and one to a maximum term of seven years. The minimum sentences, taking into account behavior in prison, was two years for two of the jocks and ten months for the third.

The scariest thing about some boys' assumption that they are entitled to, for example, masturbate in the middle of class and pin and grind girls against their lockers is that girls sometimes come to believe in the boys' entitlement. The boys who turn school into their sexual playground, after all, are usually popular athletes who win trophies, applause, and pats on the back from coaches, parents, and school administrators. Whatever they're doing is obviously considered acceptable, otherwise they'd be kicked off teams or suspended from school or, at the very least, ordered to stop. But since in many schools reprimands are far and few between, these boys rule the social scene. A girl is left with the lesson that if she wants to be socially accepted, she must be submissive to these boys' demands, even though sexual submissiveness leads to being called a slut.

NINETEEN-YEAR-OLD TAMIKA HARPER, currently a college student in Atlanta, was a deliberate tease in high school. She aggressively pursued sexual relationships in order to feel in control of her sexuality. Many teen girls follow her example. But consider this: The only reason Tamika was so forward in the first place, she tells me, was that she was raped in the eighth grade and, as a result, felt robbed of a sense of control. Her working theory was that willingly having intercourse with a number of boys would make her feel in control. It didn't.

I've lived with my grandmother and great-grandmother since I was two. I have a younger sister, but she stays with my mom.

My mom is a hair stylist and my grandmother was a school-teacher before she retired. My father died last month of a heart attack, but I didn't really know him since my parents were never married.

I went to elementary school in Atlanta, where I was a tomboy and a nerd. I climbed trees to get away from every-body so I could study. And I played basketball. I was mostly friends with boys from the neighborhood. I loved school and had very good grades. Before eighth grade I didn't know what a B was. I was very happy and I had a lot of friends. They were smart and kind of goofy and outgoing. We were all playful and loud. In class we were quiet, but once class was over we were all in the playground having fun. There was a bakery down the street from school and we would all walk down to the bakery and get doughnuts. My grandmother taught at my old elemen-tary school and my friends' mothers worked down the street, so we all played together for hours until they got off from work. We had sleepovers at my house and I got to stay at other peo-ple's houses. There weren't many restrictions. It was a nice childhood and my best friend from elementary school, Evelyn, is still my best friend.

In sixth grade I switched to a different school in a suburb of Atlanta where I live. My old school was almost entirely black but the new one was very mixed because it has this program that tries to get black and white kids together, though my friends were always black. When I got to the new school, there was a real fashion thing. We were young, so we were still wearing what our parents told us to wear. But everyone was wearing Starter coats—it's an athletic-looking jacket with the Starter logo that costs like $150—and that was the hip thing to wear. I found the fashion thing annoying because I always liked wearing plaid skirts and blouses or dresses. But the popular people in my suburb all wore high tennis shoes and athletic gear. I guess I became popular because everyone knew me and I was the pres-ident of the sixth- and seventh-grade classes. I was outgoing and hung around with the popular crowd.

After basketball practice in November of eighth grade, I was raped. I was twelve years old and a virgin. My grandfather had come to pick me up because practice ended at eight P.M. I was downstairs in the locker room taking my shower. And there was this guy hanging around downstairs that I sort of recognized from football games but I didn't know him. He didn't go to my school, but he was friendly with some of the tenth-grade guys from my school. So I took my shower very quickly and got my things and started to go up the steps. I was about to turn a corner on the staircase when he grabbed my hand. No one else was around. I said, "My grandfather's upstairs so I have to go." He said, "No, wait, I want to tell you something." And I said, "I can't, I have to go."

He tried to kiss me and then he took off my basketball shorts. He was very strong and muscular and I couldn't move. He put his hand over my collarbone so my neck was down. And with his other hand he pulled my hand behind me. I couldn't breathe or anything because he kept biting on my mouth. He penetrated me and it really hurt. He came on my stomach and got up and walked out through a side door. I pulled up my shorts and went upstairs. I don't think it lasted that long because my grandfather didn't say anything like, "You've been gone a long time, what happened?" I had these bite marks on the side of my mouth and I didn't want him to see, so I walked with the opposite side facing him.

When I got home I called Evelyn and asked her to come over for the night. Her sister brought her over because we weren't old enough to drive. I cried the whole night. My grandmother didn't know anything because she was sick and always went to bed by eight P.M. Evelyn was like, "You need to tell the police." But I didn't want to because I was afraid. I don't know. I thought they'd think it was my fault because I always wore skirts and all the other girls wore pants. They weren't short skirts, but they weren't long either. They were like knee-length. I thought the police would say that I was asking for it. Now I don't think they would have said it and I know it wasn't my fault, but at the time I thought they would blame me. Now I feel kind of stupid that I didn't say anything.

Evelyn kept saying that I should put aside my clothes in a bag and not wash them, but I did wash them. My skin was red because I kept rubbing it real hard. I felt dirty and nasty, so I wanted to feel squeaky clean. I rubbed my arms and legs and my stomach and my neck and my face and all that.

The next day was another school day, but Evelyn and I go to different schools, so her sister came and picked her up. I went to school and found out that the guy who raped me had said something to some of his friends who went to my school. Not that he raped me, but that he had sex with me. So I kind of felt some of the tenth-grade guys looking at me when I walked down the hallways. They found a way to be in the same halls that I was in, even though I had never seen them before. That day I saw them the whole day. They kept looking at me like they wanted to have sex with me too.

I stopped talking to people. I went from being an A student to a D and F student and I had to go to summer school after eighth grade. I stopped talking in class and stopped doing my homework. I didn't do tests; I just put my name on them and handed them in. I was depressed and just confused. I stopped going to church. The only thing I kept doing was basketball. I'd come home from school and go into my room and cry every night when I should have been doing homework. My grandmother didn't notice because she was getting sicker and sicker. Then I'd come out and run around the neighborhood to exercise and shoot some baskets. Then I'd eat, take my shower, and go to bed. I didn't talk to my mom at all that year. I lost a lot of weight; I went from 125 to 95 pounds, but everybody thought it was because of basketball.

I also started to change the way I dressed. I was ashamed of my body and I thought people could look at me and see the scars he left. So I stopped with the skirts and started with overalls and baggy jeans. I felt like with the skirts, guys could see my legs. With my new clothes I felt comfortable and I didn't have to worry about them trying to look at me.

At school I was still considered popular. People were like, "She's so cool. She sets her own rules and does what she wants to." They thought my behavior was some kind of statement. No one knew how I was really feeling. One teacher came up to me and said, "I know something is going on," even though she didn't really know. She was real arrogant about it. "Do you want to talk about it?" I said no. She thought it had something to do with my grandmother because all the teachers knew I lived with her. I just kept saying, "I don't want to talk about it."

I also became a tease: I felt that I would rather give it away then have it taken. I wanted to be in control. My whole attitude changed. So I messed around with a bunch of people, but I didn't have actual sex. I enjoyed it and had orgasms, so I got something out of it. I started with guys from the neighborhood—these were the same guys I played basketball with and was in the trees with from my tomboy days. Then I switched to guys from school. How many guys did I mess around with? Lord, I'd say for the rest of eighth grade it was about a dozen guys, six from the neighborhood and six from school.

In ninth grade was the first time I lost my virginity willingly. I had sex with something like three guys in the first month. But one of the guys had a big mouth and told everyone in the whole school. I found out because a guy came up to me and said, "I heard what you did. Can I be next?" I was like, "What?!" That kind of shocked me, that he was so bold. I had a lot of offers like that—you know, "Can I be next?," "Can I be a lucky one?" They assumed I was really easy. People called me a freak. Freak is a universal term—it means ho, slut, tramp, whatever. A girl who has sex a lot is a "freak."

During lunch hour my friends and I always sat at the same table; I don't want to say it was the best table but it was where the popular people sat. Guys would bring us notes. They were basically unsigned letters and they were brought over to individual girls. The notes I got all said things like, "Do me" or "Fuck me." Some of the other girls got a few of these notes, but I got a lot of them. Some days nothing would happen, and maybe on Friday I'd think to myself that I was having a good week, but then I would get another note. And I think the guys were serious. Like if I had ever said yes, I think they would have gone for it.

My first reaction was relief. I guess it was the control thing. Because they asked. I was like, "Yeah, they ask now." It was like things had leveled out. I felt like I had proven my point, but it got too out of hand, like I had proven my point too well. I got sick of it and started to have regrets, so I stopped having sex. I was afraid of people saying stuff about me. But the only way I could clear up the whole thing would be to say that I was raped, and I couldn't do that.

In tenth grade once again my personality and style changed. I went from wearing big clothes to preppie clothes—Polo slacks and golf shirts and sweaters and preppie shoes. I don't want to say that everybody followed me, but when I changed to baggy clothes, they changed to baggy clothes, and when I changed again, they changed again also. They were so dumb, because I was crying out for help and they thought it was a fashion statement. I started to attract a different breed of guys. They weren't the "Hey yo" type of guys. They were more respectful. They were the best athletes and the best students—not the nerdy guys but smart guys who were also cool. Most of the older guys had graduated, so these guys didn't care about the reputation, and I wasn't having sex. So I sort of had the opportunity to start over again.

But then I got this other type of reputation in eleventh grade. There was one gay girl at our school and she was interested in me. She had gotten into an argument with her girlfriend on the football field and said, "That's why I'm looking at someone else and her name is Tamika"—and she said it really loud. I didn't know the girl at all, but it got back to me that she was interested, and everyone found out. So that's when people started calling me "gay girl." It started off as a joke, but then people really did start believing it. They'd say, "There goes gay girl." Once again the way I dressed got me in trouble. I thought I was doing something good by wearing the slacks and shoes and sweaters, but everyone said, "She's dressed like a little white boy, so she must be gay." True enough, after I was raped, I thought a woman would treat me better, but I had never been with one and I had never made any advances.

I was mad because it wasn't true and I couldn't control it. The other thing—being called a slut—I could control because all I had to do was stop having sex and then everybody shut up. I was upset because I didn't know why they were doing this. Guys and girls both did it, but girls were worse. They did it right to my face. We'd be sitting at the lunch table and one day a new girl sat with us. I guess she didn't know it was me because she said, "Where's the gay girl you've all been telling me about?" Everybody was trying to kick her under the table because I was right there.

By senior year there were about a hundred rumors. People were really bold about it. Like, I don't drink because I don't like alcohol unless it's frozen and tastes like fruit. And if I'm tired, I leave when I want to leave, so I'm the one who always drives. But one guy made up this story that I was at this party and I got drunk and I sat on top of a table and told everybody, "Hey everybody, I'm gay." And people believed him. I just stopped speaking to the whole class—white, black, Chinese, Puerto Rican, everybody.

Now I'm a freshman in college and I still live with my grandmother. Nobody knows anything about the reputations. I'm really happy here because it's like a big high school where people don't bother you. I was lucky: I didn't get any STDs and I was never pregnant, but I did manage to get the name "slut," so go figure. Now I'm trying very hard to become a nerd again.

Guys might look nice, but you never know what they're thinking, so I don't walk anywhere by myself, even on campus in broad daylight. When I first registered for school and I had to walk around campus and I didn't know where I was going, I was a little fearful. I still feel uncomfortable when I have to stay in a room with a guy too long, like in a classroom. So I always sit in the very front, closest to the door. I don't hate men or anything, but I don't have a lot of trust. Every time I see a guy, I wonder if he finds me attractive, smart, or just another piece of ass. Will he ask for it or will he take it?

NOBODY BELIEVES YOU

The rape victim is caught in a double bind. First, she may not be believed when she claims she's been raped. If she has been sexually active, many people may find it hard to believe that she is capable of saying no (or that she has a right to say no once she has said yes). And since the sexual double standard stigmatizes "bad" girls, any girl who has been sexually active and then reports being raped may be accused of lying to avoid the social stigma. Second, people now regard her as "easy" and "slutty," leaving her vulnerable for another act of sexual violence.

The prevailing attitude among teens of both genders is that any girl who says she was raped invited it, deserved it, or is a liar. After Emilie Morgan was lured by a stranger into a small room in a shopping mall and raped at the age of thirteen, she told a few friends at school. Big mistake. "Junior high can be pretty tough when you acquire a reputation for being a slut," she reveals. "I was suddenly the most desirable girl in the school. It didn't matter that I still considered myself a virgin. To all the boys in school I was 'experienced,' and to all of the girls I was cheap."[41]

It may seem hard to believe that no one stood up for Emilie. After all, in the 1996 movie *Girls Town*, three high school girls go on a rampage after one of them has been date-raped by a football player. They destroy the rapist's car and spray-paint "rapist" on the hood. But real-life rapists have little to fear; such vigilante feminist acts are rare. Most girls distance themselves from the girl who says she's been raped. Literature instructor Pamela Fletcher explains why. When she was a high school student in the 1970s, a classmate named Rachel was gang-raped.

> The story was that she let a group of boys pull a train on her in the football field one night. I remember the snickers and the looks of disgust of both the girls and boys around campus.... But the word rape never entered my mind. After all, she knew them, didn't she? There was no weapon, no blood. She survived, didn't she? And, just what was she doing there all by herself, anyway? Now I know what "pulling a train" is. Now I know they committed a violent crime against her body and her soul. Now I know why she walked around campus with that wounded face, a face that none of us girls wanted to look into because we knew intuitively that we would see a reflection of our own wounded selves. So the other girls did not look into her eyes. They avoided her and talked about her like she was "a bitch in heat." Why else would such a thing have happened to her?[42]

Fletcher and her girlfriends avoided Rachel's gaze because on some level they were afraid that the boys could gang-rape them too. And so they explained away the gang-rape as the initiative of a "slut." It could never happen to them: They were good girls. Right? Ostracizing a raped classmate by calling her a slut is a way of protecting the status quo. In so doing, the ostracizers feel protected. In fact, however, these girls become even less safe because the rapist is not punished and therefore is able to rape again.

But you can't separate yourself from the school "slut"

without smothering your own sexual curiosity. In order to be truly rape-proof, you have to shut down your sexual desires. You must make sure that you can never be accused of inviting sexual encounters. You must be sexually passive. You must always say no. You must never say yes.

Ironically sexual passivity can lead to the very circumstance that it's supposed to dodge. Passivity, after all, can be misinterpreted as consent. If someone always says no and never says yes, how do you know when she truly means no? Sexual refusal loses all meaning. In this sexual script, girls and women go through the motions of seeming reluctant, whether or not they truly are; as a result, boys and men feel that it's okay to persuade or coerce their partners into acquiescence. Some boys and men go so far as to assume that they can have sex with someone who is passed out. Indeed, on some college campuses, 90 percent of sexually coerced encounters involve alcohol.[43]

The only way to ensure true consent is if both partners verbalize their desires. That way no always means no—and just lying there is not synonymous with yes. If sex requires the verbalization of desire, there's never a question about when rape has occurred. No one can accuse the rape victim of having "asked for it." But as long as girls are afraid of seeming "slutty," as long as they feel uncomfortable saying yes, there will be an ambiguous gray zone between consent and coercion.

It's the existence of this gray zone—when the woman says neither no nor yes yet feels pressured to have sex—that makes it so hard to collect information about rape and to punish the attackers. This gray zone makes men feel entitled to take what they can, often unaware that they are transgressing private boundaries. This gray zone makes women who have been victimized feel responsible for their victimization. We lack a vocabulary to describe encounters in this gray zone because, with the "slut" stigma hovering over them, women lack the vocabulary to assert their desires.

There's a flip-side type of sexual passivity too: always saying yes and never saying no. The girls who were eager to raise the point scores of Spur Posse members and to "Hoover" the popular Glen Ridge jocks were so desperate to fit in and be accepted into the popular crowd that they were reluctant to refuse sexual overtures. Sometimes, when you're feeling insecure, it's just easier to say yes and give in. Maya, the Saint Paul's graduate, explains, "When I had intercourse the first time, it was a social thing where I couldn't say no. I sort of surrendered because I couldn't handle the isolation if my boyfriend would break up with me or be angry with me, or if I weren't part of the group of girls who by that time had all had sexual relationships with their boyfriends. It was too much trouble to say no or to explain. It was easier just to say, 'Okay, climb on.'"

When girls possess the power to refuse or accept sex, and really mean it, they feel in equal control during sexual encounters. For Maya, the sexual act was not rape, but it wasn't entirely consensual either. Tellingly she adds that during the act she felt "like a whore."

CHAPTER 5

"NOT ONE OF US"

The Outsider

Growing up, I desperately wanted to wear the same fashions the other girls in my grade wore. A physician with a busy schedule, my mother had no clue about preadolescent trends. Her shopping philosophy was to refuse anything designer since she could get essentially the same thing without the label for less money. And since I was chubby, buying clothes was something of a tortured event: I hated trying things on in front of a mirror and would race through the chore, only to get home and realize I couldn't stand what I'd be wearing for the next school year.

Throughout sixth grade I pined for a Lacoste collared shirt with the alligator insignia. Everyone in my class had at least several; one girl had over a dozen. I saved my allowance for over two months to buy one—pink-and-aqua-striped—at a tennis shop; I wore it when I wanted to look extra nice. When knickers (yes, knickers) were the rage in seventh grade, I was one of three girls in my entire grade left wearing long pants. Never mind that the fashionably aware looked like leprechauns: I would have done anything to become a fellow leprechaun. But knickers didn't fit me; I had lost my baby fat but was still short, and knickers landed halfway down my calves. Then there was a brief moment when all the cool girls wore braided, brightly colored, elastic headbands across their foreheads. Finally: an affordable, one-size-fits-all item. Using my allowance money, I could go out and buy a headband on my own. But by the time I got to the store in a neighboring suburb that sold this prized gem, the trend was over.

Everyone knows that children and teens want to blend in and follow the crowd. And from whom do they learn this lesson? Adults of course. Let's face it: Americans follow the herd. If you want to be successful, we are told in myriad ways, conformity is the way to go. Look at corporate America, with its "team player" ethic and all the strict rules delineating what you can and cannot wear on Casual Fridays. Consider the cycles of women's fashion, which dictate when square-toed, chunky-heeled shoes are out and when pointy-toed, ankle-straining stilettos are in. And what about best-seller lists and electoral horse-race polls and movie box-office postings? Everyone wants to know what everyone else is reading and seeing and thinking—so that they can go out and read and see and think the very same things themselves.

If adults possess this tendency to efface themselves in this way, teenagers have it magnified to the thousandth degree. But studying and following the fashions of the times are not enough; teens also feel a need to be associated with fashionable people—the popular people. Their goal is to crack the glass ceiling that separates mere mortals from the "in" crowd. If they are unsuccessful, and most are, they console themselves with a clique of their own. Even an unpopular clique, the thinking goes, is better than no clique at all. This sentiment was nicely summed up by Anthony Michael Hall in the 1984 movie *Sixteen Candles*. A freshman geek, he defends his loser friends to the sophomore he obsesses over, Molly Ringwald. "The thing is that I'm kind of like the leader," he tells her, "kind of like the king of the dipshits." "Well," Ringwald responds, "that's pretty cool."

Being a member of a clique, a cohesive social group, gives a teenager a certain power, a status, a value. The more exclusive and elitist the group is, the more power it confers on its members. But all cliques are larger than the sum of their members. They endow their members with a smug sense of insularity that sets them apart from the "real world" of parents and siblings and teachers. Members radiate a sense of belonging and security.

But being part of a clique often exacts a heavy price: uniformity of thought and action. The clique tends to flatten out idiosyncrasies and signs of individuality. To be accepted into a clique, one generally has to minimize conflicts with the other members. And too often the glue that bonds clique members to each other is the practice of making fun of outsiders.

An extreme example of the damage done by conformity can be found in Japanese schools. Many Japanese boys who don't quite fit in with their peers or who have broken some school rule suffer from *ijime* (bullying) practically every day, according to the Ministry of Education, Science, Sports and Culture. Every year an alarming number of Japanese students commit suicide because they can't handle going to school where bullies beat them up, extort money, call them names, and peek in on them when they go to the bathroom—while teachers powder their heads with chalk dust or hit them with bamboo swords. Other students stand by passively, terrified that they will become the next victim.[1]

On our side of the Pacific, individualism among teenagers is sometimes appreciated. There's always some quiet, late-bloomer, loner-type kid who spends hours after school toiling alone on a science or art project that no one else knows much about. If she wins a prestigious Westinghouse award or a visual-arts school scholarship, everyone in the community will excitedly and proudly embrace her. On the other hand, what happens if the student never receives public recognition for her work or, for whatever reason, just isn't liked? All too often, if you are a boy or girl who deviates from the norm, if you are considered an "outsider," if your family is not upwardly mobile, if you are the most visible member of the "loser" clique, if you are gay in a school that's homophobic (and most schools are), forget about it: you may as well just kiss good-bye any chance at a reasonably contented adolescence. No wonder fifteen-year-old Amy Robinson, a Manhattan teenager, told *The New York Times* that "I just hate being a teenager. When people say it's the greatest years of your life, I think they should be shot."[2]

Many popular clique members, of course, are genuinely sensitive people who would never intentionally humiliate anyone. But many others can be like silicone breast implants: attractive and perky but also fake, hard, and poisonous. All too often, they make fun of girls who are on the very edge of the social and middle-class fringe—who can only afford ill-fitting hand-me-downs or who are overweight or who are rebel types who question authority—and call them sluts. (Meanwhile boys who aren't athletic or who like classical music or who wear funny-looking glasses are "fags"; and awkward teens of both genders are ridiculed as "geeks.") "Slut" serves as an all-purpose insult for any female outsider. All the social distinctions that make a teenage girl "other" are collapsed into a sexual distinction.

In junior high I was fortunate. Despite my less-than-fashionable clothes, my classmates accepted me and I enjoyed the psychological riches that come from possessing a group identity. I may have felt like an outsider, but I didn't come across as one. In high school, however, my interior assessment matched my external environment. My school was considered prestigious, and most of my new classmates came from wealthy, high-powered families; my more modest class background put me in the minority. I was also very physically developed—my body was jarringly different from those of my female classmates. I was different and vulnerable, and on the social fringe. This is why, to my mind, it was easy for classmates to think of me as a "slut."

The women who share their stories here likewise were marked as different in some way. They prove, better than anyone else, that it's not a girl's sexuality per se that gets her called a slut; it's who and what she represents. As a result of their reputations, two fulfilled their "slut" prophecy by sleeping around, and all engaged in self-destructive behaviors.

LAURA KRUPILSKI, NOW TWENTY-SEVEN, had three strikes against her in high school: She lived on welfare, was a new student, and was busty. Everyone thought she was easy, including the nuns and priests who ran her Catholic school. One teacher made a pass at her. One nun insinuated in front of an entire class that Laura was a sinner. And another teacher pointedly gave Laura an essay assignment on sin. Without friends or family to turn to, Laura was an outsider from every angle.

I was raised by my maternal grandparents, and my grandfather had a theory that if you walked down the block and ran into three people you knew, it was time to move. We lived that theory, so I went to two different high schools. The first was in New Jersey, and I was there through my freshman and sophomore year. But then my grandfather died and we moved to Scranton, Pennsylvania, and I didn't know anybody.

I had a lot of problems at my new high school, which was Catholic. It was a very small school and everyone knew everyone else. Most of the people who went to this school had families that had lived in Scranton a long time. They were mostly from working-class or upper-middle-class backgrounds. I think a lot of the problems came from the fact that I was from the wrong side of Scranton, living in a housing project. I was one of only a handful of students in my grade who received a scholarship to attend the school. So I got this reputation as being someone who was really easy, that I wasn't too particular about who I dated, that all you had to do was buy me a soda and you could get your way. It started during the second week of school. I noticed that people didn't want to have anything to do with me. I found out from one of the other girls who had a similar reputation what was going on. I didn't think I deserved a reputation because I didn't even start dating until the summer before my senior year.

This was an assessment based on who I hung out with and how I looked. I was a lot more developed than the other girls were. I had a woman's figure when a lot of the other girls were still in the process of developing. I didn't have a lot of money to get clothes, so some of my clothes were hand-me-downs and some of them were tight. There was a uniform at school, but mine was really somebody else's. It was sold to me and it never fit very well. And I've always been extremely...busty. So all that helped foster this reputation.

By the time I figured out what was going on, the only people who would have anything to do with me, other than boys who thought they were going to get something in return, were people who were kind of in the same position as I was—social outcasts at the school. So there were two or three other girls that I hung around with, mainly because they were interested in the same type of music and reading I was. We all had kind of the same reputation, or didn't fit in for whatever reason. Most of the other kids who lived in the housing project went to the technical high school. And they hated me; they thought I was a snotty person for going to the Catholic school. So these people were gossiping behind my back, too.

The girls were vicious to me. A lot of what I heard about me was secondhand, or I heard when people didn't think I was listening— "That bitch" or "That slut, what does she think she's doing?" or "She's falling all over that guy." Even today I really hate cattiness and I have a lot of problems with people gossiping—"Look at that person, she's so fat" or "She doesn't wear makeup."

The reputation got all over the place and I felt it was a danger to be attractive to anybody. I got to the point where I was so sick of it that I went from looking fairly feminine to looking masculine. I cut off my hair and got a butch cut and wore baggy clothes all the time. It was a way of hiding from people when I was walking down the street because I was afraid of being harassed. And it worked too. But I couldn't wear baggy shirts and coats to school because we had a uniform. It was a plaid miniskirt, right above the knee, white oxford shirt, and a maroon vest. And the vest definitely accentuated my bust. To this day I find it hard to dress up. I feel more comfortable in jeans, something that hides my body. I was so masculine-looking by the end of my junior year that I couldn't believe anyone would believe the stories anymore. But they did. The reputation lasted all the way to the day of graduation. The town was way too small, and everybody was in everybody else's business too much.

I had one history teacher who was a slimeball; oh God he was a slimeball. He made a couple of passes at me and I'm sure it was because he had heard stories about me. He made a lot of insinuating comments. He never touched me personally, but he did touch this other girl who was in the same situation I was. I would never let myself be in a room by myself with him. Had he been alone with me, he probably would have tried to do something else besides make comments.

When I was a junior, I found out that the people whom I'd been led to believe my whole life were my parents were in fact my grandparents. And the woman who I thought was my sister, Paula, was really my aunt. At around this time Paula got kicked out of the housing project and I didn't want to live with her after I found out the truth. So my grandmother and I rented an apartment on the west side of Scranton. My grandmother spent half of her time with Paula and half of her time with me. But I was basically living on my own because Paula needed her for child care. My grandmother kind of left me to my own devices. When she came by, for a few days each month, she'd sleep in a chair. She would give me money to pay for the rent and the food, but toward the end of the month there wasn't much left.

I met my first boyfriend when I was working at Arbie's the summer before senior year. He was the first person I was ever intimate with and the first person I had intercourse with. I think I was pretty much starved for affection because basically I felt that my grandmother had abandoned me at that point. He was six years older than I was and gorgeous. I was amazed that this gorgeous guy found me attractive—and this was when I had my butch cut. He helped the reputation along because it turned out that he was known for sleeping around. So people at school figured that if I was going out with him, I had to be doing stuff in order to keep him around, even though I was probably less sexually active than they were. Some of the popular girls in school were interested in this guy too, so when people at school found out, they were very spiteful about it.

Planned Parenthood was the only place where you could get birth control. I went there one day in the beginning of senior year and unfortunately I ran into somebody from school. By the time I got back to school the next day, everybody was whispering that I was pregnant, which wasn't true. And because it was a very small community of nuns, things did go back and forth.

When it came out that I supposedly was pregnant, one of the nuns at school really tried to make my life miserable. One day we were reading some passage in the Bible and it was about the concept of sex being a sin and why you shouldn't do it and how those who have sex without the covenant of marriage are sinners. And she wanted me to explain it, knowing full well what was going on and knowing full well that the rest of the class knew what was going on.

So there was all this gossip going around, and the principal felt that it was interfering with her management of the school. She called me into her office and wanted to know what was going on so that she could put an end to the discussion. I told her I wasn't pregnant and she believed me, but she didn't really have any sympathy for me. She scolded me for the fact that

I needed contraceptives and was basically like, "You're not old enough to make this decision." She wanted me to talk to one of the priests and to go to Catholic youth counseling services.

I started dating my second boyfriend in the middle of senior year, and that caused other problems. He was in a grade lower than I was and we were both social outcasts, which people found kind of amusing. He was rather homely actually. People just did not like him at all. He wasn't a great athlete. He was a nice guy, really sweet. We were definitely the talk of the school.

At the end of my senior year I did get pregnant, and had a miscarriage. My boyfriend told a friend, who told another friend, and then the news got out. And because of the incident the year before, people just started talking as soon as they heard, and then it just went from there. I missed about two weeks of school because I had been in bedrest. The theology teacher called me in and said, "Well, you missed this test. I'm not going to make you take it, but I want you to write a paper on your experience and how it affected you and how it affected your boyfriend and how it affected your relationship with God." I was also supposed to write about whether or not I thought I had sinned and how I would conduct my life differently from then on. That really got to me, and I basically broke down and started crying.

When I turned eighteen, I just had to get out of there. I moved to Detroit and I had one long-term relationship that was a complete disaster. I was used to feeling poorly about myself and I expected to be treated poorly. He was very insulting and said that I could never do anything right. He never hit or pushed me or anything like that, but he did a lot of things that made me feel even worse about myself than before. I pretty much let him use me. I was still getting used to the fact that I was a person.

Right after I broke up with him, I worked for three years as a process server—I served legal papers and filed them. The job was like a return to high school in some ways. There were only three other women besides me in the whole office. And I guess the guys thought I was the cutest one, because they were all over me and would make comments. They would tell me things they wanted to do with me, or make comments about what I was wearing. These were guys in their thirties and forties. I would tell these guys to cut it out, but to them it was kind of a joke. This was before Anita Hill, so I had never heard the term sexual harassment. But about three months after I left the job I realized that that was exactly what it was. I found out a few years later that the business was shut down because someone did file a sexual-harassment suit. But the atmosphere actually helped me, because I got to the point where I was able to tell these guys to fuck off. In a strange way it made me feel a lot better because I could deal with these guys on my own terms and they knew they should not do more than what they did.

"I'M SORRY"

Ask any adolescent, girl or boy, if they worry about what others think of them; chances are you won't have to wait one second before receiving an affirmative reply. (Adults, alas, are not much different—though they presumably possess at least a little more self-assurance.) This insecurity is the fuel that drives the conformist impulse. After all, high school students instantly form opinions of classmates they see or meet just once. Impression is everything. Better to dress the same as everyone else and hide contrary opinions or feelings than to risk social alienation. A lot of girls think that the more homogeneous they are—the more they look alike, the more they act alike—the more appealing they are and the more likely that they will be considered "in" or popular.

In the classroom one strategy is to slump down in one's seat, to never raise one's hand. Aligning one's shoulders directly behind the student in front of her—the student's equivalent of burying her head in the sand—is another way of avoiding being humiliated. But outside the classroom, when peers rather than teachers are the ones giving out the grades, most teens don't want to be ignored. They want to be noticed, as long as they're doing and saying the "right" things.

Many girls become pros at conformist habits—such as saying "I'm sorry" whenever they worry about dissing or disturbing a higher-status friend. "I'm sorry" is probably the most commonly uttered sentence in the teenage girl population (with "so it was like, whatever" coming in for a close second). Nicole, fifteen, from Rochester, New York, explains the rationale of the unnecessary apology. "When I was younger, I didn't like to have confrontations. If it looked like there was one coming, I'd be like, 'Oh, I'm sorry,' and then it would be over." Catherine, seventeen, from Manhattan, adds, "If I don't know a person well, and I'm trying to be friends with them and I want them to like me, and I do something that I realize might offend them or might be stupid, I'll immediately start apologizing. And then I'll apologize for apologizing." It's a vicious cycle.

Many girls aren't even aware of the fact that "I'm sorry" slips through their lips at the rate of oncoming space invaders in a video game. They only realize how truly self-effacing "I'm sorry" sounds when a friend shares the same habit. "I know it annoys people," admits Catherine. "It annoys me when people do it to me."

Like "I'm sorry," saying "You decide" whenever a decision needs to be made is a common ploy that girls use to veil what they really think and want. "Sometimes I think that my opinion sounds so stupid and people will say, 'Yuck, what's the matter with you?'" Anne, from Manhattan, worries to me. "Like if I want to go somewhere and I tell my friends, they'll be like, 'What's your problem? You want to go *there?*' So I always say, 'You decide. We can go wherever you want to go.' And I end up in places I don't want to be." When her girl-friends are deciding where to go or what to do, the stakes feel too high. She is afraid of being responsible if everyone has a bad time. She is afraid of losing her friends. She is afraid of becoming an outsider.

On the other hand, a girl can't be too much of a suck-up, or she won't ever be popular. The desperate desire to be accepted can be smelled a mile away. Popular kids know how to make their popularity seem effortless; anyone who tries too hard is clearly not one of them. A girl must walk a fine, thin line between going along with the crowd and maintaining an autonomous identity, between conformity and individuality. As Sharon Thompson, author of *Going All the Way,* observes, "Popularity requires conforming for the most part while making and publicizing an occasional distinction—being 'your own person,' expanding the ground of conformity rather than crossing the boundary. A girl who can't make a distinction doesn't have the social power to be popular. A girl who makes too many can't fit in."[3] No wonder the market for teenage girl products—Hard Candy nail polish, baby-look barrettes—is so tremendous: Girls buy things in a relentless effort to look like everyone else while also appearing just a little bit funky.

No matter how hard girls work at achieving popularity, though, it's inevitable that some will be considered "in" and others "out." The social hierarchy exists in every high school. "If you're not that popular," points out Andrea Marr, the sixteen-year-old protagonist of *Girl,* Blake Nelson's dead-on portrayal of the minutiae of teenage social divisions, "people don't want you to suddenly start going out with popular people because it screws up the social order." Andrea is critically aware of the subtleties that make or break a teenager's coolness level, but at the end of the day she affirms the power of popularity: "It was so weird because no matter how much you hate popular people, the minute they like you you like them right back."[4] In the 1989 cult movie *Heathers,* Winona Ryder explains her decision to hang out with the bitchy popular girls—so alike that they all share the name Heather—even though they require her to abandon her old, less-than-cool friends, whom she prefers. "I don't really like my friends.... It's just like, they're people I work with, and our job is being popular."

CONSENSUS THROUGH GOSSIP

More than saying "I'm sorry" and "You decide," the number-one way to generate consent is through gossip—a dart that stabs at boys as well as girls. By its very nature, gossip smooths out the lumps and bumps of disagreement and confrontation. When teens unite to criticize a fellow student, their underlying purpose is to create a harmonious sense of camaraderie and to distinguish themselves from the person they're gossiping about. They, the gossipers, are all the same and share the same values; the gossipee is different and inferior. By sharing a common object of scorn and disgust, the group becomes more cohesive, more powerful.

Gossip, according to linguist Robin Dunbar, is the reason humans learned to speak in the first place. He traces the evolution of language back to the grooming practices of our ancestors, the hominids, who would spend up to one-fifth of their days flicking their fingers through the skin and fur of their companions. According to Dunbar, grooming was our ancestors' (and today's chimps') way of expressing group loyalty; but grooming took up much too much time, especially as their lives became more complex and their groups expanded in size. Language, and particularly gossip, suggests Dunbar, evolved as a more efficient way to distinguish between different social groups.[5]

Sociologists Donna Eder and Janet Lynne Enke have studied the mechanics of teenage gossip and how inevitably it promotes consensus. Eder and Enke unobtrusively observed and listened to girls ages ten to fourteen, noting that the main topics they gossiped about were the appearance of other students and the "conceited" behavior of particular girls. (The main gossip topic for boys was the athletic performance of other boys.) After analyzing tapes of the conversations, Eder and Enke found, first of all, that gossip is an extremely easy way of participating in a group activity. Unlike other forms of talk, such as collaborative storytelling, girls participating in a group gossip session don't need to have shared in a specific experience, or even to know the girl being gossiped about.

Gossip also encourages negative evaluations. Once one girl makes an initial catty comment, it's easier to agree with her rather than challenge her. The first response after the initial comment is the linchpin. If that response supports the initial negative evaluation, all subsequent comments from the group will also support the initial negative evaluation. It's "much easier to continue to develop the expressed viewpoint of a group than it is to challenge it," explain Eder and Enke. The only time a challenge is made is immediately following the initial comment, and even that is very infrequent. "While adolescents appear comfortable challenging the evaluation made by an individual, they seem reluctant to challenge a 'group' evaluation. Once an initial evaluation was supported by another group member, it was never challenged."[6]

The gossip initiator, by the way, is always someone with high or medium status within her clique or within the school as a whole, according to Eder and Enke. And on the rare occasions when challenges are made, they come from students with a status level equal to or higher than the person they are challenging. Supportive comments, however, are made by students of all status levels, including those with the lowest status.[7]

The movie *Romy and Michelle's High School Reunion* shows what happens when one group member has the audacity to dissent from the party line. The four most popular girls ("the A group") make a habit of laughing at Romy, who's overweight, and Michelle, who wears a neckbrace. One day during lunch the first "A group" girl says, "Those weirdos are staring at us again." A second group member trumpets, "They're obsessed with us. Look at what they're wearing." A third girl asks, "Where do you even get outfits that hideous?" But then the final "A group" member defends Romy and Michelle: "They made them in home-ec from their own patterns. Actually I think they're semi-interesting." The three other girls drop their forks and stare at her, mouths agape. Hastily the lone defender backtracks. "In a freakish, off-putting sort of way," she mumbles. "Never mind."

Fourteen-year-old Kimberly from Texas admits that she shies away from sticking up for people when she gets swept up by group gossip. If she's hanging out with a group of classmates and they make it clear that they dislike a certain person, Kimberly tends to nod her head—even if the person they're talking about is a friend of hers. She knows she should defend her friend. "I feel bad about doing it," she says shyly, but she just doesn't feel at ease speaking up.

When everyone around her seems to share the same opinion, it's hard for a girl to offer her own perspective. After all, a girl who is assertive and takes a stand runs the risk of being called a bitch or too full of herself. Mary, seventeen and Puerto Rican, felt insecure in her practically all-white junior high school. "My friends were the popular girls, and everyone always wanted to hang out with them," she remembers. "Even though they were my best friends, I always felt kind of out of place. I always had to try and follow them. I always agreed with everything they said and I didn't step out of line, otherwise I couldn't be in the group anymore."

This model of intimacy—staying loyal to friends even if it means swallowing hard and nodding at everything they say—impairs everyone involved. The group as a whole becomes more and more intolerant of difference. The "lower status" girls within the clique hide their true opinions for fear of losing friends. And the girls who are damaged the most are the girls being gossiped about—the outsiders.

PART IRISH AND PART ITALIAN, LINDA GIOVANNI, born in 1962, attended an exclusive New York City girls' school on scholarship. She always longed to fit in but never did: she was seen as a different and sexual creature. Unlike her breastless, hipless classmates, Linda developed a curvy body. In seventh grade the girls started calling her a whore, which led her to act like one. Even students at all-girls' schools, we see, are quick to label girls as sluts. Today Linda is a lawyer living in New York City.

I went to a school that was very WASPy and wealthy, a private girls' school in New York that I'll call Chapman. I had transferred in from a Catholic girls' school after grade two because I had been given an IQ test that came out very high, and my parents decided to find an environment that would give me everything they thought I deserved. I got a scholarship to go to Chapman. I hated being there from the very beginning. I was a terrible student and I was considered an underachiever. Every report card I ever received said that I was not working up to my potential.

Chapman was not just upper middle class, it was really upper class. The parents were in the Social Register. My family wasn't in the Social Register and never would be because we were Irish and Italian. I didn't do the things that the other girls did. They all knew each other, they were all part of the same circle, and they all had country houses. They all went to dancing school. They had these special fancy dress balls that were for charity events. Since I lived in the wrong zip code, my friends from school had to get permission to visit me at home. And my parents did the wrong things for jobs. My mother was a schoolteacher and my father was a civil servant who worked for New York State. In seventh or eighth grade he got laid off for about two years and that was a shameful, shameful thing. The kids must have known; I just know that they knew. My father did not find a job and eventually he had to start his own business.

I clearly didn't look WASPy; I have a big nose and I don't have straight hair. The girls were blond and thin and had no busts and were blue-eyed with little noses. We had to wear uniforms, but they were expensive, so I always got them secondhand. I was conscious of being there on scholarship. I wanted to hide it, I didn't want other people to know, but they knew. I felt really awkward and dissonant. On the weekends, of course, we could wear what we wanted. It was the seventies so I wore the style of the times—bell bottoms and sneakers—but everyone else wore topsiders and straight-leg pants and Lacoste shirts and they thought I looked ridiculous. Of course I wanted to dress like them.

I started to get breasts when I was around seven, and they became really noticeable when I was nine. Certainly by the time I was eleven I was very conscious of them. I had a school jumper, which was a big relief because that kind of hid it. I walked around with my arms crossed in front of my breasts with my hands tucked up into my armpits. I walked down the street like that and sometimes also in school. I chose shirts that would cover my breasts and had pockets.

I also got my period before everyone else, when I was eleven. I hid it like crazy. It was so traumatic because I remember being in the bathroom of my school the first time I got it and I didn't have enough pads. This was 1973, so you had to use a belt and it really hurt. I remember that I was ashamed of it.

In seventh grade they started calling me slut and whore. It was something that just got around and the girls repeated it, it seemed, out of jealousy to keep a certain boy away from me. There was a boys' school near us and we spent a lot time over there. I think they became jealous when an especially desirable guy was attracted to me. A lot of what they said was behind my back, but it got to the guy who was interested in me, and I think he became fearful. I doubt that the girls really believed the stories they were saying about me—I think they were just kind of excited to have a story to tell—but I think that the guys believed them.

(Diary entry, October 31, 1974)
"You're no virgin," she said. "Linda's no virgin!" Julia screamed to the Atomic Structure class. Mrs. Atkinson turned around with an embarrassed smile on her face and said, "Could we end this discus-

*sion?" I was so embarrassed. I think she believes it.
I'd like it to be true.*

They regularly taunted me when I walked into the classroom. They chanted, "Linda's not a virgin." It started with a few people, the cooler clique of girls, and then it grew until the entire class was saying it. Girls went along with it because they were glad it wasn't happening to them. Nobody stuck up for me. I clearly remember that my homeroom teacher, Mrs. Gold, witnessed what was going on and didn't do anything about it. One day she had a hoarse, raspy voice because she had a sore throat, and she said, "Today I have something in common with Linda"—meaning that her voice was sexy. I think she meant it as a joke but I was mortified.

I told my parents and they told the school. They went in to complain about the way I was treated. I don't know exactly what the school told them, but they came away feeling humiliated. The school wanted to be able to say they were doing something nice by having scholarship students, but they didn't really care about how we were doing and they didn't seem to like me anyhow since I wasn't a good student.

*(December 3, 1974)
Julia went up to Mrs. Gold and told her I was pregnant. Mrs. Gold half believed it too. She told Mrs. Gilbert about it. Marcia and Joanna were trumpeting it around the halls. I took Joanna's bracelet and refused to give it back.*

The name-calling continued in eighth grade. Even my best friend, Amy, spread rumors about me when she felt she was losing control of me. She was very, very wealthy. She had lots of problems at school, but it didn't matter because her parents would just buy her out of them. Her family was so devoid of love and affection, and in place of showing the children love and affection the parents would give her the charge card and tell her to go buy what she wanted. I became very dependent on her because she bought me the clothes and the things to fit in, and I desperately wanted those things. I also liked her, though she was very manipulative.

I desperately always wanted to be friends with people in the "in" clique. And at certain times I would be. There was one central "in" clique and then there were various satellite groups that were comfortable in their position. But I remember that someone who followed but wasn't part of the group was called a tagger, and you didn't want to be a "tagger." At one point Amy accused me of being a "tagger."

In seventh and eighth grades we started spending time with boys more and more, and the girls told all the boys that I was a slut. But I wasn't sexually active at all. In fact their labeling me a "slut" kept me from being sexually active for several years, because I ended up keeping boys at a distance. It really built a lot of mistrust with men. I remember that boys always tried to have sex with me because they assumed that I would. I was disposable in a way that the other girls weren't because I was labeled a slut and also because I wasn't part of the social circle, so I wasn't the right girl to be with anyhow.

(April 4, 1975)
The lights were turned off and the door was closed. We lay down on the couch and made out for a solid hour.... He tried to go to second or third. I didn't really know but I didn't trust him with his hand down my pants.... He stopped Frenching me and asked me if I was a virgin. I said, "Yes." He asked me if I wanted to get screwed and I said, "No." I thought he was joking but apparently he doesn't joke about things like that.

I wanted very much to be with boys and to experiment with boys. In my first sexual experience I was used by a boy and it became a blueprint for all my relationships with guys. I was in eighth grade and he was the first guy that I really liked. His name was Jonathan and he was very popular and my kind of guy—adventuresome and into rough-and-tumble sports like hockey. We were at a party at the beginning of the year and I felt a little more sure of myself. I was excited that there was a whole new year ahead and that this guy liked me. It was a make-out party—the lights went out and the couples were in the dark kissing away. I was just thrilled to have him touch me. But he had been told that I was a "slut" and just wanted to have sex, and I said no. It wasn't so much that I wanted a whole relationship, but I thought he liked me for me. And he didn't, which was a shattering thing. He never talked to me again.

(December 22, 1975)
Cathy's been spreading rumors about me and Jonathan. She said we went to third. She also admitted that she'd purposely screw me so I wouldn't go out with him.

(January 7, 1976)
Jonathan's going around saying I'm a prude just because I didn't go to third or get laid.

It was a big deal for me. A really big deal. I remember feeling the difference between me and the other girls. Guys liked them. Those were the girls guys went out with, but I wasn't the type they went out with. And I desperately wanted to go out with someone. I never trusted guys who wanted to have sex with me after that until I met my husband. It's a pattern I had until I was in my twenties—I would meet someone and be very unsure if he liked me too, and because I was so unsure, it would destroy the relationship.

(August 12, 1976)
I am so ugly. The guy Ella has me fixed up with is going
to hate me—HATE me. Or else he'll only like me for my
tits.

I started drinking an enormous amount on the weekends. I guess because I had nothing to lose, I was more eager to drink and smoke pot and do other drugs, and I did. It was a real personality transformation. I was one kind of person at school and a different kind of person at home with my parents. I began to spend most of my time with friends who were part of the outsider fringe group.

If you're going to be branded a slut and suffer the consequences, you might as well act like one, so I started to act like a "slut." I began to drink a lot and make out with guys, any guys. I didn't have intercourse until eleventh grade, though I wanted to. We weren't really doing much—they would just basically feel me up and we'd kiss. I think I appeared more sexually aggressive than I actually was.

I think in general I liked to rise to a dare. I would do things just to show that I could do them. Acting this way made my situation easier: If I'm different, then let me be really different. It was a way to establish a personality. And then more and more it became "fuck you." I started dealing drugs in ninth grade. By tenth grade I would buy a pound or two of pot and then sell it off. I also sold pills, mostly uppers, because they were legal. There was a doctor in the building who would give me prescriptions.

In eleventh grade I transferred to a coed school, which was more liberal and double the size of Chapman. Not everyone was wealthy and the parents were much more relaxed than the parents at Chapman. I did not have a "slut" reputation there, so to some extent I was able to remake myself. Of course I got attention, as new girls always get. I was one of the few new girls and I was better-looking than some of the others. So the only reputation I had was as the cute, nice new girl. My new school was a place for truly bright kids, and kids who would have been called "nerds" at another school were the "in" crowd here, and that was really nice.

But it wasn't such a good year. I had a boyfriend, Jason, who was in the year above me and who beat me up regularly. We were together for six months and he was part of the stoner group. He was dorky and not at all attractive. I liked unattractive guys because of course they would be attracted to me. From the beginning he had uncontrollable anger and then I got slapped and then it escalated to trashing my room and hitting me. He threw me down a flight of stairs in his apartment building. I broke up with him at the end of junior year but he would follow me around—sometimes I was aware of it and sometimes I wasn't. When I was aware, I would run away as fast as I could. The scariest thing he did was he tried to strangle me and threatened to get a knife to put at my throat, but I managed to get away from him. Finally Jason was expelled because he had punched a boy, though I didn't know that at the time. So for punching a boy he got expelled, but for punching me repeatedly nothing happened.

Why was I attracted to a guy who abused me? I think I felt sorry for him because he was so fucked up and I thought, "If I love him a lot, he'll be all better." Partially I was imposing on him what I wanted someone to do for me—because I felt so damaged—to say, "You can do whatever you want and you will still be loved."

In senior year I did theater for the first time, which is something I had always wanted to do but had never the courage to do it. I had good friends who were in the theater crowd. They were nice, smart, very eclectic. By the time I graduated, I had shed a lot of the baggage that came with being labeled bad, but it's a persona that I've always come back to. Maybe I just feel comfortable with it. When I went to Toronto to college, I was definitely perceived as "bad" because I was from New York— though not a slut because it had nothing to do with my sexuality.

My persona of being "bad" was very enticing to my friends. I was used to doing things that they thought were just spectacularly "bad," like wanting to get drugged.

When I was in my mid-twenties, I started to mutilate myself. I used a razor on my face—my forehead, or my lip, or my chin. I never slashed myself, but I would just dig at my face and it would look like an abrasion. People noticed and I made up stories about falling down the stairs and things like that. It started because I hated the outer manifestation of myself, my body. I thought, "If I could just rid myself of this, I'd feel better." I was taught to hate my body and to feel ashamed of it by the kids at school, but at the same time I also knew that my body was my poster to the outside world. The mutilation was also a way of getting help from other people without having to tell them exactly what was wrong. I stopped the self-mutilation when I went on antidepressants when I was twenty-nine.

The experience of being ostracized and shamed has impacted me greatly. Those kids picked on me because I was a "slut," but I always knew that it was because I was seen as weak and vulnerable. I associated this, even as a kid, with my being less affluent, less socially "with it," and physically distinct. The whole thing really shook my confidence in a way that I am not sure I can ever fully recover from. It also tapped into a profound anger that I already had: Growing up with an Irish-American grandfather had taught me that WASPs were the ones who had kept "us" down, here as well as in Ireland. For much of my life my anger has had a destructive tone. The counterpoint to this is that my anger has made me aggressive about changing what I see as unfairness, both to myself and others.

CLASS DISMISSED

Gossip, of course, is always at someone's expense, and gossip about the class "slut" never fails to attract gleeful participants. Through the self-important drama of gossip, girls who are clearly not sexual become sexualized anyway. In the film *Welcome to the Dollhouse,* the geeky, gawky Dawn Wiener is a loser with a capital L. She wears absurdly childish outfits: elastic-waist pants in screaming-bright colors and ponytail holders adorned with two ceramic balls. In the crowded lunchroom, where she has no one to sit with, the oh-so-cool cheerleaders come up to her and ask her if she's a lesbian, then chant "Lesbo" in front of the whole school. The class bully threatens to rape her. Perhaps since all the other girls in her class are in the process of sexual development, showing off their curves in cropped tops and tight pants, Dawn's innocent asexuality seems mocking. And what sweeter revenge could there be than to take her sexuality to task?

More typically, though, the overweight girl's fleshy body is sexualized. When she was in the eighth grade, Tawnya Brawdy, now in her mid-twenties, was regularly taunted by classmates at Kenilworth Junior High School in Petaluma, California, who likened her to a cow.[8] A special-education student who was pudgy and big-busted, Tawnya endured the "mooing" sounds her classmates made. "I'd like to see her if she got pregnant," they laughed, adding, "She'd tip over." Male students regularly made references to her sex life. It happened every day: as she was walking into class, as she was sitting at her desk, as she was leaving class, as she was walking around the school. According to a classmate, students made fun of her "whenever they felt like it. If they were in the mood to tease someone, she was their target." Why was she the target of choice? "Because she was overweight.... I personally took it that they thought she was a cow, more like a milking cow, because of her chest."

Tawnya's teacher continued his lessons over the din of the insults. He made no attempt to quiet down the class, even after he saw Tawnya cry. Tawnya suffered from headaches and stomachaches. Naturally she didn't want to go to school; her grades dropped. One day Tawnya's mother, Louise Brawdy, was cleaning her daughter's room and found a will.

Her daughter had decided to kill herself. She had detailed who should get her stuffed animals and her beloved cassette collection.

Being fat, especially if you're female, is associated with being "lower class"—and being "lower class" is one manifestation of being "slutty." Remember Anna Nicole Smith, the 1993 *Playboy* playmate of the year and former Guess? jeans model? Smith, who was hugely voluptuous back in 1993 and whose curves have only expanded since then, has been publicly derided as trampy "white trash": she was featured on a *New York* magazine cover story, "White Trash Nation," depicting her reaching for a bag of Cheez Doodles nestled between her legs. (Smith sued the magazine for five million dollars, alleging that she was tricked into posing for the cover.) Smith has also been widely scorned as a "slutty" gold digger, since she married oil baron J. Howard Marshall II when he was in his late eighties and she was a twenty-six-year-old topless dancer. If Smith had been *either* overweight or a topless dancer—but not both—it's doubtful that journalists would have gone out of their way to humiliate her to the extent that they have.

More than anyone else, the lower-class girl is dismissed as a "slut." Even before she is sexually active, she is characterized as the type of girl a boy can sleep with but should never marry. "It is assumed that loose sexual morals or deviant desires placed [women on welfare] in the shameful status of poor," comments Tammy Rae Carland, who grew up on welfare and was labeled a slut by the time she was nine years old, "but not just poor—poor women that no man wants or that men only want for one thing."[9]

August Hollingshead, who did groundbreaking research on the social lives of adolescents in the 1940s, found a strong correlation between economic class and social status. Disturbingly, his conclusions seem no less applicable today. Hollingshead found that adolescents within a given class learn similar definitions of acceptable and unacceptable behavior, and that families within the same class provide their children with a social code of acceptable manners and behavior. Teens are guided, and sometimes pressured, by their parents to choose friends with the same social code. Popular kids don't simply fall into their role—they are born into and groomed for it. Those in the middle and upper middle classes are taught by both parents and teachers that they deserve a higher status, while those who are lower middle class and poor are taught that they deserve a lower status. Too often the whole community, not just kids, identify "lower class" as "no good."

SOLIDLY WORKING-CLASS SUSAN HOUSEMAN, thirty-one, was slapped with the "slut" label because she really *had* been sexual—she had slept with the boyfriend of a friend. But once everyone at her West Virginia school knew her as a "slut," she consciously began acting like a proverbial "bad girl"—smoking, cutting classes, having one-night stands with guys she met at parties. The "slut" label and her sexual behavior melted into each other.

I'm an only child and I was a real daddy's girl. I think my mother was startled that I wasn't just a cute little thing to dress up. I was very much a tomboy, which my father was fabulous about. But it bothered my mother that I didn't want to be a cheerleader or majorette or play with my toy oven. I played football and I broke things. I was also kind of a geek, because I read a lot, and understood things more than my age level would indicate. I was in the Talented and Gifted Program from second grade through sixth, when the program ran out of funding. My dad was a firefighter, and my mom was a bookkeeper who worked at home most of the time.

Up until high school I was one of the good girls and I was probably like second-level popular. I was always troublesome, but I had managed to hang out with people who were socially acceptable, so I was socially acceptable by extension. When I was in elementary and junior high school, my teachers recognized me as an intelligent person. When I went to high school, a few of them continued to recognize that. There were a few teachers who sucked up to the popular kids and treated me very badly.

My high school was all white people—no blacks, Asians, Jews, or any ethnicity—and I had known the majority of them since kindergarten. The popular kids were athletic and dressed fashionably and the girls were good-looking. I don't think that in general they were any more socially adept than anyone else, but they just fell into the popular role. In ninth grade I was kind of boring. I was just sort of settling in, and didn't hang out with many people in general. But then, starting in tenth grade, I hung out with the bad girls mostly. I don't know if it was a conscious decision on my part or not. I went through an anarchist hippie stage and started to buy all my clothes at Goodwill and dress like a freak. I took scissors and sliced off chunks of my hair on one side. I started dying my hair. Then I started frosting it. I don't even remember what color it was when I graduated. When I saw Cindi Lauper, I felt so vindicated.

The first time I had sex with a boy was in the beginning of tenth grade, and it was somewhat calculated on my part. It was with a friend's boyfriend, and in retrospect, it was probably not such a good idea. He was a student at Marshall University in Huntington, which is about a half hour away from where our school was. It's a small, primarily liberal arts college. My friend Barbara had a boyfriend whose father was a professor there. So Barbara's boyfriend introduced us to all the campus boys. Barbara and I and my other friend Stephanie all hung out, and Barbara's boyfriend introduced us all to this guy Rick. Stephanie started dating him and had sex with him. Any guy who's in college who's going out with high school girls is kind of a sleezeball. But back then it was like, "Oh wow, this guy likes me, and he's in college, he's so cool and he wants to hang out with me."

Most of my friends had already had sex by this point. And

then I had intercourse with Rick too. It was mostly curiosity on my part. You know, he was someone I liked. He was cute, accessible, all that. We were both at a house party one weekend, and Stephanie had gone home. He initiated it. I didn't see it as a big deal at all. But I had been expecting sex to be a fabulous experience, and it was a real disappointment.

Rick told Stephanie, and she was not happy. She saw it as a betrayal on my part. But I didn't intend it to be. It was curiosity, boredom, maybe a little jealousy because she had done something that I hadn't done. I had always been something of an experimenter. She was also mad at him; she ditched him. So Stephanie was pissed and told everyone.

I hadn't been attending school every day at this point; I would cut at least two of the five days a week and hang out, get high, read library books, and try to figure out what Nietzsche meant—not really acceptable things for Wayne County. So the next day that I went to school, nobody would talk to me. Most people were really rude to me. They were like, "How could you do this?" They meant how could I do this to Stephanie. But when I tried to explain that it wasn't meant against her, that it was just casual, it was considered an affront. I think my attitude really inflamed people, and made them more hostile to me.

After that there were a lot of rumors about me behind my back and people stopped being friends with me. The girls wouldn't talk to me. I was hurt. I had one friend who was very similar to me, who was very questioning of everything, and she remained my friend. But the other people I'd hung out with up until that point dropped me. I found that shocking and hard to believe.

My friends were just as sexual as I was, but they didn't have reputations because they had sex within parameters of dating people, whereas I wasn't dating Rick and I was very casual about it. Most of the people in my high school were in relationships, some of which lasted only two weeks. The reputation was also a convenient method for identifying me. "Well, we don't like

having
sex with
(o my only ones
boy friend   *"Not One of Us"* / 185

her. It's not because she reads strange books or because she doesn't think or dress the same way we do. It's because she's a slut. Yeah, that's it." I think part of it was social outrage—"You're not like us"—but it was a very convenient method of defining who I was rather than saying, "She disregards our social boundaries." It was more about the fact that I behaved like someone outside the norm, and slut was the closest word they could find to describe me.

A lot of times I think girls fall into being like "sluts" because of the same mentality. They think, "Well, I don't fit into the mold." Acting like a "slut" is a real easy method of fitting into some sort of mold, some sort of reference point, because at that age you don't have a lot of role models. So you just fall into being a "bad girl," which is easily identifiable to you or to other people.

I started smoking after that. Most of the people at my school probably smoked cigarettes at one time or another, but smoking on the high school campus was considered really bad. I developed new friends and started hanging out with the smokers. These were friendships out of necessity. None of these people was terribly bright and I felt intellectually superior. That bothered me. But what bothered me most was the fact that I was so limited in the people I could hang out with and communicate with. There were very few people in general I felt I had much in common with intellectually. The girl who was my best friend was one of them, but she was dating a guy, so she was never around. So I was basically forced into a social milieu that I wasn't really so thrilled with.

When I wasn't at school, I hung out at the university with college students. At the time I thought they were really cool. They were mostly musicians. We would go to keg parties or stay up all night. I would tell my mom that I was spending the night with Karen or Barbara or whoever. So when I wasn't going to school, I had a wonderful time. I always knew that I had other options that I could get out of smoking pot and hanging around with university students. I knew that it was just a temporary place, that I wouldn't be hanging around with these people for the rest of my life.

My parents are very 1950s. They had no clue at all. They never knew I was cutting school. I would forge notes and they never got called. On the one hand, I was very much a troubled adolescent, so it would have been nice if someone had noticed what was going on and had tried to do something about it. But on the other hand I managed to work out my life very well.

I had a lot of one-night stands, for the most part with boys I met at parties at the university. Over the course of tenth, eleventh, and twelfth grades, I messed around with about ten guys. I think that being sexually active and not really making any bones about it made it real easy to turn me into a "bad girl." It also made it easy for people to discount other reasons for not wanting to associate with me. It became self-fulfilling.

There was only one time that I had sex with someone from my own age group, when I was in eleventh grade. He went to a different school and it ended up being a very unpleasant incident. He called and asked me out. I was like, "Sure, whatever." He probably asked me out because of my reputation. He was sixteen or seventeen, a high school boy from one of the nearby schools. I'd never gone out with anyone that young before. I ended up being sexually assaulted by him and two of his friends.

He said we were going to the house of a friend of his. So we went there, and his friends were hanging out in the living room. It's possible that I may have been a little stoned. He and I were in the bedroom, and then his friends came in and, what's the phrase? "Pulled the train"? They each had intercourse with me. They didn't hold me down, but I felt intimidated. I wasn't sure where I was, since we were in a house in a neighboring town. I never reported it. I knew that they felt they could get away with it because of my reputation. At the time I felt like it was definitely my fault. "If I didn't have this reputation, if I hadn't agreed to go out with this guy..." I felt it was very much deserved.

If I were an adult who had never gone through something like this, I'd be like, "No woman deserves to have anything happen to her against her will." But was it against my will? It was more an environmental pressure than anything else. I got into a situation and I didn't know a way of getting out of it gracefully. To some extent I felt too intimidated to say no. It was not a situation that I would put myself in now, and if I were to hear about a young woman in the same situation, while I would feel sympathy for her for being hurt or feeling bad, my immediate response would be "God, what was she thinking?" So looking back, I think, "Geez, that was a stupid situation to put myself in." I don't have a lot of sympathy for myself. What a dumb thing to do.

During my last semester of high school, in 1985, I met a woman a year older named Barbara and ended up in a relationship with her. Once I got together with her, I wasn't promiscuous any longer. We were together for a year and a half, and my parents were clueless again. When I met her, it was such a revelation: "Oh, that's why sex with men isn't much fun." The truth is that when I was with guys in high school, I didn't really like sex. I didn't have orgasms. I didn't really think about sex with guys as pleasurable at that time. It was a power thing, an identity thing. It was a way of making myself exist in the world. And it was primarily an act of rebellion. But it had never occurred to me to try to have sex with a woman.

I went to Marshall for a few years, then dropped out and I traveled a lot on the East Coast and followed the Grateful Dead for a while. It was real fun. I ran up my parents' credit card bills. Barbara moved to California, so I lived in San Francisco with her for a few months. I went to a lot of concerts. Then after about two years I went back to Marshall. I moved back home with my parents for a year and a half. This was a good thing in some ways. I got to know my mom as a human being.

Since high school I've had sex with maybe only five or six people. I never again had sex unless it was within a relationship, though for me personally I see sex as kind of recreation. Maybe occasionally it's mystical and fabulous, but for the most part it's just fun. I had been bisexual and now I'm married. Before I married, my husband and I had the big discussion about monogamy. I was like, "You mean, you expect monogamy?" And he said, "Of course I expect monogamy! We're getting married!" Men can be way more traditional than women. I haven't done drugs in years. I'm so boring now.

In a sense my reputation was a freeing experience. The reputation put me outside the boundaries of accepted behavior. Once you've crossed a line or stepped outside of what is accepted, then you have much more freedom to experiment with who you are because you don't have the same social pressures that most girls and women have. You can think about yourself outside of the "good girl" roles—cheerleader, girl scout—and you can find other boundaries for yourself. It gave me more perspective. Because if I'd been a good girl, I never would have considered having sex with a girl, who was someone I cared about. I probably would have thought about getting married right after graduation. Even though it was a rural high school, it was expected that if you were a girl, you would go to college to either get a degree in elementary education or meet a nice boy and get married. But neither of those options appealed to me. I could see how limited those options were. I had more freedom. I could hang out with my friends and read unpronounceable books and do drugs. I felt like my life was more expansive. So having the reputation gave me more options with my life.

ARE YOU A JOCK OR A DRUGGIE?

When sociologist Penelope Eckert spent three years observing students at five Detroit suburban high schools in the 1980s, she found that the categories of Jocks and Burnouts (her term for "druggies") were "adolescent embodiments of the middle and working class, respectively; their two separate cultures are in many ways class structures; and opposition and conflict between them define and exercise class relations and differences."[10] Nearly every public high school—and many private oncs—has a group of Jocks, in their coordinated Gap and Banana Republic outfits, who do sports and cheerleading and the band. The Druggies, meanwhile, cut classes and wear thrift-store clothes and work at Dairy Queen because they can't afford to work at résumé-enhancing, nonpaying internships. Most students, obviously, fall into neither category; but in the schools Eckert observed, all students identified themselves in relation to these two dominant, and highly visible, groups ("I'm in the drama club, so I'm not really a Jock, but I'm more like a Jock than a Druggie.")

The thing is that everyone at Eckert's schools—students, teachers, coaches, administrators—was aware of the very deep social division between the Jock and Burnout groups, yet no one ever overtly correlated them to their class status. No one ever commented on the near inevitability that children of middle-class parents were drawn to school-sponsored extracurricular activities while children of working-class parents tended to distance themselves from everything the school stood for. Instead observers viewed affiliation with either the Jock or Burnout group as a matter of personal choice. "The prevailing attitude in the school," says Eckert, "is that Jocks become involved in school because their families have instilled in them confidence, ambition, and academic skills, while Burnouts become alienated from school because their families have failed them. Burnouts' rebelliousness is seen as resulting from problems at home and from frustration at their lack of academic ability."[11]

There is no denying that when teens who are working- or lower-class are thrown into high schools with teens of more prosperous means, they are at a tremendous disadvantage. The entire community assumes that these teens are headed to a dead-end future, and that it's their own damned fault—because they have made bad choices about who they hang out with and what they do with their time. Middle-class kids define themselves as Not-Burnouts; they have a future, thank you very much, filled with years of college and graduate school and home ownership. Barbara Ehrenreich, in her social history of the middle class *Fear of Falling,* notes that the professional middle-class is deeply anxious and insecure because, without the inherited security of the upper class, it knows it can slide downward at any time.[12] Sensing this anxiety and perhaps feeling it themselves, middle-class kids are obsessed with maintaining boundaries between themselves and those "others," whom they look down on as grungy and stupid and tasteless—and, if they are girls, sexually promiscuous.

Being an outsider can lead to devastating consequences. Or it can result in benefits. Or both. It can free you from the soullessness of going along with the crowd and help you survive high school with distinctive quirks, ideas, and philosophies intact. So many insecure and conforming high school girls grow up to be insecure and conforming women—desperately searching for a man, getting married as soon as possible, swallowing personal ambitions for the sake of their families. They would do better to follow the example of the girls they torment, many of whom emerge from adolescence and enter adulthood with an admirable resilience.

ALL GIRLS ARE OUTSIDERS

But aren't all girls "outsiders" to some extent? Aren't all girls marginalized? After all, being female is widely considered to be a liability. When sociologist Barrie Thorne followed elementary school students in California and Michigan, she discovered that the children independently separated themselves by gender in the classroom, lunchroom, hallways, and especially on the playground. The gendered groupings were separate and unequal. Thorne also observed elaborate rituals used to designate the girls as pollutants, such as declaring that they are contaminated by "cooties."[13] Girls shrewdly use boys' fear of contamination for their own ends, as a source of power: A girl can threaten to kiss a boy, thereby implanting him with cooties, forcing him to run away. Nevertheless it's always preferable to be contaminable than contaminated. A boy usually can escape cootie poisoning, while a girl has to live with it.

Children understand the nature of power in our society. They know that being male has advantages. Educators Myra and David Sadker posed this question to hundreds of students across the country: "Suppose you woke up tomorrow and found you were a member of the other sex. How would your life be different?" Forty-two percent of the girls could think of reasons why it would be advantageous to be male—but only 5 percent of the 565 boys questioned could find any advantage whatsoever to being female.[14]

"Boys took imaginative, desperate measures to get out of being girls," the Sadkers report in *Failing at Fairness: How America's Schools Cheat Girls.* "A twelve-year-old wrote: 'To have my boy body I would walk off a cliff. I would bungee jump without a bungee cord off the tallest mountain.'" Another twelve-year-old said he would "walk around the world on hot coals," while another boy offered to "jump out of a plane into a glass of milk to get my boy body back."[15] The boys' evocations of despair are as disturbing as they are clever and funny. They know all too well that the worst form of derision is to be called a girl.

These early roots of misogyny are nourished by teachers, according to the Sadkers. They discovered over and over again, as they observed more than a hundred classrooms over three years, that teachers respond to boys more than to girls. Their research shows that white males receive the most teacher attention, followed by minority males, then white females and, lastly, minority females. It's not necessarily that teachers seek out boys for extra attention; boys call out eight times more often than girls. Although teachers universally value hand-raising as a means to control classroom chaos, the Sadkers found that they tolerated boys who called out of turn, but not girls. "When girls call out, there is a fascinating occurrence: Suddenly, the teacher remembers the rule about raising your hand before you talk. And then the girl, who is usually not as assertive as the male students, is deftly and swiftly put back in her place."[16]

Even when they aren't yelling out answers or asking questions out of turn, boys devise clever strategies to call attention to themselves. The Sadkers colorfully describe one fifth-grade boy who, desiring to speak, would wave and pump his entire arm—not just his hand—for five long minutes. That tactic ineffective, he would get out of his seat and wave some more, with elaborate sound effects, for another four and a half minutes, until the moment of truth: recognition from the teacher and the chance to have his say. Post-teacher-recognition repose would last only four minutes, and then the whole drama would be reenacted. Those who are well behaved— mostly girls—quite understandably receive less attention.[17] (Even the Sadkers themselves, in an unfortunate irony, devote more space in their book to descriptions of bad-boy behavior than they do to female decorum. That's the nature of decorum: It's forgettable.)

Given this boy-dominated school atmosphere, you would think that girls would gravitate toward each other to create a support system, to show the boys and teachers that they, too, have intrinsic value, that they are not pollutants, that their remarks are worthy of being heard. But that's not what usually happens. Instead girls assimilate the pervasive belief that they are inferior. They come to believe it as truth. As a result many girls disavow their entire gender. If all girls are inferior outsiders, then what's the point in associating with them? To distance themselves, many girls become competitive with other girls.

There's nothing inherently wrong with competition. If channeled properly, it is an admirable and necessary trait. Competing to gain admission into an advanced-placement math class or to become class president means working hard, sharpening skills, and summoning up savvy—activities that

are worthwhile in and of themselves, regardless of the outcome. But girls and women are at a particular disadvantage
in a classic damned-if-you-do, damned-if-you-don't situation.
When they are overtly ambitious, especially with each other,
they are derided at best as unladylike and at worst as bitches.
As the Cinderella, Snow White, and Sleeping Beauty fairy
tales teach us, passive women are beautiful and virtuous, and
competitive women are undesirable and unworthy. But not
competing at all is also not an option.

So what's a woman or girl to do? She must hide her ambition—by secretly competing. The competitive impulse is
rerouted rather than smothered. But women and girls are supposed to be sisterly and "relate" to each other. Competition is
considered unfeminine: it's, well, not nice. Girls and women
are socialized to be polite, to say "please" and "thank you"
and "you're welcome." If they don't have anything nice to
say, they shouldn't say anything at all. (I, for one, still have
trouble telling telemarketers that I'm not interested in whatever it is they're selling.) This tension between covert competition and the social pressure to be nice to other women and
girls pushes the competitive spirit into the surreptitious realm
of gossip and backstabbing and undermining.

By fifth and sixth grades, girls gossip about each other end-
lessly, a practice that is not discouraged. A popular activity is
to sit around and just talk about other girls, putting down losers for not wearing the right clothes and not being invited to
parties. A 1992 ad for Candie's Shoes depicted two fluffy-
haired girls squealing in laughter. The caption? "She was the
only girl in high school that didn't own Candie's... maybe
that's why she never had a date." Remember "slam books,"
immortalized by Judy Blume in *Otherwise Known as Sheila
the Great*? Girls pass around these notebooks, anonymously
recording brutally uncensored opinions of other girls. Popular
categories of judgment are "Hair," "Body," "Face," and
"Brain."

By the time a girl is a teenager, it's been drummed into her head—by romance novels, teen magazines, TV shows, and movies—that she needs a boyfriend in order to have value. Catching the interest of a boy is a competitive project because there are only so many boys willing enough or confident enough to publicly go out on dates, and of that group there are only so many boys who are considered desirable. When the scrambling is complete, most girls will be left standing alone. And so every other girl is, by virtue of her gender, a rival. One girl's gain, according to this logic, becomes another girl's loss.

It's a sentiment commonly held by adult women as well as by teenage girls. The 1994 movie *Four Weddings and a Funeral* says it all. Andie MacDowell plays Carrie, a classy, beautiful, sexually assertive woman who attracts the attention of Charles (Hugh Grant) at a wedding. Instantly Charles's friend Fiona has her antennae up. Charles turns to Fiona—who has been secretly and unsuccessfully pining for him for years—to inquire about the graceful, svelte stranger in the classic, crisp white suit and the black, broad-brimmed hat. "Her name is Carrie," Fiona replies, spitting out each word with venom. "American. Slut."

Hollywood has always been fascinated by woman-against-woman competitiveness. In *All About Eve,* Anne Baxter schemes to become a great actress like her idol, Bette Davis, and even to take her place on the stage, in the theater-gossip columns, and in her husband's heart. In Clare Boothe's *The Women,* Joan Crawford plays a classic tart stealing the husband of dewy-eyed, demure Norma Shearer. In addition to fast-paced volleys of bitchy comments among Shearer's so-called friends—"Chin up. That's right, both of them"; "Good grief, I hate to tell you, dear, but your skin makes the Rocky Mountains look like chiffon velvet"—we are treated to the sight of women punching, pummeling, and biting each other as they pull each other's hair and roll around on the ground with their skirts hiked up and their panties exposed. In *Rich and Famous,* Candice Bergen and Jacqueline Bisset, once best friends, become competing writers; each seethes with a sense of self-righteous injustice because one woman earns critical acclaim while the other enjoys commercial success. In *Single White Female,* the dowdy Jennifer Jason Leigh is so jealous of her roommate, played by Bridget Fonda, that she murders Fonda's boyfriend and attempts to kill Fonda. Fonda is a glamorous, successful, stylish entrepreneur—*of course* Leigh has to do her in.

The list goes on and on. *The Hand That Rocks the Cradle* presents women as instinctive enemies who have nothing better to do than fight over men. After Annabella Sciorra is sexually molested by her gynecologist during an exam, she presses charges; the doctor commits suicide and his pregnant widow, Rebecca de Mornay, has a miscarriage. Against whom does de Mornay plot her revenge as a fiendish baby-sitter? Inexplicably, against Sciorra—a woman, a victim—rather than against her dead husband, an assaulter. In *My Best Friend's Wedding,* Julia Roberts hates on sight the very blond and sunny Cameron Diaz, who is engaged to marry Roberts's best friend (whom she never even considered a possible romantic partner until he became unavailable) and maliciously schemes to break up the engagement. And finally, who can forget *Working Girl?* Sigourney Weaver plays a hotshot Wall Street executive who offers to mentor the ambitious but naive Melanie Griffith. "I consider us a team," Weaver tells Griffith. "I welcome your ideas and I like to see hard work rewarded." Later she appropriates Griffith's media-merger idea and passes it off as her own creative insight. With a mentor like that, who needs corporate spies?

Hollywood does a disservice with its cartoon-like characters and high-drama mise-en-scène: It conveys the untrue impression that every day women are throwing china at each other and ripping out hunks of each other's hair. Tabloid talk shows, such as *Jerry Springer* and *Jenny Jones,* do their part, too, in showcasing women as violent competitors. Ice skater Tonya Harding's role in the knee-whacking of Nancy

being called a
slut by a
girl

Kerrigan aside, however, most acts of female competitiveness are subtle: a cutting comment here, a sizzling scowl there.

But let's be frank: Too many of us feel competitive with any attractive, ambitious, successful woman who comes along. Deep down we know that our knee-jerk dislike is unfair: How can we reject someone just for being good-looking and successful? Well, we rationalize, if she is a "slut," then her success is illegitimate and undeserved. *She's* head of the department because she slept her way to the top; *she* wouldn't be anything special if she hadn't snagged that millionaire investment banker; *she* may have knockout breasts and long legs, but ask her what she thinks about welfare reform and watch her stammer with pitiful incoherence. Positioning the envied woman as a "slut" is an easy way out of the sinking, self-conscious worry that one doesn't stack up. "It's not that I'm inadequate," the thinking goes, "it's that she has an unfair advantage. She possesses a smarmy sexual power that men are too weak to resist, but that *I* can see right through. She is bad; I am good. She is a 'slut'; I am an angel." For many teenage girls as well, picking on a "slut" is a form of solace; it relieves insecurities about weight, looks, and grades.

When a teenage girl is called a slut by another girl, it hurts more than when the name-caller is a guy. Kira Mitchell, a high school senior in Massachusetts, was called a slut in ninth grade by her boyfriend's friend, who was envious of the relationship and resentful that he was left out. The friend created sexual rumors about her that spread throughout the school. Kira was the subject of graffiti on school desks and on the boys' bathroom walls—"Kira Mitchell is a whore," "Kira Mitchell is a fucking bitch," "Kira Mitchell is a slut." People laughed at her when she walked by; they would throw things at her during lunch. Her own friends began to make fun of the way she dressed and the music she listened to.

Although her reputation was instigated by a guy, it was girls who ran with it. "None of the girls liked me," Kira tells me, her voice breaking. "I think it's because I don't go to the mall and wear makeup and stuff like that, and because I don't pretend to be stupid. The guys didn't like me either, but the girls were really, really cruel. Girls know what will hurt a fellow girl, so they really use that. For example, this year the girl with the locker next to mine is one of those popular mall types. All the guys are always after her and everyone is always like, 'She is so hot.' She just started insulting me one day. She started flipping out on me. 'You're such a slut'—she just went off on me in the hallway. This drew a really large crowd of people. She knew exactly what she wanted to say."

Whenever she was harassed, Kira stifled tears. She put on a front of indifference. "But the girls were beating up on me so bad with what they were saying that it was worse than being physically beaten up. It was so emotionally damaging. I don't even know if they knew the power of their words."

"SHE'S SO PRETTY, LET'S KILL HER"

Nearly every American teenage girl longs to look thin and attractive. Not only that, she generally wants to look thinner and more attractive than the other girls, so that she can grab the attention of the best-looking, most popular boy. Plus she should also make sure not to hang out with any girls who are overweight or ugly since there is guilt by association. In our culture, beauty is equated with virtue, ugliness with a character flaw.

Is it any wonder that teenage girls, particularly white girls, are so preoccupied with losing weight? By age nine, one half of all girls have dieted. By age ten, the percentage of girls who have cut down on calories zooms to 80 percent, according to the Council on Size and Weight Discrimination.[18] Black girls, however, are apt to be more satisfied with their bodies than white girls, according to University of Arizona nutritionist Sheila Parker and anthropologist Mimi Nichter, who led a three-year longitudinal study involving nearly three hundred white and black high school girls, because "white images of style [are] built around a more restricted set of beauty ideals," which leads most white girls to "express dissatisfaction with their bodies, especially in terms of their desire to lose weight as a way to 'be perfect' and popular."[19] The white girls described the "perfect" girl as five foot seven, weighing between 100 and 110 pounds, with long, flowing blond hair—that is, a Barbie doll. While 70 percent of the black teens told Parker and Nichter that they were satisfied with their weight, 90 percent of the white girls were dissatisfied.[20]

The "beauty myth"—Naomi Wolf's term for the concept that beauty is an objective, universally recognized quality that women want for themselves, with men wanting the women who have it—stirs up an ethic of sisterhood, since all girls are subject to it together. "Commiserating about the myth is as good as a baby to bring strange women into pleasant contact, and break down the line of Other Woman wariness. A wry smile about calories, a complaint about one's hair, can evaporate the sullen examination of a rival in the fluorescent light of a ladies' room."[21] Wolf is right: There is nothing more effective to jumpstart a conversation between two girls than complaining about tripping over platform shoes or finding just the right shade of blue nail polish. Anthropologists Mimi Nichter and Nancy Vuckovic have found that "fat talk"— repeatedly using expressions like "I'm so fat"—is a way of being part of a group, since it requires the listeners to jump in and say, "No, you're not."[22]

But sharing a common enemy leads only to an evanescent kind of solidarity. Too many girls become absorbed with the task of always trying to look better—better than what they currently look like, since whatever they look like is never good enough ("Does this shirt look stupid? Is my butt too big?")—and better than the other girls ("Are her jeans cooler than mine because the hems are wider?" "Where did she get those barrettes?"). Too often girls prove their own worth by diminishing others. Girls and women "can tend to resent each other if they look too 'good' and dismiss one another if they look too 'bad,'" notes Wolf.[23] And can you blame them? They know all too well that boys and men are praised for what they accomplish, while girls and women are praised for what they look like. And since they have generally not been exposed to feminism, it does not occur to them to contest the beauty ideal rather than each other.

Dieting is one way of trying to gain control in a world with unrealistic standards and unfair advantages. Food is a powerful metaphor. Controlling one's caloric intake says something that many of us cannot say with words: that one feels powerless. "I'm so fat" is a subtle way of saying, "I'm unhappy with myself."

Slut-bashing likewise is a sad attempt to wield power by those who feel they don't have any. It is a way for a girl who does not attain the beauty ideal (and how many do?) to establish her superior femininity. Her target? Girls whom she fears are prettier and shapelier. Parker and Nichter discovered that black girls respect those who embodied their version of the beauty ideal but that white girls resent those who matched their own ideal.[24] When she sees a girl she thinks is prettier than she is, confesses Paula, a white ninth-grader from Manhattan, she says, "She's so pretty, let's kill her." Paula's best friend Samantha volunteers, "If she's pretty, I loathe her." Paula cites the example of a new and really cute girl in her class. "When my friends and I first met her, we were like, 'Oh great, there's the end of our social life.'" Paula and her friends also assumed that the new girl was "dumb or shallow or obnoxious."

No wonder self-confidence plummets among adolescent girls. Two large-scale studies—conducted by the American Association of University Women and the Commonwealth Fund—show that girls ages nine to fifteen experience a "crisis in confidence."[25] In childhood, girls tend to be carefree—putting on playlets with their friends in full costume, climbing trees, skipping and somersaulting with abandon. But as they grow into preadolescence, according to the

Commonwealth Fund report, "girls were particularly likely to be critical of themselves, and one-quarter of older girls reported that they did not like or hated themselves. In contrast, only 14 percent of boys said they felt this way."[26] The Commonwealth Fund report goes on to link risky behaviors such as cigarette smoking, drinking, and using drugs with low self-esteem, suggesting that girls who like themselves are less likely to engage in these behaviors. Meanwhile the use of anti-depression medicine for young patients has soared—in 1996 nearly 600,000 children and adolescents were prescribed anti-depressants[27]—and of the two-million-plus American self-mutilators, most are women who begin cutting themselves at the age of fourteen.[28]

The conventional wisdom is that teenage girls suffer from low self-confidence because of the patriarchal pressures to look pretty, be polite, and become involved in a defining heterosexual relationship—the social expectation, in other words, that they conform to the feminine role model. Psychologist Mary Pipher, author of the best-selling call to arms *Reviving Ophelia,* writes, "Adolescent girls experience a conflict between their autonomous selves and their need to be feminine, between their status as human beings and their vocation as females." This is why, "just as planes and ships disappear mysteriously into the Bermuda Triangle, so do the selves of girls go down in droves."[29]

But too often girls are not innocent bystanders in some grand, patriarchal battle for their souls. They are complicit in bringing each other down. The behavior of other girls is a major cause of one's diminishing self-confidence. Girls habitually drop a member of their clique if she's deemed not popular or cool enough, and they can make life hell for a girl whom they've decided, for no particular rational reason, to hate.

It's true that girls' competitiveness sprouts from circumstances beyond their control: the pervasive idea that girls are inferior to boys; mixed messages about being both feminine and ambitious; a ludicrously restrictive beauty ideal. It's true that girls often turn on each other because of the social pressure to "get the guy." And it's true, as Letty Cottin Pogrebin has so cogently put it, that "our competitiveness is not a dirty act of treachery but the survival tactic of a second-class human being. Lacking confidence, bereft of self-esteem, we play the only game in town that seems to offer a payoff."[30] Women and girls lash out at other women and girls when they recognize that no matter how hard they work, and no matter what sacrifices they make, they will always have more to prove than men and boys do.

Nevertheless girls who shout out insults like "slut" and "bitch" to other girls must be held accountable for their behavior. They may be victims themselves, but that should not give them license to victimize others.

CHAPTER 6

FROM SEXISM TO
SEXUAL FREEDOM

I didn't cut myself. I didn't develop an eating disorder. I didn't turn to drugs or alcohol. I didn't OD on sleeping pills.

Instead, I cried. And when I say I cried, I mean that plump, salty tears blurred my vision, splotched my face, slid down my neck, and settled into the hollows of my collarbones. I cried on the commuter train home from school (in the morning, on my way into Manhattan, I was too tired to muster the energy). I cried at home at night, of course, behind my locked bedroom door. In school I cried in the library, where I spent my free periods. And I cried in the middle of class, in full view of my teachers.

The teachers saw everything: how could they have missed it? They witnessed the students who cast me scornful once-over looks when I entered a classroom, and who snickered audibly when I raised my hand. (Somehow, through my tears, I always managed to participate in class. The verbal volleys of classroom discussions served as a good distraction from my depression.) Yet not one teacher asked me what was wrong. And not one teacher reprimanded the students who made me the target of their vindictive adolescent humor.

One day a high-level school administrator called me into her office. Finally, recognition from above! But instead of being concerned, she was confrontational. She told me that my crying was disruptive to the other students. If I didn't see a therapist, she warned me, she might have to consider asking me to leave the school. Then she softened and asked me why I was so sad. I told her that the other students were making fun of me, but I did not disclose the details of the slut-bashing. For one thing, having just handed me a callous threat, the administrator did not exactly inspire my trust. Besides, I didn't have a clue that what I was undergoing could have been considered harassment, sexual or otherwise. I had chalked it up to adolescent meanness, plain and simple—and remember, I felt that I deserved it. And so, after promising to make an appointment with a psychologist, I raced for the door. Thus ended my one and only meeting with a faculty member to discuss my slut-bashed school life.

In a national survey of teenage girls published in *Seventeen* in 1993, only 8 percent of the girls who responded reported that their schools had, and enforced, a policy on sexual harassment. Even when girls told a teacher or administrator about the harassment, nothing happened to the harasser in 45 percent of the incidents reported.[1] It's not that teachers and administrators are oblivious. They just don't consider slut-bashing a serious problem. They tend to dismiss it as typical adolescent cruelty and a rite of passage. Even when adult observers do recognize the name-calling as improper behavior, they often do not consider it a form of sexual harassment. To most people, "sexual harassment" is a problem exclusive to the work world—an act carried out by a male boss to intimidate a female colleague. But repeatedly making fun of a girl as a "slut" (or a boy as a "fag"), even when carried out by another girl, is also a form of sexual harassment. It is unwanted and unwelcomed sexual attention that creates a hostile environment and reduces a girl to a sexual category.

"SLUTS" AND SUITS

If a girl believes that she is experiencing sexual harassment at school, she should complain to her school administration. (See Appendix A for advice on how to file a complaint.) If a girl's school is unresponsive, she can file a complaint with the U.S. Department of Education's Office for Civil Rights (OCR) within her state. The OCR enforces Title IX of the Education Amendments of 1972, which prohibits discrimination on the basis of sex in education programs and activities in schools that receive federal money. Since 1989, the OCR has investigated claims of peer sexual harassment. If a school fails to respond to instances of peer-to-peer sexual harassment once it has been put on notice, the OCR can find the school monetarily liable. In many states a student may also file a complaint with the Department of Human Rights, which similarly oversees state laws on sexual harassment in education.

Katy Lyle, who filed a complaint with her state's Department of Human Rights, was the first public school student ever to receive a monetary settlement for sexual harassment. Katy is attractive, with fluffy blond hair, kittenish features, and a pert nose, the kind of girl you would probably describe as "cute." In the fall of her sophomore year at Central High School in Duluth, Minnesota, one and a half months after entering the school as a new student, Katy became the object of graphic sexual graffiti.[2]

Katie Lyle is a slut.

One day in October 1987, a senior came up to her. He and Katy were friendly because they shared locker space. "I don't know you that well," he said, "but you seem like a really nice girl. Do you know what they're writing about you?" He told her that there was some graffiti in the second-floor boys' bathroom, but he didn't get very specific.

"I thought he was just kidding. It seemed ridiculous. I hadn't dated anyone. But then he came up to me a second time a few days later and told me some of the things that were written—that I was a 'slut'—and that I should try to do something to get the writing off. Then I realized he must be serious." He told her that she was the only girl singled out.

Because of logistics, Katy had chosen not to attend the more prestigious high school in town, where her city friends from junior high went. Instead she attended Central, where most of her classmates were country kids. "I was a country kid too, but I lived on a lake. Some of the other kids might have been resentful of me. Somebody picked me for some reason and put it up there. And then, when it wasn't removed, it gave other guys an incentive to top it. The comments about me just kept going and going. Since they spelled my name wrong—with an *ie* instead of a *y*—it leads me to believe that whoever started it didn't know me that well."

I fucked Katie Lyle. Katie Lyle gives good head.

She had started Central with "good girl" values written all over her: she was enrolled in advanced classes, and her new friends were the well-liked, all-American types who became cheerleaders. She was just beginning to feel comfortable with her new surroundings. And she was doing well—though quiet, Katy wasn't shy. She went to football games and played piano and saxophone in the school band and jazz ensemble. Friends came over to her house to swim, water-ski, or ice-skate. But the relationships that were in formation never had a chance to gel.

Katie Lyle fucks farm animals.

People stopped talking to her. Soon she started getting comments in the halls from the guys: "Katy, I took a shit in your stall this morning." "Why don't you come to my house and show me if it's true." "Are you as good as everyone says?" "Oh Katy, do me." The girls treated her like she had a contagious disease. It was clear that she was no longer welcome among them.

Katy complained to a guidance counselor, a woman, who promised that the graffiti would be removed immediately. But no one did anything about it, and the comments became progressively more obscene. Having spent months only hearing about the graffiti, Katy decided to slip into the boys' room to have a look. Nothing prepared her for what she saw: The second stall was entirely covered with permanent-ink scrawls, the comments spilling over the door as well as both walls. A few guys had actually carved their comments with a razor blade. Katy stood there, staring and reading. On the bus ride home she couldn't contain her tears.

Katy quietly went about trying to get the graffiti removed. She's not the kind of person who seeks attention or publicity; she just wanted the whole thing to disappear. She went to two more guidance counselors and then the principal. "Boys will be boys," he told her—literally—and added that the experience would make her a stronger person; after all, "graffiti is a fact of life." But because he considered it a building-maintenance problem rather than an issue of sexual harassment, he didn't aggressively pursue its removal, and the graffiti remained.

Katie Lyle sucked my dog off. Katie Lyle sucked my dick after she sucked my dog's dick.

It took two months to work up the courage to confide in her parents. "It was really hard with my dad, since he was a guy once, too, you know. He would know what kinds of girls they write stuff about, and I didn't want him to think about me that way. But I knew right away that they were going to support me because they said, 'It's not your fault and we'll do everything we can to help you.'"

Two weeks before her senior year Katy and her mother drove to Central to find out if the graffiti had been removed once and for all. Katy's mother parked the car in the lot and went inside. Katy remained in the car; she refused to enter the building. A janitor escorted her mother into the bathroom and the infamous stall. When she returned a few minutes later, she was crying. "So I knew the graffiti was still there, two years after it had begun." That day, Katy and her parents had a new resolve: they confronted the school board and for the first time after eighteen months and sixteen separate complaints, the bathroom was finally cleaned. It was also the day they decided to file a complaint of sexual harassment through the Minnesota Department of Human Rights. "I wanted the school to know that what had happened to me was not right," explains Katy. "The thing I wanted most was an apology from my principal."

Katy and her family kept the complaint "super quiet" during her senior year. She didn't even tell her best friend about it. "I was really hoping that I would be able to write policy changes and implement a good policy in Duluth about this. So it went back and forth all through my senior year of high school and then all through my freshman year of college. Then we had a mediation session with the school board, in the spring of my freshman year in college. At the end of September in my sophomore year in college, the complaint got settled. We didn't tell anybody."

But after the settlement, for which Katy received fifteen thousand dollars, the school district leaked the news. It was written up the next day, in September 1991, on the front page of the Duluth local paper. A couple of days later, Katy received calls from a number of reporters at other newspapers, including *The New York Times*. During the next year she appeared on the talk show circuit and all the morning shows.

"People started to treat me differently," Katy recalls. "They thought I was a terrible person for suing the school district. They thought it was a stupid, petty thing to try to get money out of, and I put up with a lot of grief in college. I've had to deal with a lot of people who think I was looking for press, which I wasn't. People would come up to me and say nasty things: 'Oh, we talked about you in my psych class today,' or 'We talked about you in women's studies today.'

There was a real backlash, and dealing with it is even harder than just having to justify that I'm not a 'slut.' Now I have to justify that it's okay for me to bring the complaint."

Clearly, formal complaints and lawsuits are important and necessary: They send a strong message to schools that they are obligated to try to halt the cruel behavior and develop and enforce sexual-harassment policies. The complaints and lawsuits also make it clear that verbal harassment can be just as damaging as physical attacks. And they infuse young women with the determination to prevent slut-bashing and the damage it causes to other potential victims.

"My grandma at first told me that the complaint was a dumb idea, and that I should try to get violence off TV instead—that I should make that my cause," Katy relates with a chuckle. "And then all of a sudden she looked at me and said, 'You know, back in 1932'—and then she started crying. She went on to tell me about what some guy had done to her and said to her. She didn't get very explicit, but from what I can tell, it sounds like it was sexual harassment. And here it's sixty-something years later, and she's crying about it. It sticks with you for a long time."

But essential as they are, lawsuits also have some serious shortcomings. For one thing, I believe that if the school does not know about the harassment, or does know and makes serious, good-faith attempts to quell it, it should not be held liable; instead the harasser should be. (In 1999 the Supreme Court ruled that school districts receiving federal money can be liable for monetary damages if they fail to prevent severe persistent sexual harassment among students.)

Also, the charge of sexual harassment implies that the problem is strictly gendered—that boys alone are responsible for harassing girls as "sluts." Yet, as we have seen, girls can be vicious name-callers and rumor-mongers. When the "slut" reputation is shoehorned into a legalistic framework, guilty girls tend to get off the hook. (In one OCR case in San Jose, California, a girl was subjected to repeated sexual rumors, taunts, and graffiti, but the school did not investigate the complaint because it did not consider the conduct sexual harassment: The harasser was also a girl.[3])

It's also not always so evident what is sexual harassment and what is simply an instance of sexual teasing, and I worry about the two being confused. Sexual teasing can be hostile, of course, but sometimes it's nothing more than playful and curious behavior on the part of both boys and girls. When in 1996 two young boys—a seven-year-old in Queens and a six-year-old in North Carolina—kissed classmates, they were charged with sexual harassment.[4] No one questioned whether the boys' intent was malicious or playful or somewhere in between. In fact no one analyzed their behavior at all. In both cases their behavior was instantly classified as sexual harassment and they were suspended accordingly.

Sexual harassment sometimes becomes a catchall term for a wide variety of obnoxious behaviors. Laurie, a high school student in the Midwest, brought a sexual harassment complaint against her school through the Department of Human Rights in 1993 after her name appeared on a list of the "twenty-five most fuckable girls."[5] One of the charges in her case was that a male student had pasted sexually explicit photographs of women on a manila folder. She was also upset that, during a Winterfest skit, two students were dressed as Pee Wee Herman and his girlfriend. The Pee Wee Herman character had a mirror on his shoe and used it to look up the dress of his girlfriend, who said, "Oh, don't look up my dress; I don't have any panties on." Certainly Laurie was right that the Pee Wee Herman joke belittled girls and women by reducing them to their sexuality, and did not belong in a school skit. But was it a form of sexual harassment under the law? Laurie seemed to have confused sexual harassment with sexism, and along the way she made sexuality her target. Her case was settled out of court for forty thousand dollars.

Laurie's confusion, by the way, is distressingly common. Nearly one third of Americans find sexual references or images in advertising "offensive," according to a study conducted by *American Demographics*. Women ages thirty-five to fifty-four in particular are likely to be offended by advertising that features sex.[6] Many sexually charged ads are sexist, to be sure, but somehow I doubt that it's the sexism that Americans find "offensive." If that were the case, they would also find car commercials "offensive," since these commercials nearly always showcase female models draped over the merchandise as if they were part of a package deal. I suspect that it's the commodification of sex, not sexism, that troubles most of the offended.

An even deeper problem with the lawsuits is that they may actually promote, rather than inhibit, the targeting of girls as "sluts." Litigation tends to reinforce the attitude that leads to girls being labeled sluts in the first place. Given the way suits are structured, with clear-cut victims and aggressors, it is nearly impossible to fight the "slut" label on the grounds of sexual harassment without strengthening the boundary between "good" girls and "bad" ones. When a girl is waging a legal battle against being identified as sexually active, she inevitably defends herself by claiming to be "good." The girl harassed as a "slut" can't be an innocent victim, the logic goes, unless she is sexually innocent.

My own story is instructive. I never considered suing—I didn't even realize I could—but my reaction was typical of those who sue: I escaped into the persona of a celibate "good" girl. I feverishly sought to be known as a smart girl, not a sexual one. The trade-off: I excelled academically but I was miserable and inhibited. Looking back, I realize that my defense was a tacit endorsement of the sexual double standard. In an irony that was lost on me at the time, those who defined me by my sexuality caused my sexuality to become stunted.

Paula Pinczewski underwent a similar process. The summer before her junior year, she began dating a boy in college. "But I wouldn't let him touch me. All I let him do in the beginning was put his arm around me. He would be like, 'Why can't I kiss you?' I was like, 'I don't know why, but my mind tells me it's bad.' I was afraid that he was going to turn me into the whore I supposedly was, and that was the last thing I needed."

The question is: How do you contest being labeled a slut without criticizing what it means to be a "slut"? In other words, how do you uphold the notion that girls should have more sexual freedom, not less, when you are waging a battle against being identified as a sexually active girl? It seems that those who appeal to the law go to enormous lengths to prove their "good girl" status. "I'm not the type of girl boys write that stuff about," Katy told me. The implication is that it is acceptable to ostracize the type of girl whom boys *would* write that stuff about.

When your sexuality is used against you, the temptation is to distance yourself from it. It is precisely this mind-set that led Katy to present herself as a virginal "good" girl when she appeared on the talk shows. "At the *Maury Povich* show, they had one guy stand up and ask me, 'Well, just because you weren't dating someone doesn't mean you were a virgin.' My parents were there and everything. I got this cute little innocent look on my face like I was totally appalled. And Maury came to my rescue. He said, 'Oh now, come on, you apologize to her.'" Phil Donahue hushed an audience member who inquired about Katy's sexuality. ("If you weren't dating these guys," the audience member asked, "how did this all come about?") The complaints of a "slut" would never be taken seriously, the show seemed to suggest, if she were sexually active. Similarly, in an ABC "After-School Special" broadcast in 1994, a character based on Lyle was portrayed as totally asexual, her figure hidden beneath baggy madras shirts. The program, which is used in schools across the country as a training tool, portrayed boys (with the exception of Lyle's brother) as oversexed perverts.

Katy embraced the asexual identity of the "good" girl in

her personal life as well, both before and after the lawsuit. "When I met new people, I felt the incredible need to make myself seem like a prude." During tenth and eleventh grades she didn't even try to date anyone. But in her senior year she started to date the captain of the football team and goalie of the hockey team—"Mr. Joe Stud on campus." He had to put up with rude comments from the other guys—things like "I don't know why you're going out with her." But he was supportive, and Katy was finally able to relax and enjoy school. There was only one problem: She was still acting like a prude. She explains, "I didn't want him to think I was 'like that.'"

Katie Lyle is a sex slave.

Even in college Katy worried about her dates thinking that she was "like that." She told me about one night when she invited a new guy she had met to join her while she house-sat. They cooked a pizza and watched TV. Then he kissed her. "I didn't want to see him again because I figured he was only interested in that part of me. I brought him home right after that. The next day I said, 'I was kind of mad about that, and didn't appreciate that very much.' He wanted to know why. I said, 'Because you didn't ask.' It's stupid stuff like that I get hung up on still." Should he have asked? "Maybe. It depends on the situation. In that given situation I think he should have."

Katy didn't want to be thought of in sexual terms, even in sexual situations. Being asexual gave her self-confidence because it made her feel like the "good" girl she knew she was all along. She liked to be in control: No one was going to kiss her without her prior consent. "It takes me a very long time to trust a guy. It's like he has to prove himself to me so that I know he's interested in me and not in some preconceived notion he has of me."

Even Nan Stein, director of the Sexual Harassment in Schools Project at Wellesley College's Center for Research on Women—the most visible feminist in the country speaking out against sexual harassment in schools—is concerned that contesting sexual harassment can lead to restrictions on sexual expression. "In some states, in some circles," she points out, "the following statement is viewed as sexual harassment, no matter the age of the speakers: 'I see London, I see France, I see Susie's underpants.'"[7] In 1994, Millis High School in Millis, Massachusetts, banned hand-holding, hugging, or any other physical contact between students on school grounds. The school enacted the rule in response to a lawsuit brought against a football player who had raped or sexually assaulted eleven female students. Stein complains that the rule is an overreaction to the fear of lawsuits, and that "there's not enough hand-holding in high school."[8] In its zeal to protect female students, Millis High administrators seem to have confused sexual harassment with female sexuality. If girls are "good," if they remain asexual, the policy implies, then they won't be harassed.

Small wonder that some former "sluts" themselves pick on others as "sluts." One college student who, like Katy, settled her lawsuit out of court, told me about a classmate whom she and her friends pick on for being a "slut." But come to think of it, there isn't any hard evidence that the classmate has slept around. "We just assume. But if the gossip starts to get graphic, then I get uncomfortable, and I let my discomfort be known. It's gotten me into trouble a few times, because people think I'm really bitchy." It seems that everyone, the school "slut" included, can always find someone less "good" than herself to police.

The way things stand now, lawsuits put "sluts" in a double bind. For real progress to occur, teachers and school administrators need to be trained about sexual harassment, but they also need to be taught that teenage girls have just as much a right to be sexual as boys do. Lawyers and others involved in sexual-harassment claims need to remember that sexuality is not the same as sexism. Otherwise girls involved in lawsuits may win lucrative settlements and awards, but at the cost of denying girls' sexuality.

JUST SAY NO TO ABSTINENCE-ONLY EDUCATION

The turn of the millennium is a sexually conflicted time for teenagers. On the one hand, teens seem incredibly sexually sophisticated: They get into R-rated movies with ease, openly joke about Viagra, and discuss the minutiae of President Clinton's sex life. But for many the facade of maturity belies serious sexual ignorance. Our government, after all, contends that graphic sexual facts, no matter how informative, must be shielded from teens. Surgeon General Joycelyn Elders was forced out of her job because she condoned the idea of teaching schoolchildren, in sex-education classes, to masturbate as a way of avoiding the spread of the AIDS virus.[9] Donna Shalala, Secretary of Health and Human Services, wrote a letter to Ann Landers begging the advice columnist's readers to preach abstinence to the young men and women in their community. And what do teens need to help them remain sexually responsible? Shalala did not breathe a word about birth control or informative sex education. Instead, she wrote, the only things teens need are "healthful activities such as sports, art programs and jobs."[10]

Then, in 1997, Bill Clinton denounced comprehensive sex education, which provides information about birth control and safe-sex practices even while it encourages students to postpone sex. The premise behind comprehensive sex education is that students should be prepared and responsible whenever they do decide to initiate sexual activity. Clinton, worried that this curriculum might encourage teens to have sex, urged school districts to offer instead abstinence-only curricula, which do not present any information about contraception and safe sex.[11] Advocates of abstinence-only curricula claim that comprehensive sex education offers a mixed message: "It's like saying don't drink and drive, but here's a beer and here are the car keys," says Chris Ardizzone, executive director of the conservative group Eagle Forum.[12]

Yet a mixed message may be the most honest message we

can convey when it comes to teenage sex. The bottom line is that most teens will not delay intercourse until they are married—especially given the fact that many of them won't marry until they're twenty-six or older (if they marry at all). Telling teens to abstain from sexual activity is as hopelessly ineffective as all-day lipstick. In my opinion we would do better to discuss openly with teenagers that there is more to sex than intercourse; if they truly feel mature enough and ready to have sex, they should limit themselves to sexual activities that do not pose the risk of pregnancy or HIV transmission. Too many teens believe that anything besides intercourse is simply foreplay and therefore not "real" sex. They have a very narrow perspective on what sex is. We could lower the rate of pregnancy and sexually transmitted diseases if we were open with teenagers about the wide range of pleasurable sexual activities.

In any event there is no evidence that comprehensive sex education encourages teens to have sex. After analyzing thirty-five studies of comprehensive sex education programs around the world, the World Health Organization concluded that they did not lead to an increase in sexual activity.[13] In the United States two separate studies revealed that making condoms easily accessible to public high school students does not increase rates of sexual activity (though it does increase condom use among those already sexually active).[14] And there is no evidence that preaching abstinence actually works. U.S. teens are much less likely to have access to free or low-cost contraceptive services than their counterparts in other industrialized countries, and live in one of the most sexually conservative of Western countries, with sex widely regarded as sinful and dirty. Is it a coincidence that they also have the highest pregnancy, abortion, and birth rates?[15]

If anything, abstinence-only programs can cause more harm than good. An estimated four thousand school districts currently use abstinence-only curricula, according to Phyllida Burlingame, a researcher for the Public Media Center and the

Applied Research Center. The most widely taught course is called *Sex Respect,* which has been purchased by approximately two thousand school districts nationwide. The text states that "There's no way to have premarital sex without hurting someone," and in an accompanying video a student asks, "What if I want to have sex before I get married?" The instructor replies, "Well, I guess you'll just have to be prepared to die. And you'll probably take with you your spouse and one or more of your children." Abortion is referred to only as "killing the baby." In the narratives presented in *Sex Respect,* premarital sex always leads to pregnancy or disease; there is no mention of contraceptives or abortion. Even in the best-case scenario, the curriculum says, premarital sex will cause severe emotional pain ("There's no condom strong enough to protect my heart").[16] Other abstinence-only curricula exaggerate the failure rate of condoms and suggest that after sex when a condom is used, the genitals should be washed with Lysol.[17]

Sex Respect features scare tactics aimed at teens of both sexes, but it does particular damage with its misinformation about female sexuality. Girls are taught that they don't feel sexual desire the way that boys do. A chart indicates that boys become genitally aroused as soon as they begin "necking," whereas girls don't feel aroused until the next stages, "petting" and "heavy petting." *Sex Respect* also argues that a boy only pretends to be in love with a girl in order to have sex with her, and that a girl only pretends to enjoy sex with a boy in order to feel loved. "A male can experience complete sexual release with a female even if he doesn't particularly like her," the text reads. "A female, however, experiences more sexual fulfillment with a person she trusts and who is committed to her. Some people describe the difference this way: Boys tend to use love to get sex. Girls tend to use sex to get love."[18] A girl who feels aroused during "necking" and who enjoys being sexual is told that there is something fundamentally wrong with her. She learns that sex is something to be resisted. She does not learn how to take control of her own desire and her own sexual choices.

In addition, a drawing of the female reproductive anatomy included in the Student Workbook features the vagina, ovaries, uterus, cervix, fallopian tubes, and endometrium—but no clitoris. The clitoris is literally erased; nor is it mentioned in the glossary.[19] Girls in *Sex Respect* classes are kept shamefully ignorant of their own bodies.

The curriculum confirms the anxieties of girls who have sexual desires but are worried about being "bad." One girl is quoted in the accompanying Student Workbook as saying that she was very insulted when someone offered her birth control pills at the age of fifteen. She replied, "Thanks, but no thanks. What do you think I am?"[20] The text says, "You think sex will be 'safe' if you use contraceptives. You wonder if they really work. You feel guilty beforehand because now you are 'planning' to do something wrong for you, and you can't pretend anymore that 'it just happened.'"[21] It's twisted logic like this—which encourages boys but especially girls not to plan ahead by acquiring a contraceptive—that leads to unplanned pregnancy. After all, a girl who has been fitted for a diaphragm or is on the Pill or has bought a pack of condoms is, according to *Sex Respect,* a "slut." No wonder that fewer than half of sexually experienced teenagers said they always used contraception when they had sex.[22]

Campaigns to promote abstinence always seem to pay particular attention to the virtues of female chastity. True, the simplistic slogan "Just Say No," which was everywhere in the late eighties and nineties, was targeted to both boys and girls. And billboards across the country—depicting hip-looking couples with the message, "Abstinence makes the heart grow fonder. (You can go farther when you don't go all the way.")[23]—have been seen by teens of both genders. But in television, movies, and music, the ubiquitous happy virgins have been universally female. Prime-time female characters defined by their virginity were featured in *L.A. Law* and *Beverly Hills*

90210, in *Blossom* and *Clueless.* Rock musician Juliana Hatfield admitted publicly that she was still a virgin, as did Kennedy, the host of an MTV show. Virginity is a valuable commodity for all teens, we are told, but for girls its value skyrockets.

True Love Waits, an evangelical organization preaching teen abstinence, tells girls that the only way they can experience true love is if they remain chaste. The appeal of True Love Waits, which boasts more than 220,000 members, is its concept of "secondary virginity": If a nonvirgin pledges abstinence, it's as if she were a virgin. She can be reborn, as it were. True Love Waits members attend rallies in sports stadiums and sign a pledge card bearing the organization's covenant: "Believing that true love waits, I make a commitment to God, myself, my family, my friends, my future mate, and my future children to be sexually abstinent from this day until the day I enter a biblical marriage relationship." At a 1994 abstinence rally in Anaheim, California, the teens were separated by gender for simultaneous seminars. At the "For Guys Only" seminar, the boys were taught that premarital sex was wrong, end of story; they spent their allotted time chanting, "We are real men! We are real men!" Meanwhile, at the "Girls Only" session, the speaker implored the girls to save their virginity until their wedding night, otherwise they would never achieve true and eternal love.[24] When selling chastity to girls, love is always the bait.

The love-sex connection for girls should come as no surprise. Most Americans believe that female sexuality is based on romantic, mushy feelings, rather than lustful ones. When it comes to sex scenes in the movies, for instance, *The New York Times* reports that "male and female tastes differ sharply.... Typically, women are happier with the metaphors for sex on screen (and the coy banter of seduction), while men prefer watching the act itself, or creative variations of it." I don't doubt for a minute that females and males relate different preferences, but isn't it possible that the teenage girl or woman who is turned on by, say, the steamy sex in a movie like *Basic Instinct* is uncomfortable with her arousal, and therefore either represses or denies it? Certainly this outcome is a strong possibility, given all the messages she has absorbed about the inherently different natures of female and male sexuality. As film critic Molly Haskell told the *Times,* "The problem is that deep down we still believe that a sexual woman is a bad woman. I think female desire is very threatening because it means that Mother is sexual… women are afraid of female sexuality too."[25] Haskell's razor-sharp insight was buried three-quarters into the article: The idea that we are threatened by sexual women is itself threatening. And the idea that women as well as men like sex is alarming. We still don't even know whether women are aroused by explicit talk of sex. To date, no one has come up with a reliable way to measure female arousal. "For most medical professionals, a woman's genitals are still 'down there,'" confesses John Gagnon, a sociology professor at the State University of New York at Stony Brook.[26]

As long as being a "good" girl means being asexual, the slut label will thrive. Honest sex education—which discusses female desire rather than false and scary scenarios about "bad" girls who go too far—is a prerequisite for eliminating the word slut from our vocabulary.

A SUPPORT SYSTEM

Volumes of books have been written about the sinking confidence levels of preadolescent and adolescent girls, about how so many girls are meek and hesitant and afraid of saying or doing anything daring. Essayist Sallie Tisdale was struck by the distinction between boys and girls on the cusp of adolescence when she taught writing to 110 freshmen and sophomores at a big inner-city high school. The assignment: that her students write an autobiography of their future—any possible future. One sophomore girl queried, "Is this legal?" She clarified, "I mean, is it legal to write about something we don't know anything about?" The boys, Tisdale reports, handed in outlines dealing with adventure, crime, and inventions. One student expected war with China. Another invented a time warp. Another resurrected Jesus. And another is shot by a robber. The girls, on the other hand, imagined very different futures. "One after the other writes of falling in love, getting married, having children, and giving up—giving up careers, travel, college, sports, private hopes, to save the marriage, take care of the children. The outlines seem to describe with remarkable precision the quietly desperate and disappointed lives many women live today."[27]

Given the mixed messages girls receive about their sexuality, it's no wonder that so many of them feel so paralyzed that they can't even imagine a future beyond marriage and motherhood. And if they can't imagine an exciting future, what kind of future will they create for themselves?

Many parents and educators believe that the panacea is all-girls schools. The theory is that since boys dominate classroom discussions and gym activities, girls receive an inferior education as a result, and that they are therefore more likely to blossom if they are segregated from the boys. But I have always suspected that all-girl environments are not necessarily superior to coed ones. Abstinence-only curricula, with their damaging lessons about female sexuality, are not limited to coed schools. Girls as well as boys are apt to perpetuate double standards. And slut-bashing, as we have seen, tends to be instigated by girls. Indeed, one of my interviewees, Linda Giovanni, was called a slut in her exclusive Manhattan all-girls private school and ended up transferring to a coed school to escape the harassment. I also believe that girls and boys need to learn to interact with one another and see each other up close as human beings; segregation can cause one group to become alienated from or fearful of the other group—leading to more double standards. Even the American Association of University Women, after studying single-sex education programs, concluded that single-sex schools might reinforce stereotypical roles for girls and boys.[28]

If parents really want to help their daughters through adolescence, they should simply pay attention to them. No matter what is troubling them, teens need to know they can confide in their parents. Teenagers who have strong emotional attachments to their parents are less likely to use drugs and alcohol, attempt suicide, engage in violence, or become sexually active at an early age, according to the largest study ever conducted of American adolescents. More important than the amount of time parents spend at home, and more important than whether one lives in a one- or two-parent household, the study found, is the attention and love that parents give to their teenage children.[29]

Of all the girls and women I spoke with, those who had close relationships with their parents were best equipped to fight back against their "slut" reputations. Carla Karampatos, a high school senior, reports that when she told her parents that the girls in her tenth grade class called her a slut and a bitch, "they were always there for me" and went to meet with her teachers several times. When Paula Pinczewski told her parents, "They were very supportive. I'd come home with tears in my eyes and my mom would give me a hug and say, 'Do you want to talk about it?' I'd say, 'That's the last thing I want to do right now' and she'd be like, 'Okay, you want to watch a movie?' She did anything to keep my mind off of it."

For real changes to occur, girls need to change the way they relate to one another. If they can contest slut-bashing as a group rather than as individuals, they stand a fighting chance of exposing the sexual double standard—after all, they can't *all* be "sluts." To that end, I encourage girls to overcome their competitive impulses and to form girl groups that meet after school or on weekends. Girl groups are not intended to shut out boys; they are simply meant as a forum for girls to discuss the issues that affect them—everything from slut-bashing to how they feel about the *Sports Illustrated* swimsuit issue. If there are boys who are interested in the subjects being discussed, and can offer respectful and meaningful comments, they can be invited to some of the meetings. Carla Karampatos relates that she formed a women's-issues group at her school. At the first meeting, held at the end of the school year, twenty girls came, which was a promising turnout because her school is small. "I realized that I'm not the only girl who's had problems," she says excitedly. "I learned through the group that some others were called bitches, too. Next year we're going to talk about body image and sexism and sexual harassment. We're going to have Awareness Days where we put up posters about these issues. I hope to make some friends through the group."

Similarly, Jackie Garcia attends a women's group at her community college, where the participants "talk about issues and relationships. Sometimes we go to the cafeteria and invite guys and discuss things with them. I think talking in a group helps better than talking one-on-one with a therapist. When I went to a therapist, all she did was ask questions and that was it. In a group you get more feedback and everybody thinks differently and has their own opinion. I like to listen to the other people's stories and what they went through."

Through sharing personal stories, girls in girl groups learn that they are not the only ones who have experienced harassment, extreme dieting, or abusive boyfriends. They come to recognize that a situation that might seem "normal" (because they've never seen anything else to compare it with) is in fact oppressive. And they resolve to work together to overturn the oppressive situation.

One group of fourteen-year-old girls in Ames, Iowa, decided to do something about the Hooters T-shirts that several boys in their middle school wore to school and that they felt parodied girls' breasts. The T-shirts, which advertised the Hooters restaurant chain, featured owl eyes peering out from the nipple areas, inside the O letters, along with the slogan

"More Than a Mouthful." The girls responded by creating their own T-shirt with a picture of a rooster on it and the slogan "Cocks—Less Than a Mouthful."[30]

In response, the principal, who had never punished the boys for wearing the Hooters shirts, suspended four students (including three boys) for wearing the Cocks shirts. They were told that the Hooters shirts referred to a legitimate commercial business, whereas the Cocks shirts did nothing more than make fun of boys' anatomy. In the end, the school administration banned both the Cocks and the Hooters shirts, even though the girls never wanted censorship. They intended only to make the Hooters shirts "socially unacceptable rather than legally unacceptable," in the words of one exasperated eighth-grader.[31] The girls lost this battle; nevertheless their time was well spent. They were able to publicize their message with a good dose of humor and creativity. They taught others about the sexual double standard. They also learned a sad, important lesson: that schools commonly impose censorship instead of confronting sexism and dealing with sexual expression.

A girl group that did see positive results is the Teddie Bears from Santa Clara High School in Santa Clara, California. The Teddie Bears is the name of an all-female squad that for eighteen years kept statistics at Santa Clara Bruins football games. The girls attended every game and compiled statistics on the players for the school and the local newspapers, which helped them win scholarships to attend college. The all-female group also carried water to the players and sold programs at the games.[32] In October 1995 all fifteen members of the Teddie Bears resigned in protest after the principal did nothing to stop repeated verbal and physical sexual harassment from boys on the team, who had circulated sexual rumors about them, grabbed their breasts, and spat on them.

The resignations resulted in retaliation by the football players and indifference by the administration. The athletes defaced football programs containing the girls' pictures with sexual drawings and circulated a slam book that listed the girls along with descriptions of them as sexually promiscuous. Still nothing was done to discipline the boys involved. Instead, the girls say, the principal threatened them with disciplinary action for "playing an equal part in the problem" and told them the school could not guarantee their safety at football games. The director of personnel for the school district said, "From my point of view, statisticians are very important to the team, but I don't know that they have to run around on the sidelines in short skirts. They perpetuate this thing: 'Look at me, I'm a cute little thing in my short skirt with my fanny hanging out.'" Interestingly, the girls didn't wear skirts; they wore sweatsuits.[33]

Finally, five of the fifteen girls filed a sexual-harassment complaint against the school district. (It was later settled out of court for an undisclosed sum.)[34] Only then did the school begin suspending some of the football players, and it expelled one. And only then did the harassment stop.

When one girl fights back against being sexualized, inevitably she feels compelled to defend her honor: she is a "good" girl, she wants us all to know. (Other girls may be "sluts," but not her.) When girls fight back together, they don't feel the need to justify their "goodness" because they don't feel pitted against each other. As a result they are able to point out that, when it comes to sexuality, girls are not treated equally or fairly. And because they speak up together, their voices get heard.

When we say that a boy or man is "bad," we generally mean that he drinks, or can't make a commitment to a woman, or can't hold down a job. Perhaps he is a womanizer, but "bad" for a male doesn't necessarily translate into "womanizer." When we say that a girl or woman is "bad," however, we always mean that she has an active sex life.

We can overturn this linguistic connection, and we must start with teenagers. This means encouraging girls to demand sexual equality and educating them about birth control. It means gently persuading girls who hunch over their breasts to stand up straight and strong. It means pointing out to boys the hypocrisy of devaluing girls who "fool around" at the same time that they brag to their male buddies about how far they got last night. It means being sympathetic to the girl who says she had unwanted sex, even if she wasn't raped in the legal sense, and explaining to the boy involved that silence does not equal consent. It means revealing to girls that other girls are potential allies, not enemies, by teaching them from the youngest ages that it's okay to compete publicly, that wearing size-16 leggings is nothing to be ashamed of, and that they can have a great time spending Saturday nights with the girls. And it means showing rather than telling boys and girls that conformity can be stifling: we must set an example by speaking our own opinionated minds.

After decades of telling girls that they have the same abilities as boys, isn't it time we started treating them as equal to boys?

AFTERWORD
to the Perennial Edition

Most people who meet me for the first time are surprised by two things: that I am the type of person who would ever write a book with a title like *Slut!*, and that I was once known as a "slut." I have been described in print as "demure" and as "a petite brunette with wire-rimmed glasses"—code words for nice, shy, bookish. On the Oprah Winfrey show, I was presented as a nice, middle-class woman married to a nice, middle-class man. Over and over I am told, "But you're so clean-cut—you don't seem like a slut at all."

My point exactly: Any girl or woman can be labeled a "slut." Looks and attitude often have nothing to do with it. Yet the word continues to evoke for most people an image of someone trampy and pathetic—the kind of girl or woman who wears short, tight, cleavage-enhancing clothes, always makes a beeline for the guy who enters the room, and can't string two sentences together without making a non sequitur. In short, she deserves to be called a "slut."

In presenting the stories of a wide range of accomplished and intelligent girls and women labeled "sluts," I have attempted to dispel the stereotype of the sleazy "slut" with

227

whorish hormones. Yet when journalists contacted me in the aftermath of the publication of the hardcover edition of this book in 1999, I discovered that even with all the evidence in front of them, they *still* had a lot of trouble swallowing the idea that "slut" rarely indicates anything more than the sexism of the name-caller. In fact, a number of reporters told me that they wanted to write an article about slut-bashing, but that the newspapers they worked for were too "conservative" and "family-oriented," and therefore wouldn't allow such an article to appear. Two different *New York Times* reporters from two different sections expressed an interest in interviewing me, but then called back to say that they wouldn't be able to after all: their editors were concerned about using the word "slut" in the pages of the esteemed paper of record. Journalists from other papers ran into the same obstacle, but luckily they succeeded in running stories that included the dreaded four-letter word—though *Newsday* felt compelled to add that the title of this book "is one that you might discreetly cover with another coffee table book."

"Slut" is, of course, a disturbing insult. But it is part of the vocabulary of adolescents—and adults—and a key word in the vocabulary of the sexual double standard. The severity of the word might offend some people, such as a racial or ethnic insult would, but refraining from using it in serious discussion serves only to reinforce its power. After all, "nigger" is a profoundly disturbing word, but can we have an honest conversation about racism without using it? I don't think so. Likewise, we must use the word "slut" and openly discuss its ramifications in order to eliminate the sexual double standard.

Below are some of the comments I've received from men and women in bookstores and radio call-in shows, and from television and radio show hosts. It's clear that most people are far more concerned with the sexuality of girls than with that of boys. My responses point out that females as well as males should be entitled to express their sexual desires. Hardly a radical concept, but it can stir up a lot of hostility.

SLUT-BASHING IS A TERRIBLE THING, BUT LET'S FACE IT: IT AFFECTS ONLY A SMALL NUMBER OF GIRLS. WHY WRITE A WHOLE BOOK ABOUT IT?

A reputation acquired in adolescence can damage a young woman's self-perception for years. She may become a target for other forms of harassment and even rape, since her peers see her as "easy" and therefore not entitled to say "no." She may become sexually active with a large number of partners (even if she had not been sexually active before her reputation). Or she may shut down her sexual side completely, wearing baggy clothes and being unable to allow a boyfriend to even kiss her.

It's true that most girls escape adolescence unscathed by slut-bashing. Nevertheless, just about every girl is affected by it. Every girl internalizes the message that sex is bad—because it can earn you a reputation. The result is that even years later, when she is safely out of adolescence, a woman may suffer from a serious hangup about sex and intimacy—even if she was not herself called a "slut." Second, the fear of being called a "slut" makes many girls unlikely to carry or use contraceptives, leading of course to the risk of pregnancy or disease.

Slut-bashing also affects boys. It fosters a culture of sexual entitlement that says that "easy" girls are expendable while only "good" girls deserve to be treated well. And that means that only some girls are treated with the respect that they all deserve.

YOU MAKE IT SEEM AS IF WE'RE LIVING IN THE 1950S. BUT THIS IS THE TWENTY-FIRST CENTURY. LOTS OF GIRLS ARE HAVING SEX; MOST OF THEM ARE NOT CALLED "SLUTS."

Of course, a girl today has many freedoms that her 1950s counterpart did not possess, including the license to sexually experiment before marriage. But even today, the prevailing attitude is that there is something wrong with the girl who behaves just as a boy does. Compare, for example, the fate of two recent movies about teenagers and the pursuit of sex, one involving girls, the other involving boys. *Coming Soon,* a witty comedy set in the world of wealthy teen Manhattanites and boasting a star-filled cast (Mia Farrow, Spalding Gray, Ryan O'Neal, Gaby Hoffman), follows a female high school senior who has never had an orgasm and wonders why her boyfriend leaves her sexually unfulfilled. She worries that there is something wrong with her; after all, her girlfriends report that *they* feel completely fulfilled. (It turns out they're lying.) The movie is actually far from raunchy. There is no nudity, and the raciest scene involves only the protagonist and a Jacuzzi. It garnered positive reviews from *Variety, The Hollywood Reporter,* and many prestigious film festivals.

Yet the Motion Picture Association of America gave *Coming Soon* the dreaded NC-17 rating, effectively barring it from theaters—until director Colette Burson agreed to cut several scenes that the MPAA deemed "lurid." Now it has been granted a "respectable" R rating (and has been released by a small distributor in a few theaters), but at the expense of a serious exploration of female sexuality. Burson explains that the MPAA "really didn't like the idea of girls and orgasm."

While Burson was busy tranquilizing *Coming Soon,* kids lined up at theaters across the country to see the vulgar antics of four teenaged boys desperate to lose their virginity in *American Pie.* In a weak nod to the notion that one's partner should enjoy sex too, one of the buddy-boy characters works hard to give his girlfriend an orgasm—not because he cares about her satisfaction, but because that will induce her to go "all the way" with him. The movie is far more sexually explicit than *Coming Soon* ever was and utterly contemptuous of girls (the tag line is "There's something about your first piece"), yet it merited an R rating. *American Pie* has grossed over a hundred million dollars in United States box-office receipts alone.

Put side by side, these two movies demonstrate that the idea of females exploring sex is taboo, while the idea of males exploring sex is an opportunity for slapstick and knowing guffaws. With this double standard in place, it's no wonder that any girl who asserts her sexual desire (or is presumed to) is treated like a freak. Her behavior is considered so deviant that it can't even be represented in the same theaters that screen bloody, ultra-violent films like *Reservoir Dogs* or incest-themed films like *Spanking the Monkey*. (For information about *Coming Soon*, go to *www.comingsoonmovie.com*.)

The sexual double standard was also in full force in the summer of 1999 when a dozen Virginia junior high school girls were discovered to have engaged in oral sex throughout the school year during parties and at local parks. *The Washington Post* broke the story, which was subsequently picked up by the Associated Press and reprinted in newspapers across the country. Parents, health educators, and guidance counselors weighed in with a loud chorus of condemnation. Certainly it was disturbing that kids so young were engaging in meaningless sexual encounters. But much more disturbing was that, first, the girls had been nothing more than sexual servicers to the boys; and second, that all of the censure was directed to the girls. It turns out that the school principal had called the parents of the girls to a special meeting to discuss the matter—but none of the boys or their parents was approached. Boys will be boys—but girls will be "sluts."

GIRLS TODAY DRESS SO PROVOCATIVELY, EVEN TO SCHOOL, IN SKIMPY OUTFITS THAT EXPOSE A LOT OF FLESH. THEY PRACTICALLY *INVITE* PEOPLE TO CALL THEM "SLUTS" AND OTHER NAMES.

I have to admit that I am often appalled by some of the outfits I see young girls wearing these days: It's one thing for an adult woman to showcase her sexual appeal and a different thing entirely for an eighth grader to do likewise. But I don't blame the girls. On the contrary, I am sympathetic to them. These girls believe that if they attract a boyfriend and fall in love, their lives would be better and they would be happier. Sadly, many of these girls believe that their sexuality is the only power or appeal they have, and so they play it up to the hilt. They also feel competitive with other girls in a battle for the most desirable guys, so they feel the need to out-dress their peers. Dressing in sexy outfits, then, is both a strategy to obtain romance and a competition with other girls. But just because a girl dresses in a sexually provocative way doesn't mean that she is sexually promiscuous. In reality, she may not be any more sexually active than the prissy girl in tailored pants, loafers, and sweater set.

SOME OF YOUR INTERVIEWEES WERE CALLED "SLUTS" EVEN THOUGH THEY WEREN'T SEXUALLY ACTIVE AT ALL. THEY WERE INNOCENT VICTIMS. BUT THE GIRLS WHO WERE SEXUALLY PROMISCUOUS ARE A DIFFERENT STORY: THEY DESERVED WHAT THEY GOT.

I don't believe that there should be a distinction between those who deserve a bad reputation and those who don't. Because frankly, I don't think that any girl deserves to be called a "slut." After all, boys who are sexually active are congratulated as studs.

Dividing "sluts" into the innocent and the guilty merely reinforces the sexual double standard. This is why, when I have been asked about my own sexual history—believe it or not, radio show hosts, aping Howard Stern, have felt perfectly comfortable quizzing me about the details of my sex life—I have refused to respond. Besides the fact that the answers are no one's business, they would serve only to buttonhole me as either "innocent" or "guilty," and I reject both categories.

SLUT-BASHING MAY HAVE HARMFUL REPERCUSSIONS, BUT IT'S A NECESSARY DETERRENT SO THAT GIRLS WON'T BE SEXUALLY ACTIVE.

But slut-bashing is ineffective as a deterrent. The girl who is called a "slut," I found, tends to become more sexually active than she was before the reputation. As many girls told me, their thinking is: "Well, if people are going to think I'm a slut, I may as well act like one."

In any event, the proportion of high school students having intercourse has been declining for the last decade, with fewer than half of the country's high school students engaged in sexual intercourse.[1] And, since its peak in 1991, the teen pregnancy rate has dropped 15 percent.[2] The teenage birth rate has dropped too—a full 16 percent since 1991—pushing the country's overall birth rate to the lowest point since the government began keeping records in 1909.[3] So there is no need for alarmist and destructive "deterrents" such as slut-bashing in the first place.

OUR CULTURE IS TOO OPEN ABOUT SEX.

It's true that anyone with eyes is bombarded by sexual images. But while in many ways Americans are very open about sexual images, they are, at the same time, profoundly uncomfortable discussing the realities of sexuality. Last year, a popular sexuality course was nearly eliminated from the curriculum of a New York community college because of Catholic opposition. The course, which was not required, addressed abortion, birth control, and homosexuality—all standard fare for a college-level human sexuality course. The college ultimately won the battle because a federal district court judge found in its favor, but it is amazing that the opponents, who were represented by the American Catholic Lawyers Association, got as far as they did.[4] Yes, mostly naked women appear everywhere from bus shelters to *New*

York Times lingerie ads, but at the same time we live in a culture that accepts and promotes moral and sexual policing. When it comes to sex, this is very much a divided culture.

IF FEMALES PRACTICED AN ETHIC OF SEXUAL MODESTY, MALES WOULD BE MORE LIKELY TO TREAT THEM WITH RESPECT.

Ideally, I think sex should be harnessed within a romantic relationship, but that ideal isn't possible or desirable for everybody. There are young women who perhaps would like to wait and initiate their first sexual encounter in a loving relationship, but for whatever reason, they have desire and want to act on it before they've met the "right" person—or they may never meet the "right" person. I worry that these young women are going to feel guilty and ashamed of their own sexual desire. I'm also concerned that they are going to make bad choices about who their mate is going to be, perhaps marrying too young. A sex drive is a natural appetite for males and females. If you say that females are innately modest, then you're also saying that a girl or woman who isn't modest is doing something unfemale and wrong.

In her book *A Return to Modesty,* Wendy Shalit argues that girls have to be "good" in order for boys to behave properly—to stop sexually harassing them. But I worry about the implications of being a "good" girl. Once you start characterizing some females as "good," you inevitably label others as "bad." And once you start thinking of some girls as "bad," in essence you are saying that those girls don't deserve to be treated with respect. The irony is that so many girls who are regarded as slutty aren't even particularly sexually active, and they are rarely more sexually active than their peers are. So the whole good girl/bad girl thing is a sham. Its purpose is to elevate some girls and to degrade others, and in the long run it hurts everyone. Boys will treat girls with respect, and loveless, casual sexual encounters will decrease, when we have one standard for both sexes—that is, when we have sexual equality.

YOU WRITE IN THE INTRODUCTION THAT NONE OF THE "SLUTS" YOU INTERVIEWED IS A VICTIM. YET A NUMBER OF THEM WERE RAPED, SOME EVEN GANG-RAPED, AND ALL WERE TREATED BADLY. DOESN'T THAT MAKE THEM VICTIMS?

I never meant to suggest that slut-bashing doesn't have serious repercussions. It's obvious that the girl who is labeled a "slut" is victimized. But at the same time, I wanted to point out that slut-bashing has some unintended positive consequences. Every one of the adult women who looked back on her experiences of being known as a "slut" told me that in a perverse way, she was glad that the slut-bashing had happened to her. It taught her about gender roles, the sexual double standard, cruelty, and what it's like to be an outsider. Also, some girls and women have embraced the word as a badge of honor; they turn the insult on its head to proclaim that they've done nothing wrong and they have no reason to be made to feel ashamed.

SCHOOL SEXUAL HARASSMENT LAWSUITS ARE GETTING OUT OF HAND. HOW CAN A SCHOOL BE MONETARILY RESPONSIBLE FOR SEXUAL HARASSMENT? THESE LAW-SUITS HURT EVERYONE, SINCE THEY TAKE MONEY AWAY FROM EDUCATION.

The Supreme Court ruled in May 1999 (*Davis v. Monroe County Board of Education*) that school districts receiving federal money can be liable for monetary damages if they fail to prevent severe, persistent sexual harassment among students. The ruling was in response to a case brought by the mother of a fifth-grade girl in rural Georgia. The girl, LaShonda Davis, was harassed by a male classmate who made repeated unwanted sexual advances over the course of five months. At least two teachers, as well as the principal, were aware of the incidents, but no disiciplinary action was taken against the boy. Meanwhile, Davis's grades dropped and her father discovered that she had written a suicide note.

The ruling is important because it sends the message that schools must be vigilant in halting sexual harassment—which includes slut-bashing, a verbal form of sexual harassment. I agree that a school should be liable if the sexual harassment is severe and persistent and if the school is aware of the behavior but does not take steps to halt it. If, on the other hand, the school makes a good-faith effort to stop the behavior, then I don't believe it should be liable.

It's unfortunate that a ruling against a school results in a monetary loss, but it's also unfortunate that the threat of monetary payment is the most effective wake-up call to school administrators. As for the argument that these payments take money away from education, sexual harassment also impedes the ability of teachers to effectively educate and the ability of students to effectively learn.

THE AVERAGE AGE WHEN TEENS BEGIN TO HAVE SEXUAL INTERCOURSE IS FIFTEEN. THAT IS MUCH TOO YOUNG.

I think all teenagers, boys and girls alike, should be encouraged to wait until they are in a serious relationship, and they should wait until they are emotionally ready. By and large, fifteen-year-olds do not meet both those criteria. In schools, sex education is often lacking. All teenagers should be exposed to comprehensive sex education, which encourages teens to wait until they initiate sexual activity but offers them information about birth control and abortion so that they are prepared whenever they do become sexually involved.

Yet sex education in public schools is increasingly focused on abstinence, with more than a third of districts using an abstinence-only curriculum that permits discussion of contraception only in the context of its unreliability. Fewer than half of public schools offer information on where to get birth control (45 percent). Only slightly more than a third mention abortion (37 percent) or sexual orientation (36 percent) as part of the curriculum.[5] (The decline in teenage sexual activity is not the result of abstinence-only sex education programs, which have become prevalent only at the end of the 1990s.)

Parents, meanwhile, must also communicate with their children about sex. I think that this should start from birth. The key is to engage in discussions that are age-appropriate. Ten-to-twelve-year-olds in particular are very hungry for sexual information, and they need it. Half of them say that they want this information. Yet approximately half of their parents have not discussed how to handle peer pressure to have sex, and 60 percent have not discussed how to prevent pregnancy or HIV.[6]

When parents do open up discussions about sexuality and sexual risk with their children, it increases the likelihood that their children will in turn communicate with their partners about sex and using condoms. Only 57 percent of sexually active teenagers always use a condom, and only 45 percent report that they have discussed sexually transmitted diseases with their current or most recent sexual partner. Yet approximately four million teens get a sexually transmitted disease each year.[7]

We should learn from the example of our European counterparts, who tend to be far less inhibited about adolescent sexuality and who openly discuss contraceptives and responsible decision making with their teens. In those countries, teens initiate sexual activity at a later age. For instance, the age of first act of intercourse in the Netherlands is seventeen—two years older than in the United States.[8]

Admittedly, many parents find it awkward and difficult to raise these issues. One great bit of advice that sex educators offer is to talk about sensitive issues while riding in a car, since you have a captive audience but you can avoid potentially embarrassing eye contact.

WHY ARE GIRLS OFTEN WORSE THAN BOYS WHEN IT COMES TO SLUT-BASHING?

All of us yearn for one arena in which we can wield power. For girls, this desire is often thwarted. After all, girls may get better grades—but boys, especially athletes, by and large receive more attention and congratulatory pats on the back from school administrators and teachers. Boys call out more in class and get away with it. They rule the playground. Many feel a sense of entitlement to grope girls' bodies. With these depressing realities, it's no wonder that many girls develop a sense of self-hatred. Sensing that femininity is devalued, they may feel, at some level, uncomfortable with being a girl, and therefore are reluctant to bond with other girls. Instead, they latch on to one small sphere of power they can call their own: the power to make or break reputations. Slut-bashing is a cheap and easy way to feel powerful. If you feel insecure or ashamed about your own sexual desires, all you have to do is call a girl a "slut" and suddenly you're the one who is "good" and on top of the social pecking order.

WHAT CAN WE DO TO STOP SLUT-BASHING?

Parents should be open about sexuality with their kids—and that means being open about female sexuality as well as male sexuality. They should teach their daughters and sons that girls as well as boys have sexual feelings, and that sexual feelings are entirely normal. That way they won't have to pin their sexual anxieties on a scapegoat and then distance themselves from her.

Teachers must recognize that slut-bashing is a serious problem. Too often, they dismiss it as part of the normal fabric of adolescent life. But slut-bashing is a form of sexual harassment, and it is illegal under Title IX, which entitles students to a harassment-free education. If a teacher witnesses slut-bashing, she must make sure that it stops. She must confront the ringleader and other name-callers. Of course, teachers and school administrators shouldn't wait for slut-bashing to occur. They must create and publicize awareness through sexual harassment policies for their schools.

Schools and youth programs have an obligation to talk to kids about the harm in sexual labeling. One of the best programs I've ever seen in this regard, Project Respect (www.yesmeansyes.com), was developed in Canada by the Victoria Women's Sexual Assault Centre in Victoria, British Columbia. (Don't confuse Project Respect with Sex Respect, the frightening abstinence-only curriculum used nationwide in the U.S.) The Project Respect "social marketing program," as its creators call it, includes a video (for classroom use), workshops (held in schools and intended to encourage communication with respect), as well as a multimedia campaign.

Project Respect makes the connection between stereotypes and sexual assault without being at all pedantic (not an easy feat). The program features teenagers talking honestly—and rivetingly—about their feelings on sexual attitudes, values, peer pressure, and miscommunication. Project Respect has already had a tremendous impact on young men and women in British Columbia. A number of young women have actually stood up in the middle of the workshops to tell the young men present to stop labeling them "sluts," that the word is degrading and demeaning, and they don't like it. A number of young men have suddenly realized how hurtful and powerful the word is. For me, the most exciting aspect about Project Respect is that it is a sex ed curriculum that does not self-righteously preach abstinence and is not about how having sex will ruin your life. Yet, it is very much about consequences that stem from sexual stereotypes and the sexual double standard, not from sexual expression. We can learn a lot from our northern neighbors and we should try to emulate their example by creating similar programs across the U.S.

(For more information about Project Respect, write to projectrespect@hotmail.com or Project Respect, 754 Broughton Street, 2nd Floor, Victoria, BC V8W 1E1, Canada. Project Respect needs funding to expand its reach. Please contact them if you can provide assistance.)

But the most important thing that all of us need to work on is this: to stop calling or thinking of women as "sluts." Face it: At one time or another, many of us have called a woman a "slut." We see a woman who's getting away with something we wish we could get away with. What do we call her? A "slut." *not always*

We see a woman who dresses provocatively, and maybe we wish we had the guts to dress that way ourselves. What do we call her? A "slut."

If we think of a woman or girl as a "slut," it's like she's not one of us. She's one of *them*. She is other. "Slut," like any other derogatory label, is a shorthand for one who is different, strange—and not worth knowing or caring about. Unlike other insults, however, it carries a unique sting: the stigma of the out-of-control, trampy female. Most of us recognize that this stigma is unjust and unwarranted. Yet we have used the "slut" insult anyway: Our social conditioning runs too deep. We must will ourselves to be aware of the sexual double standard and of how we lapse into slut-bashing on an everyday level. If we become aware of our behavior, then we have the power to stop.

And never again be slut-bashers or self-bashers.

WHAT TO DO

Sexual harassment in schools is against the law as defined by Title IX of the 1972 amendments to the Education Act. To receive federal money, schools must be vigilant against teacher-to-student and student-to-student harassment. Nan Stein, director of the Sexual Harassment in Schools Project at Wellesley College's Center for Research on Women, advises a systematic approach. "Schools need to resist the temptation to treat sexual harassment symptomatically—a videotape here, a workshop there."[1] First she recommends that schools offer training programs on sexual harassment for staff. If teachers, coaches, and school board members aren't able to recognize sexual harassment, they aren't able to report it. Students should also be included in the discussions—through orientations, assemblies, student handbooks, peer advising, and classroom lessons. As author of the first curriculum created about sexual harassment in schools, Stein urges schools to use curriculum materials, including videos, that highlight prototypical case studies to shed light on the complexities of sexual harassment.

Most important, Stein and the NOW Legal Defense and Education Fund counsel every school to develop and enforce a sexual-harassment policy, sending a strong message that verbal and physical harassment will not be tolerated, that students know how to file a complaint, and that punishments are speedy but fair. The policy should include definitions of sexual harassment involving student-to-student, adult-to-student, and same-sex harassment. "Ultimately," says Stein, "a strategy to attack sexual harassment in schools needs to aim at a transformation of the broader school structure."[2]

Stein also offers concrete advice to girls who have been sexually harassed. The first step is to tell someone what is going on. If that person doesn't seem to care, the girl should find someone else who can provide emotional support. Next she should keep a written record of the incidents: what happened, when, where, who else was present, and how she reacted. She should save any notes or pictures.

If there is one primary harasser or an identifiable ringleader, a girl might consider confronting him or her through a letter. Stein and the NOW Legal Defense and Education Fund encourage those girls who feel comfortable doing so to write a letter to the harasser describing the behavior, explaining that it bothers her, and saying that she wants it to stop. She should have an adult help her write it and keep a copy of it. It's a good idea to have the adult hand-deliver the letter, so that the harasser takes it seriously.[3]

If the girl doesn't feel comfortable writing a letter and the harassment persists, she should schedule a meeting with the person at her school who is responsible for dealing with complaints about sexual harassment. She should bring a friend or parent to attend the meeting with her. The school is responsible for investigating the harassment and taking steps to ensure that it stops.

After Massachusetts sophomore Kira Mitchell was repeatedly called a whore, bitch, and slut, as well as the subject of graffiti on school desks, she received a letter threatening physical harm. She knew who was behind all of the harassment: her boyfriend's friend, who felt jealous of the relationship, and four of his male buddies. Kira decided to go to her vice principal, Mr. Leeds. She brought the letter with her and told him, "This is distracting me from my schoolwork. I don't want to come here anymore." Leeds took the letter from Kira (without making a copy for her to keep) and promised to make the harassment stop. But half an hour later Kira heard his voice on the school loudspeaker calling her name and the names of the five boys she had mentioned, instructing them to come to his office. Once there, the boys denied everything. "I said, 'Right, like I'm calling myself a whore and writing on the desks myself and putting up my number in the guys' bathroom,'" Kira says dryly.

Leeds ushered Kira and the boys into a conference room with the school psychologist, "the stupidest woman I have ever met in my life, Miss Laslo. She was like, 'Well, they're not really threatening you. It's an empty threat,'" recalls Kira. "I said, 'I think a threat is a threat.' Besides, I really did think they would carry it out. So I said to her, 'So they're allowed to say they want to hit me and that's okay in this school?' She got really mad at me and told me I was provoking them. She said, 'Sometimes women provoke men to the point where the men want to hit them.' I said, 'And that makes it okay?'"

Kira was so upset that she called her mother from school. Her mother called Leeds, who told her that dealing with the issue was a "waste of his time." But her mother insisted on meeting with Leeds, along with Kira and her father. At the meeting Leeds refused to return the threat letter to Kira—"I bet he was afraid that we would sue the school," Kira speculates. "He actually had the audacity to tell my parents, with me sitting right there, that 'These boys are good kids. They're in the school band.' I didn't know how to take that. It was okay for them to harass me because they are 'good' kids? What did that make me—a bad person because I'm the one those 'good' kids chose to harass? My parents couldn't believe that he would say that to me." Kira started to cry, and Leeds continued, "This is just a high school soap opera. I don't have time for this sort of nonsense. My job here is to make sure that the eight hundred fifty students in this school have a safe and comfortable learning environment, and get a good education." Kira shot back: "They get to feel safe and comfortable here and get a good education and I don't because you don't feel that this is worth the time or effort to change what is going on?"

Leeds had nothing to say, though he finally did agree to tell the boys that they had to stop their behavior. The final upshot? "They did stop for a while, because Mr. Leeds told them to, but they've started again," Kira tells me. "The other day they said things about me when I walked past them. They still call me a whore. It's the same as before, except they don't write things anymore because they know that will get them in trouble. I'm not going to even waste my time going to Mr. Leeds."

Paula Pinczewski from Wisconsin saw better results when she turned to her guidance counselor. In the eighth grade Paula was called a slut, whore, and hooker because she was physically more developed than the other girls. "During the time the harassment was going on," she says, "I felt lower than amoebas on ants." She suffered from chronic stomach cramps and wanted to stay home from school all the time. But her guidance counselor was very supportive. He met with Paula for fifteen minutes every day and tried to boost her ego. He then organized a meeting with the principal and the district administrator to discuss the matter. The principal promised to have the police speak with every student who had harassed Paula. When she gave the principal a list of names— including nearly everyone in her class—the principal believed her.

"I knew what 'sexual harassment' meant," says Paula, "but I wasn't sure if it pertained to me. When my guidance counselor told me that it was sexual harassment, I said,

'That's a good way to put it.' All of a sudden I was like, 'Now I can put a name to it.' Before that I had figured that I had done something wrong but nobody would tell me what it was. The term made me realize that I didn't do anything wrong."

A few days later the sheriff and one of his deputies visited the school. Paula's classmates were called out of class one by one to speak with them. Paula watched each student go in and then come back out five or ten minutes later, beet-faced. The sheriff mailed a letter to the students' parents warning that if the harassment continued, formal charges would be brought. "After that the parents cracked down because I barely heard anything, except the kids punctured my bike tires a couple of times. The week after the cops were there, sexual-harassment policy sheets were hung up in every classroom in the school. They were on bright orange paper and said that sexual harassment is a violation of Title IX, and they listed the repercussions if you did it and gave information about the psychological damage it can have. I'll tell you, I felt a lot stronger when I saw them up on the walls."

What about a girl whose school does not resolve the complaint in a way that satisfies her? She may realize that the only way to shed a "bad" reputation is to leave the environment in which it festered. That's what Julie did, and it saved her from years of humiliation. Julie, you may recall, is the woman who was raped after she passed out from drinking at age thirteen and immediately became known as the school slut. She says, "My junior high ended in ninth grade, and I decided I didn't want to go to high school with these people. I didn't want to have this reputation for the rest of my life. I wanted to end it. So I switched to a special school for the sciences. I went there to basically escape my reputation. And it was so nice. Nobody knew me, because I was the only one from my neighborhood to go." Transferring to a different school is not running away; it can often be a smart move of last resort.

If a girl can't or doesn't want to transfer, she can turn to the government. A student who believes that sexual harassment has denied her the opportunity to equal education can file a complaint with the Department of Education's Office for Civil Rights (OCR), in which case she may be entitled to monetary damages from the school district and a court order barring sexual harassment. In 1999 the Supreme Court ruled that school districts receiving federal money can be liable for monetary damages if they fail to prevent severe, persistent sexual harassment among students. A number of states also have laws specifically prohibiting sex discrimination and sexual harassment in schools. For more information about Title IX complaints, refer to the Department of Education's web site, www.ed.gov, and search for "Title IX." For information about the law, contact the NOW Legal Defense and Education Fund, 99 Hudson Street, New York, NY 10013-2871. Request their legal resource kit on sexual harassment in schools, which contains a blueprint for action, a sample letter for filing a Title IX complaint, and legal background, for $5.00.

RECOMMENDED RESOURCES

FOR GIRLS AND YOUNG WOMEN

Magazines for Teenage Girls

NEW GIRL TIMES
215 West 84th Street
New York, NY 10024
1-800-560-7525

$12/twelve issues (1 year)
Newspaper written entirely
by teenage girls. Very highly
recommended.

TEEN VOICES
Women Express, Inc.
515 Washington Street,
6th Floor
Boston, MA 02111
617-426-5505

$20/four issues (1 year)
Written, edited, and produced
by a collective of teenage girls.
Very highly recommended.

Magazines for Women in Their Twenties

BITCH: Feminist Response to
Pop Culture
3128 16th Street, Box 201
San Francisco, CA 94103
www.bitchmagazine.com

$15/four issues (1 year)
Very highly recommended.

BUST
P.O. Box 319
Ansonia Station
New York, NY 10023
www.bust.com

$11.95/four issues (1 year)
Very highly recommended.

On-line Zines

All have a hip attitude, catchy graphics, and a feminist edge. They are of interest to both girls and young women.

Cybergrrl (www.cybergrrl.com)
gURL (www.gurl.com)
Maxi (www.maximag.com)
Minx (www.minxmag.com)
Riotgrrl (www.riotgrrl.com)
Wench (www.wench.com)

Organizations

GIRLS INC.
120 Wall Street
3rd Floor
New York, NY 10005-3902
212-509-2000

Provides programs, research, and advocacy for teenage girls around the country, with an emphasis on mentoring girls to become leaders, who themselves go on to mentor younger girls.

THE THIRD WAVE
FOUNDATION
116 East 16 Street
7th Floor
New York, NY 10003
212-388-1898
ThirdWaveF@aol.com

The only national young feminist orgaization. It offers public education campaigns and leadership training and provides grants to teenage girls and young women

FOR PARENTS AND EDUCATORS

Organizations

AMERICAN ASSOCIATION
OF UNIVERSITY WOMEN
(AAUW)
1111 Sixteenth Street N.W.
Washington, DC 20036-4873
202-785-7700

A membership organization of college graduates that promotes education and equity for women and girls. It has published a number of important works on gender bias in education, including *Growing Smart: What's Working for Girls in School* (1995, $35.95); *Hostile Hallways: The AAUW Survey on Sexual Harassment in America's Schools* (1993, $11.95); and *How Schools Shortchange Girls* (1995, $12.95). For telephone orders, call 1-800-225-9998, ext. 327. The AAUW also sponsors the National Coalition for Women and Girls in Education, which promotes national policies assuring educational equity for females.

EDUCATIONAL EQUITY
CONCEPTS
114 East 32nd Street
Suite 701
New York, NY 10016
212-725-1803

Develops educational materials
addressing sex and race
discrimination in early childhood education.

THE NATIONAL COALITION
FOR SEX EQUITY IN
EDUCATION (NCSEE)
P.O. Box 534
Annandale, NJ 08801-0534
908-735-5045

A national organization of
educators and advocates
who work to create learning
environments free of sexism
and racism.

SEXUALITY INFORMATION
AND EDUCATION COUNCIL
OF THE UNITED STATES
(SIECUS)
130 West 42nd Street,
Suite 350
New York, NY 10036-7802
212-819-9770
www.siecus.org

An excellent source of sexuality
information. It publishes *The
SIECUS Report,* the leading
journal in the field of sexuality
education; fact sheets on topics
such as "Sexuality Education:
Issues and Answers,"

"Adolescence and Abstinence,"
and "Sexually Transmitted
Diseases in the United States";
and many useful booklets, reports,
and teaching guides on all
aspects of sexuality education.

Educational Materials

Merle Frosche, Barbara
Sprung, and Nancy Mullin-
Rindler, *Quit It! A Teacher's
Guide on Teasing and Bullying
for Use with Students in
Grades K-3.* Wellesley, Mass.:
Wellesley College Center for
Research on Women, 1998,
$19.95. Send orders to
Publications Office, The
Wellesley Center for Research
on Women, Wellesley College,
106 Central Street, Wellesley,
MA 02181-8259.
Tel: 781-283-2510.
www.wellesley.edu/WCW/inde
x.html. A shipping and han-
dling cost is added to each
order.

Marylin A. Hulme, *Sexual
Harassment in Schools: A
Selected, Annotated
Bibliography.* Free For Further
information or a copy of the
bibliography, contact Marylin
A. Hume, Equity Assistance
Centers, Rutgers University, 36
Street 1603, Piscataway, NJ
08854-8036. Tel: 732-445-
2071. Fax: 732-445-0027.
Email: hulme@rci.rutgers.edu

or visit website: www.nyu.edu/education/metro-center/eac.eac.html.

Melissa Keyes, *Sexual Harassment and Student Services Personnel*. Developed for the American School Counselors' Association. Contains general and specific information for all educators and anyone interested in preventing sexual harassment and assault. $13.50 (includes tax, s/h). Order from Keyes Consulting, Inc. 300 N Pinckney Street, Madison, WI 53703-2134 or call 608-256-2156.

Lisa Sjostrom and Nan Stein, *Bullyproof: A Teacher's Guide on Teasing and Bullying for Use with Fourth and Fifth Grade Students*. Wellesley, Mass.: NEA Women and Girls Center for Change and the Wellesley College Center for Research on Women, 1995, $19.95. See above for ordering information.

Nan Stein and Lisa Sjostrom, *Flirting or Hurting? A Teacher's Guide on Student-to-Student Sexual Harassment in Schools* (for grades 6 through 12). West Haven, Conn.: NEA Professional Library and Wellesley College Center for Research on Women, 1994, $19.95. See above for ordering information.

A companion video to *Flirting or Hurting?*, produced in 1997 by WGBY-TV in Massachussetts, is available for $79.95 (plus $5.59 in shipping and handling) through Great Plains Nations (GPN). Call 1-800-228-4630 to order. 60 minutes.

Nan Stein, *Classrooms and Courtrooms: Facing Sexual Harassment in K-12 Schools*. New York: Teachers College Press, 1999, $18.95 plus $3.50 s/h. Contains summaries of legal cases, findings of major surveys, and words and experiences of students themselves. Order from Teachers College Press, P.O. Box 20, Williston, VT 05495-0020 or call 800-575-6566.

National Women's Law Center, *Do the Right Thing: Understanding, Addressing, and Preventing Sexual Harassment in Schools* (for parents and educators) and *Righting the Wrongs: A Legal Guide to Understanding, Addressing, and Preventing Sexual Harassment in Schools* (for attorneys, educators, and school administrators). *Do the Right Thing* is $15 and *Righting the Wrongs* is $35. Both available from the National Women's Law Center, 11 Dupont Circle NW, Suite 800, Washington DC 20036. 202-588-5180.

Susan Strauss with Pamela Espeland, *Sexual Harassment and Teens: A Program for Positive Change*. Minneapolis: Free Spirit, 1992. $17.95 (plus $4.25 in shipping and handling). A comprehensive program for grades 7 through 12 designed to prevent harassment. Send orders to Free Spirit Publishing, 400 First Avenue North, Suite 616, Minneapolis MN 55401. 612-338-2068.

Women's Sport Foundation, *Prevention of Sexual Harassment in Athletic Settings: An Educational Resource Kit for Athletic Administrators*. $10.00 plus $3.00 s/h. Order from the Women's Sports Foundation, Eisenhower Park, East Meadow, NY 11554 or call 800-227-3988.

INTRODUCTION

1. Felicity Barringer, "School Hallways as Gantlets of Sexual Taunts," *The New York Times*, June 2, 1993, p. B7. The poll, conducted by Louis Harris & Associates for the American Association of University Women Educational Foundation, surveyed 1,632 students in grades eight through eleven in seventy-nine schools across the country.

CHAPTER 1: INSULT OF INSULTS

1. In Jordan in 1993 a sixteen-year-old girl who had been raped by her older brother was killed by her family because, it was said, she had seduced him into sleeping with her. Kristen Golden, "Rana Husseini: A Voice for Justice," *Ms.*, July/August 1998, p. 36; Tali Edut, "Global Woman: Rana Husseini," *HUES* , Summer 1998, p. 41. In Afghanistan, where women must remain covered from head to toe in shrouds called *burqas,* the General Department for the Preservation of Virtue and Prevention of Vice beats women for wearing white socks or plastic sandals with no socks, attire that is said to provoke "impure thoughts" in men. John F. Burns, "Sex and the Afghan Woman: Islam's Straitjacket," *The New York Times*, August 29, 1997, p. A4. And in Turkey in 1998 five girls attempted suicide by eating rat poison and jumping into a water tank to avoid a forced virginity examination. An unmarried woman discovered not to be a virgin risks being beaten or killed. The virginity tests were carried out as the girls recovered in their hospital beds; when one girl did succeed in killing herself, her father had the exam performed on her corpse. Kelly Couturier, "Suicide Attempts Fuel Virginity Test Debate," *The Washington Post*, January 27, 1998, p. A18.

2. Lauri Umansky, "Breastfeeding in the 1990s: The Karen Carter Case and the Politics of Maternal Sexuality" in Molly Ladd-Taylor and Lauri Umansky, eds., *"Bad" Mothers: The Politics of Blame in Twentieth-Century America* (New York: New York University Press, 1998), pp. 299–309. Karen Carter is a pseudonym.

3. Tamar Stieber, "Viewpoint," *Glamour*, August 1996, p. 138.

4. Stieber, p. 138.

5. Jon Jeter, "Woman Who Sued Ex-Husband's Mistress Is Awarded $1 Million," *The Washington Post*, August 7, 1997, p. A3.

6. Tim Weiner, "C.I.A. To Pay $410,000 to Spy Who Says She Was Smeared," *The New York Times*, December 8, 1994, p. A1; Tim Weiner, "Woman Who Was C.I.A. Chief Requests Criminal Investigation," *The New York Times*, July 18, 1995.

7. David Brock, "The Real Anita Hill," *The American Spectator*, March 1992, p. 27.

8. Alix Kates Shulman, *Memoirs of an Ex-Prom Queen* (Chicago: Cassandra Editions, 1985; first published 1972), p. 61.

9. Erica Jong, *Fear of Flying* (New York: New American Library, 1973), pp. 156–157.

10. *Sex and America's Teenagers* (New York and Washington: The Alan Guttmacher Institute, 1994), p. 20.

11. Laurie Goodstein with Marjorie Connelly, "Teen-Age Poll Finds a Turn to the Traditional," *The New York Times*, April 30, 1998, p. A20. The poll, of 1,048 teenagers ages thirteen to seventeen, was conducted by telephone in April 1998. The poll also found that only 18 percent of thirteen- to fifteen-year-olds said they had ever had sex, as against 38 percent of sixteen- and seventeen-year-olds.

12. Ethan Bronner, "Lawsuit on Sex Bias by 2 Mothers, 17," *The New York Times*, August 6, 1998, p. A14. A year later, however, after the American Civil Liberties Union sued on the students' behalf, the society was odered to accept them. Michael Pollak, "Honored, a Year Later," *The New York Times*, May 19, 1999, p. C30.

13. "All in a Name" (Letters page), *Seventeen*, November 1995, p. 12.

14. Lorne Manly, "Off the Record," *The New York Observer*, June 23, 1997. (Messenger was ultimately awarded $100,000 by a jury that found that YM was "grossly irresponsible" for using the photo without "valid consent."—Greg B. Smith, "'Trashed' Model Wins Mag to Cough Up $100,000," New York *Daily News*, March 28, 1998, p. 6.)

15. Tamar Lewin, "Kissing Cases Highlight Schools' Fears of Liability for Sexual Harassment," *The New York Times*, October 6, 1996; David Stout, "Schoolgirl's Harassment Complaint is Rejected," *The New York Times*, November 22, 1996.

16. "Girl, 14, Wins Case Charging Sex Harassment" (AP), *The New York Times*, October 4, 1996.

17. "School District in California Settles Sex Harassment Suit," *The New York Times*, December 27, 1996, p. A24; Tamar Lewin, "Students Seeking Damages for Sex Bias," *The New York Times*, July 15, 1994, p. B7.

18. Janie Victoria Ward and Jill McLean Taylor, "Sexuality Education for Immigrant and Minority Students: Developing a Culturally Appropriate Curriculum," in Janice M. Irvine, *Sexual Cultures and the Construction of Adolescent Identities* (Philadelphia: Temple University Press, 1994), p. 63.

19. Lillian B. Rubin, *Erotic Wars: What Happened to the Sexual Revolution?* (New York: HarperPerennial, 1991), p. 119.

20. Shere Hite, *Women and Love* (New York: St. Martin's Press, 1987), p. 205.

21. Tamar Lewin, "Boys Are More Comfortable With Sex Than Girls Are, Survey Finds," *The New York Times*, May 18, 1994.

22. Barrie Thorne, *Gender Play: Girls and Boys in School* (New Brunswick, N.J.: Rutgers University Press, 1993), p. 141.

23. The Commonwealth Fund Survey of the Health of Adolescent Girls, Washington, D.C., September 30, 1997. The survey included 6,748 girls and boys in grades 5 through 12 in public, private, and parochial schools.

24. Jennifer Wolff, "Named and Shamed," *Marie Claire*, March 1998, pp. 108–112.

25. Jonathan Alter and Pat Wingert, "The Return of Shame," *Newsweek*, February 6, 1995, p. 24.

26. Pam Belluck, "Forget Prisons. Americans Cry Out for the Pillory," *The New York Times*, October 4, 1998, Week in Review p. 5.

27. Katharine Q. Seelye, "Gingrich Looks to Victorian Age to Cure Today's Social Failings," *The New York Times*, March 14, 1995.

28. Katha Pollitt, *Reasonable Creatures: Essays on Women and Feminism* (New York: Knopf, 1994), p. xiii.

CHAPTER 2: "THEN THERE WERE THE TRAMPS":
THE "SLUT" LABEL IN THE 1950s

1. Susan J. Douglas, *Where the Girls Are: Growing Up Female with the Mass Media* (New York: Times Books, 1994), p. 81.

2. Louise Bernikow, "Confessions of an Ex-Cheerleader," *Ms.*, October 1973, p. 67.

3. Lawrence Stone, *The Family, Sex and Marriage in England 1500–1800,* abr. ed. (New York: Harper & Row, 1979), pp. 315, 334–337.

4. Ibid., p. 315.

5. Ibid., pp. 315–316.

6. Ellen Rothman, *Hands and Hearts: A History of Courtship in America* (New York: Basic, 1984), pp. 46–49.

7. Ibid., pp. 54, 122, 124.

8. Abraham Flexner, *Prostitution in Europe* (New York: Century, 1920), p. 64. Cited in Judith R. Walkowitz, "Dangerous Sexualitics," in Geneviève Fraisse and Michelle Perrot, eds., *A History of Women Vol. IV: Emerging Feminism From Revolution to World War* (Cambridge, Mass.: Harvard University Press, 1993), p. 372.

9. Walkowitz, pp. 371–372.

10. See Nancy F. Cott, *The Grounding of Modern Feminism* (New Haven: Yale University Press, 1987).

11. Rothman, p. 295.

12. Joan Jacobs Brumber, *The Body Project: An Intimate History of American Girls* (New York: Random House, 1997), p. 155.

13. Rothman, p. 242.

14. Mary McCarthy, *The Group* (New York: Signet, 1963), p. 28.

15. Molly Haskell, *From Reverence to Rape: The Treatment of Women in the Movies,,* 2d ed. (Chicago: University of Chicago Press, 1987; first published in 1974), pp. 117-118, 92.

16. McCarthy, p. 138.

17. Herman Wouk, *Marjorie Morningstar* (New York: Pocket, 1955), pp. 604, 739, 755.

18. Wini Breines, *Young, White, and Miserable: Growing Up Female in the Fifties* (Boston: Beacon, 1992), p. 3.

19. Ibid., p. 10.

20. Ibid., p. 104.

21. Rickie Solinger, *Wake Up Little Susie: Single Pregnancy and Race Before Roe v. Wade* (New York: Routledge, 1992), pp. 5–55.

22. Sylvia Plath, *The Bell Jar* (New York: Harper & Row, 1971), p. 66.

23. Haskell, pp. xii, 181.

24. Alfred C. Kinsey, Wardell B. Pomeroy, Clyde E. Martin, and Paul H. Gebhard, *Sexual Behavior in the Human Female* (Philadelphia: W.B. Saunders Co., 1953), p. 286.

25. Robert T. Michael, John H. Gagnon, Edward O. Laumann, and Gina Kolata, *Sex in America: A Definitive Survey* (New York: Warner, 1994), p. 21.

26. Kinsey et al., pp. 251–259, 263.

27. Ibid., p. 242

28. Ibid., p. 263.

29. Roy Dickerson, *So Youth May Know: Sex Education for the Teen-Age,* rev. ed. (New York: Association Press, 1948), p. 113.

30. Douglas, p. 25.

31. Andrew Cherlin, *Marriage Divorce Remarriage.* Cambridge, Mass., 1981, chap. 1, cited in Rothman, p. 288.

32. John Bushnell, "Student Culture at Vassar," in *The American College,* ed. Nevitt Sanford (New York and London, 1962), p. 509f. Cited in Betty Friedan, *The Feminine Mystique* (New York: Dell, 1963), pp. 143–144.

33. Nora Johnson, "Sex and the College Girl," *Atlantic,* November 1959, pp. 57–58. Cited in Rothman, p. 304.

34. Rona Jaffe, *Class Reunion* (New York: Delacorte, 1979), p. 63.

35. Ibid., pp. 72, 321.

36. Ira Reiss, *Premarital Sexual Standards in America* (Glencoe, Ill.: The Free Press of Glencoe, 1960), p. 97.

37. "J," *The Sensuous Woman* (New York: Dell, 1969), p. 9.

38. Benjamin Morse, *Sexual Behavior of the American College Girl* (New York: Lancer Books, 1963), pp. 102–103.

39. Morton Hunt, *Sex in the 70s* (Chicago: Playboy Press, 1974), p. 21. Cited in Rothman, p. 308.

40. Carol Cassell, *Swept Away: Why Women Fear Their Own Sexuality* (New York: Simon & Schuster, 1984), p. 95.

41. Helen Gurley Brown, *Sex and the Single Girl* (New York: Pocket, 1963), p. 2; first published in 1962 by Bernard Geis.

42. Mary Jane Sherfey, "A Theory on Female Sexuality" in Robin Morgan, ed., *Sisterhood Is Powerful: An Anthology of Writings from*

the Women's Liberation Movement (New York: Vintage, 1970), pp. 245-246. Originally published as "The Evolution of Female Sexuality in Relation to Psychoanalytic Theory" in the *Journal of the American Psychoanalytical Association* 14:50 (1966).

43. Rachel P. Maines, *The Technology of Orgasm: "Hysteria," the Vibrator, and Women's Sexual Satisfaction* (Baltimore: Johns Hopkins University Press, 1999), p. 23.

44. Ibid., p. 3.

45. Barbara Seaman, *Free and Female: The Sex Life of the Contemporary Woman* (New York: Coward, McCann & Geoghegan, 1972), p. 19.

46. Anne Koedt, "The Myth of the Vaginal Orgasm" in Leslie B. Tanner, ed., *Voices from Women's Liberation* (New York: New American Library, 1971), p. 159. Originally published in Shulamith Firestone and Anne Koedt, eds., *Notes from the Second Year* (New York: New York Radical Women, 1970).

47. Shere Hite, *The Hite Report: A Nationwide Study of Female Sexuality* (New York: Dell, 1976, 1981), pp. 230, 360.

48. *Fear of Flying* has sold more than twelve million copies in twenty-seven languages, according to Daisy Maryles, "Behind the Bestsellers," *Publishers Weekly*, August 8, 1994.

49. Erica Jong, *Fear of Flying* (New York: New American Library, 1973), pp. 9–10.

50. Ibid., pp. 274-275.

51. Barbara Ehrenreich, Elizabeth Hess, and Gloria Jacobs, *Re-Making Love: The Feminization of Sex* (Garden City, NY: Anchor, 1986), pp. 168–169.

52. Ibid., pp. 166, 171.

53. Lillian B. Rubin, *Erotic Wars: What Happened to the Sexual Revolution* (New York: HarperPerennial, 1990), p. 116.

54. Ehrenreich et al., 183–185.

CHAPTER 3: "SHE'S SO LOOSE": THE SEXUAL GIRL

1. Beth Landman Keil and Deborah Mitchell, "Intelligencer," *New York*, February 2, 1998, p. 12.

2. Maureen Dowd, "The Slander Strategy," *The New York Times*, January 28, 1998, p. A25.

3. "Victimhood," *The Wall Street Journal*, Review & Outlook section (editorial), July 9, 1998, p. A18.

4. Brendan Bourne and Tracy Connor, "Teacher Claims Monica Stalked Him Over Affair," *New York Post*, January 28, 1998, p. 5; Michelle Caruso and Helen Kennedy, "Sex-Crazed, Ex Lover Says Monica Planned Prez Seduction," *Daily News* January 28, 1998, p. 3; James Bennett, "Sympathy and Smears for Monica Lewinsky," *The New York Times* on the web January 31, 1998.

5. Philip Weiss, "The Monica You Didn't Know: Young Woman in a Hurry," *The New York Observer*, October 5, 1998, p. 1.

6. Richard L. Berke, "'That Woman' Has Turned Politics Upside Down," *The New York Times*, August 23, 1998, Section 4, pp. 1, 4. Additionally Clinton's approval rating was phenomenally high—72%—the day after the House of Representatives voted for impeachment. Adam Nagourney with Michael R. Kagay, "Public Support for the President, and for Closure, Emerges Unshaken," *The New York Times*, December 21, 1998, p. A23.

7. Samuel S. Janus and Cynthia L. Janus, *The Janus Report on Sexual Behavior* (New York: John Wiley & Sons, 1993), p. 40. Seventy-five percent of men aged eighteen to twenty-six said they "strongly agree" or "agree" that "there is still a double standard in sex regarding men and women." Eighty-seven percent of the women aged eighteen to twenty-six said they "strongly agree" or "agree." The sample population for the Janus Report totaled 2,765 and was representative of the population distribution of the United States in the areas of gender, age, region, income, education, and marital status.

8. "Poll Shows Decline in Sex by High School Students" (AP), *The New York Times*, September 18, 1998, p. A26. According to the Centers for Disease Control, which released these findings, there has been an overall decline in sexual activity for all teens, but especially for boys: Teenage boys reporting that they had intercourse dropped from 57 percent in 1991 to 49 percent in 1997. For girls the figure dropped from 50.8 to 47.7 percent.

9. "Jenny, My Daughter Needs a Makeover Bad!," *The Jenny Jones Show*, January 19, 1998.

10. Donna Eder, "Girls' Talk About Romance and Sexuality." Paper presented at "Alice in Wonderland: The First International Conference on Girls and Girlhood," Amsterdam, June 1992, p. 9.

11. Joyce Canaan, "Why a 'Slut' Is a 'Slut': Cautionary Tales of Middle-Class Teenage Girls' Morality," in Hervé Varenne, ed., *Symbolizing America* (Lincoln, Neb.: University of Nebraska Press, 1986), p. 192.

12. Marcia E. Herman-Giddens et al., "Secondary Sexual Characteristics and Menses in Young Girls Seen in Office Practice: A Study from the Pediatric Research in Office Settings Network," *Pediatrics* 99:4 (April 1997), p. 505.

13. Sandra G. Boodman, "Girls Beginning Puberty Earlier, Study Finds," *The Washington Post*, April 22, 1997, Health section, p. 7.

14. Barrie Thorne, *Gender Play: Girls and Boys in School* (New Brunswick, N.J.: Rutgers University Press, p. 141).

15. Martha K. McClintock and Gilbert Herdt, "Rethinking Puberty: The Development of Sexual Attraction," *Current Directions in Psychological Science* 5:6 (December 1996), pp. 178–83.

16. Kim S. Miller, Beth A. Kotchick, Shannon Dorsey, Rex Forehand, and Anissa Y. Ham, "Family Communication About Sex: What Are Parents Saying and Are Their Adolescents Listening?" *Family Planning Perspectives* 30: 5 (September/October 1998), pp. 218–22.

17. Shere Hite, *The Hite Report on the Family: Growing Up Under Patriarchy* (New York: Grove, 1994), p. 115. The total number of respondents to Hite's survey was 3,208, of whom 1,154 were between the ages of eleven and nineteen. Two thirds of the total respondents were female; presumably, then, approximately 773 of the adolescent reponents were female.

18. Ibid., p. 121.

19. Michelle Fine, "Sexuality, Schooling, and Adolescent Females: The Missing Discourse of Desire," *Harvard Educational Review* 58:1 (February 1988), p. 33.

20. Tamar Lewin, "Teen-Agers Alter Sexual Practices, Thinking Risks Will Be Avoided," *The New York Times*, April 5, 1997, p. A8.

21. *Market Facts* 1984, cited in Linda K. Christian-Smith, *Becoming a Woman Through Romance* (New York: Routledge, 1990), p. 104; Kathryn Falk and Cindy Savage, *How to Write a Novel for Young Readers and Get It Published* (Brooklyn, N.Y.: Romantic Times, 1990), p. 75.

22. Christian-Smith, p. 13.

23. Ibid., pp. 25–26, 34, 40.

24. Ibid., pp. 101, 102, 104.

25. Dinitia Smith, "Media More Likely to Show Women Talking About Romance Than at a Job, Study Says." *The New York Times* May 1, 1997. The study was conducted in the fall of 1996 and reviewed 23 top-rated television shows, 15 movies, three weeks of top 20 music videos and four issues of leading magazines for teenage girls: *YM, Sassy, Teen,* and *Seventeen.*

26. Tamar Lewin, "Boys Are More Comfortable with Sex Than Girls Are, Survey Finds, *The New York Times*, May 18, 1994.

27. Sharon Thompson, *Going All the Way: Teenage Girls' Tales of Sex, Romance, and Pregnancy* (New York: Hill and Wang, 1995), p. 27.

28. "Student Dispatches: Love, Sex and Other Misunderstandings," *The New York Times,* Special section on Teens, April 29, 1998, p. 8.

29. Thompson, p. 7.

30. Lena Williams, "Pregnant Teen-Agers Are Outcasts No Longer," *The New York Times*, December 2, 1993, pp. C1, C6.

31. Sharon Thompson, "Changing Lives, Changing Genres: Teenage Girls' Narratives About Sex and Romance, 1978–1986," in Alice R. Rossi, ed., *Sexuality Across the Lifecourse* (Chicago: University of Chicago Press, 1994), p. 225. Sharon Thompson, "Search for Tomorrow: On Feminism and the Reconstruction of Teen Romance" in Carole S. Vance, ed., *Pleasure and Danger: Exploring Female Sexuality* (London: Pandora, 1992), p. 363. Thompson, *Going All the Way,* pp. 29, 43.

32. Thompson, *Going All the Way,* p. 127.

33. Ibid., pp. 43–4.

34. Ibid., p. 273.

35. Barbara Seaman, *Free and Female: The Sex Life of the*

Contemporary Woman (New York: Coward, McCann & Geoghegan, 1972), p. 21.

36. Tamar Lewin, "Sexual Abuse Tied to 1 in 4 Girls in Teens," *The New York Times*, October 1, 1997. The link between early sexual abuse and early intercourse was reported by the Alan Guttmacher Institute in a 1997 analysis of a 1992 survey of 3,128 girls in eighth, tenth, and twelfth grades in Washington State.

CHAPTER 4: "SHE ASKED FOR IT": THE RAPED GIRL

1. Tamar Lewin, "Sexual Abuse Tied to 1 in 4 Girls in Teens," *The New York Times*, October 1, 1997.

2. Donna Christiano, "Rape: Do Your Fears Fit the Facts?," *Glamour*, January 1993. This statistic comes from the National Women's Study, also known as the "Rape in America" survey, of over four thousand American women over the age of eighteen. The study spanned three years and covered a wide cross-section of women from around the U.S.

3. The first survey, "Sex in America," in which 3,400 random Americans ages eighteen to fifty-nine were interviewed about their sexual practices, found that 22 percent of women "were forced to do something sexually at some time." The survey was conducted by the National Opinion Research Center. See Robert T. Michel, John H. Gagnon, Edward O. Laumann, and Gina Kolata, *Sex in America: A Definitive Survey* (New York: Warner, 1994), p. 223. The second survey, the National Survey of Family Growth, included 10,847 women ages fifteen to forty-four and was conducted in 1995 by the National Center for Health Statistics. It found that one fifth of women report that they have been forced to have intercourse against their will at some point in their lives. See Barbara Vobejda, "Survey: One-Fifth of Women Have Had Involuntary Sex," *The Washington Post*, June 6, 1997.

4. David Johnston, "Survey Shows Number of Rapes Far Higher Than Official Figures," *The New York Times*, April 24, 1992. This figure is from the National Women's Study, also known as the "Rape in America" survey, a government-financed, independently conducted survey of over four thousand American women over the age of eighteen.

5. Ibid. The Louis Harris survey was conducted for the Commonwealth Fund Survey of the Health of Adolescent Girls, September 30, 1997, and included 6,748 girls and boys in grades five through twelve.

6. Ibid.

7. Bernard Lefkowitz, *Our Guys: The Glen Ridge Rape and the Secret Life of the Perfect Suburb* (Berkeley: University of California Press, 1997), pp. 241–243.

8. Alice Vachss, *Sex Crimes* (New York: Random House, 1993), p. 90.

9. Ibid., pp. 89, 138.

10. Linda A. Fairstein, *Sexual Violence: Our War Against Rape* (New York: Morrow, 1993), pp. 81, 128.

11. Vachss, p. 31.

12. Helen Benedict, *Virgin or Vamp: How the Press Covers Sex Crimes* (New York: Oxford, 1992), pp. 18–19.

13. Ibid., chap. 6.

14. Ibid., pp. 96–107, 123.

15. Cited in Benedict, p. 131.

16. Benedict, pp. 140–142.

17. Peggy Reeves Sanday, *A Woman Scorned: Acquaintance Rape on Trial* (Berkeley: University of California Press, 1997), pp. 212–215.

18. Fox Butterfield with Mary B. W. Tabor, "Woman in Florida Rape Inquiry Fought Adversity and Sought Acceptance," *The New York Times*, April 17, 1991.

19. Yankelovich Clancy Shulman conducted this telephone survey of five hundred American adults for *Time*/CNN on May 8, 1991. The percentages of those surveyed who believe a woman is "partly to blame" if "she dresses provocatively" are 53 percent of those over the age of fifty; 31 percent of those ages thirty-five to forty-nine; and 28 percent of those ages eighteen to thirty-four. The percentages of those who say she is to be blamed if "she agrees to go to the man's room or home" are 53 percent, 29 percent, and 20 percent, respectively. The survey results are reported in *Time*, June 3, 1991, p. 51.

20. Felicity Barringer with Michael Wines, "The Accused in the Palm Beach Case: Quiet, Different and Somewhat Aloof," *The New York Times*, May 11, 1991.

21. Sanday, pp. 218–221.

22. Myriam Miedzian, *Boys Will Be Boys: Breaking the Link Between Masculinity and Violence* (New York: Anchor, 1991).

23. Felicity Barringer, "School Hallways as Gantlets of Sexual Taunts," *The New York Times*, June 2, 1993. A total of 1,632 students responded to the survey, which was sponsored by the American Association of University Women Educational Foundation.

24. Nan Stein, *Secrets in Public: Sexual Harassment in Public (and Private) Schools* (Wellesley, Mass.: Center for Research on Women, Wellesley College, 1993), pp. 2–3.

25. Anonymous, "Your Silence Will Not Protect You: A Story of High School Sexual Harassment," *Teen Voices*, 4: 2 (1995), pp. 22–26.

26. Amy Cunningham, "Sex in High School: What's Love Got to Do with It?," *Glamour*, September 1993, p. 318.

27. Ibid., p. 255.

28. Seth Mydans, "High School Gang Accused of Raping for 'Points,'" *The New York Times*, March 20, 1993.

29. Jane Gross, "Where 'Boys Will Be Boys,' and Adults Are Befuddled," *The New York Times*, March 29, 1993, p. A1.

30. Cunningham, p. 319.

31. Gross, p. A1.

32. Seth Mydans, "8 of 9 Teenagers Freed in Sex Case," *The New York Times*, March 24, 1993.

33. Seth Mydans, "7 of 9 California Youths are Freed in a Case of Having Sex for Points," *The New York Times*, March 23, 1993.

34. Albert made this comment to the *Press-Telegram*, cited in Cunningham, p. 321.

35. "Psychiatrist Calls Woman 'Bewildered' and Helpless in Glen Ridge Sex Case, *The New York Times*, December 19, 1992.

36. Lefkowitz, p. 5.

37. Ibid., p. 128.

38. Quoted in Don Terry, "Gang Rape of Three Girls Leaves Fresno Shaken, and Questioning," *The New York Times*, May 1, 1998, p. A18.

39. Lefkowitz, p. 160.

40. Ibid., p. 383.

41. Emilie Morgan, "Don't Call Me a Survivor," in Barbara Findlen, *Listen Up: Voices From the Next Generation* (Seattle: Seal Press, 1995), pp. 155–156. Emilie Morgan is a pseudonym.

42. Pamela R. Fletcher, "Whose Body Is It, Anyway? Transforming Ourselves to Change a Rape Culture," in *Transforming a Rape Culture,* ed. Emilie Buchwald, Pamela R. Fletcher, and Martha Roth (Minneapolis: Milkweed Editions, 1993), p. 429.

43. "Campus Drinking: Who, Why and How Much," *U.S. News & World Report*, June 20, 1994, p. 21. The statistic is cited in a report from Columbia University's Center on Addiction and Substance Abuse.

CHAPTER 5: "NOT ONE OF US": THE OUTSIDER

1. Nishiyama Akira, "Among Friends: The Seductive Power of Bullying," *Japan Quarterly,* October-December 1996, pp. 51–57; Murakami Yoshio, "Bullies in the Classroom," *Japan Quarterly*, October-December 1985, pp. 407–411.

2. "Eight Real-Life Experts Speak Their Minds," *The New York Times*, April 29, 1998, p. G5.

3. Sharon Thompson, *Going All the Way: Teenage Girls' Tales of Sex, Romance, and Pregnancy* (New York: Hill and Wang, 1995), p. 55.

4. Blake Nelson, *Girl* (New York: Touchstone, 1994), pp. 19, 226–27.

5. Robin Dunbar, *Grooming, Gossip, and the Evolution of Language* (Cambridge, Mass.: Harvard University Press, 1996).

6. Donna Eder and Janet Lynne Enke, "The Structure of Gossip: Opportunities and Constraints on Collective Expression Among Adolescents," in *American Sociological Review*, vol. 56 (August 1991), p. 501, 505.

7. Ibid., pp. 504–505.

8. Sources for Tawnya Brawdy's story: Correspondence from Louise Brawdy, October 27, 1994; Deposition of classmate of Tawnya Brawdy from Brawdy's hearing in the Superior Court of the State of California against the Petaluma City School District, March 24, 1992 (I am honoring Louise Brawdy's request not to name this witness); "Boys Will Be Boys," an undated leaflet put out by Parents for Title IX, run by Louise

Brawdy in Petaluma, California; Nan Stein, *Secrets in Public: Sexual Harassment in Public (and Private) Schools* (paper published by the Wellesley Center for Research on Women, Wellesley College, 1993); and Nina J. Easton, "The Law of the School Yard," *Los Angeles Times Magazine,* October 2, 1994, pp. 17–24.

9. Tammy Rae Carland, "Reflections of a Stupid Slut (Or, a Frigid Feminist—Depending on How You Look at It)," in Karen Green and Tristan Taormino, eds., *A Girl's Guide to Taking Over the World: Writings From the Zine Revolution* (New York: St. Martin's, 1997), p. 191.

10. Penelope Eckert, *Jocks and Burnouts: Social Categories and Identity in the High School* (New York: Teachers College Press, 1989), p. 5.

11. Ibid., p. 7.

12. Barbara Ehrenreich, *Fear of Falling: The Inner Life of the Middle Class* (New York: HarperPerennial, 1989), p. 15.

13. Barrie Thorne, *Gender Play: Girls and Boys in School* (New Brunswick, N.J.: Rutgers University Press, 1993), pp. 73–74.

14. Myra Sadker and David Sadker, *Failing at Fairness: How America's Schools Cheat Girls* (New York: Scribner's, 1993), pp. 83–84.

15. Ibid., p. 84.

16. Ibid., p. 43.

17. Ibid., pp. 44–46.

18. American Anorexia Bulimia Association, Inc., "Facts on Eating Disorders," p. 3. The AABA is a New York–based, national nonprofit organization dedicated to the prevention, treatment, and cure of eating disorders.

19. Sheila Parker, Mimi Nichter, Mark Nichter, Nancy Vuckovic, Colette Sims, and Cheryl Ritenbaugh. "Body Image and Weight Concerns Among African American and White Adolescent Females: Differences That Make a Difference," *Human Organization*, 54: 2 (1995), p. 111.

20. Ibid., et al, p. 106.

21. Naomi Wolf, *The Beauty Myth: How Images of Beauty Are Used Against Women* (New York: Morrow, 1991), p. 75.

22. Mimi Nichter and Nancy Vuckovic, "Fat Talk: Body Image Among Adolescent Girls," in Nicole Sault, ed., *Many Mirrors: Body Image and Social Relations* (New Brunswick, N.J.: Rutgers University Press, 1994), pp. 109–131.

23. Wolf, p. 75.

24. Parker, Nichter, et al., p. 107.

25. Jane E. Brody, "Girls and Puberty: The Crisis Years," *The New York Times*, "Personal Health" column, November 4, 1997, p. F9. The AAUW surveyed 2,400 girls and 600 boys aged nine through fifteen, while the Commonwealth Fund surveyed 3,586 girls and 3,162 boys in grades five through twelve.

26. The Commonwealth Fund Survey of the Health of Adolescent Girls, "Facts on Mental Health," September 1997.

27. Barbara Strauch, "Use of Antidepression Medicine for Young Patients Has Soared," *The New York Times*, August 10, 1997, p. A1.

28. Jennifer Egan, "The Thin Red Line," *The New York Times Magazine*, July 27, 1997, pp. 21–25; 34, 40, 43–44, 48.

29. Mary Pipher, *Reviving Ophelia: Saving the Selves of Adolescent Girls* (New York: Ballantine, 1995), pp. 20–21; 19.

30. Letty Cottin Pogrebin, "Competing with Women." *Ms*, 1 (July 1972), pp. 78–81, reprinted in Valerie Miner and Helen E. Longino, eds., *Competition: A Feminist Taboo?* (New York: The Feminist Press, 1987), p. 12.

CHAPTER 6: FROM SEXISM TO SEXUAL FREEDOM

1. Nan Stein, Nancy L. Marshall, and Linda R. Tropp, *Secrets in Public: Sexual Harassment in Our Schools* (Wellesley, Mass.: Center for Research on Women, Wellesley College, 1993), p. 11. The survey, which was a joint project of the NOW Legal Defense and Education Fund and Wellesley College Center for Research on Women, was published in the September 1992 issue of *Seventeen*. Over 4,200 girls completed and returned surveys. Girls completing the surveys ranged in age from nine to nineteen years old.

2. Sources for Katy Lyle's story: Telephone interview with Katy Lyle on July 28, 1994, when she was twenty-two; Laurie Hertzel, "No Apologies," *Duluth News Tribune*, January 12, 1993; Katy Lyle, "Sexual Harassment in the Boys' Room," *Choices*, January 1993; Katy Lyle with Mark Bregman, "'I'll Never Look at the World the Same Way Again,'" *Scholastic Update*, March 12, 1993; *Donahue* transcript #3445 (April 14, 1992): "Writing on the Bathroom Wall: New Form of Sexual Harassment?"

3. As reported by Nan Stein, "Sexual Harassment in School: The Public Performance of Gendered Violence," *Harvard Educational Review*, 65: 2 (1995), pp. 156–157.

4. Sarah Kershaw, "Kissing Pupil Is at Center of New Clash on Discipline," *The New York Times*, October 11, 1996; Tamar Lewin, "New Guidelines on Sexual Harassment Tell Schools When a Kiss Is Just a Peck," *The New York Times*, March 15, 1997.

5. According to the terms of her settlement, Laurie is not allowed to communicate with journalists. However, the facts of her case were well publicized in her local newspaper before the gag order. I spoke with both Laurie and her mother about her case. "Laurie" is a pseudonym; she requested that I not specify where the events took place.

6. Doris Walsh, "Safe Sex in Advertising," *American Demographics*, April 1994, p. 26. The magazine asked a nationally representative sample of 1,001 adults about sex in advertising and how it affected their purchasing decisions.

7. Nan Stein, "Is It Sexually Charged, Sexually Hostile, or the Constitution? Sexual Harassment in K-12 Schools," *West's Education Law Reporter*, 98: 2 (June 1, 1995), p. 622.

8. Tom Moroney, "Coming Unhinged Over Hand-Holding Ban," *The Boston Globe*, January 21, 1995.

9. Douglas Jehl, "Surgeon General Forced to Resign by White House," *The New York Times*, December 10, 1994, p. A1.

10. "Shalala Appeals for Help in Teen Pregnancy Battle," Ann Landers column, *Chicago Tribune*, August 19, 1994, Tempo section p. 3.

11. Tamar Lewin, "States Slow to Take U.S. Aid to Teach Sexual Abstinence," *The New York Times*, May 8, 1997, p. A1; "Sex Education That Teaches Abstinence Wins Support" (AP), *The New York Times*, July 23, 1997.

12. Quoted in Tamar Lewin, "States Slow to Take U.S. Aid to Teach Sexual Abstinence," *The New York Times*, May 8, 1997, p. A1.

13. Anne Grunseit and Susan Kippax, "Effects of Sex Education on Young People's Sexual Behavior," Unpublished review commissioned by the Global Programme on AIDS, World Health Organization, July 1993.

14. Mark A. Schuster, Robert M. Bell, Sandra H. Berry, and David E. Kanouse, "Impact of a High School Condom Availability Program on Sexual Attitudes and Behaviors," *Family Planning Perspectives*, 30: 2 (March/April 1998), pp. 67–72; 88. See also Lynda Richardson, "Condoms in School Said Not to Affect Teen-Age Sex Rate," *The New York Times*, September 30, 1997, p. A1.

15. Elise F. Jones, Jacqueline Darroch Forrest, et al., "Teenage Pregnancy in Developed Countries: Determinants and Policy Implications," *Family Planning Perspectives*, 17: 2 (March/April 1985), pp. 53–63. Also see Jay Friedman, "Cross-Cultural Perspectives on Sexuality Education," *SIECUS* (Sexuality Information and Education Council of the United States) *Report*, August/September 1992, pp. 5–11.

16. From the *Sex Respect* video *Why I Waited*, 1997, Respect, Inc.

17. Phyllida Burlingame, *Sex, Lies, & Politics: Abstinence-Only Curricula in California Public Schools* (Oakland: CA, Applied Research Center, 1997), pp. 5, 23. This is a joint report from the Public Media Center and the Applied Research Center.

18. Coleen Kelly Mast, *Sex Respect: The Option of True Sexual Freedom, Student Workbook*, rev. ed. (Bradley, Ill.: Respect Incorporated, 1997), pp. 7, 6.

19. Ibid., p. 106.

20. Ibid., p. 31.

21. Burlingame, p. 18.

22. Jane E. Brody, "Personal Health" column, "Sex Education Made Easier for Parent and Teen-Ager," *The New York Times* December 11, 1996, p. C13. The statistic is from a survey of 1,510 Americans aged 12 through 18 conducted for the Kaiser Family Foundation in 1996.

23. Judith Newman, "Proud to Be a Virgin," *The New York Times*, June 19, 1994.

24. Erica Werner, "The Cult of Virginity," *Ms.* March/April 1997, p. 41; L. A. Kauffman, "Praise the Lord, and Mammon," *The Nation*, September 26, 1994, p. 308.

25. Guy Garcia, "Woman=Coy Banter, Man=Nude Blonds," *New York Times*, October 23, 1994, Arts and Leisure pp. 17, 28.

26. Gina Kolata, "Women and Sex: On This Topic, Science Blushes," *The New York Times*, June 21, 1998, Women's Health supplement, p. 3.

27. Sallie Tisdale, "The Hounds of Spring," *Salon* magazine (www.salonmagazine.com), July 1, 1997.

28. Tamar Lewin, "All-Girl Schools Questioned as a Way to Attain Equity," *The New York Times*, March 12, 1998.

29. Barbara Vobejda, "Love Conquers What Ails Teens, Study Finds," *The Washington Post,* September 10, 1997, p. 1. The findings are from the first wave of data from the $25 million federal study known as the National Longitudinal Study of Adolescent Health, which surveyed 90,000 students in grades 7 through 12 across the country.

30. Erin Rollenhagen, "Shirting the Issue," *Seventeen*, October 1994, pp. 122–123.

31. Rekha Basu, "Girls Give a Hoot About Free Speech," *USA Today*, June 9, 1994, p. 11A.

32. "Pep Squad Sues for Harassment," *The Gazette* (Montreal), September 8, 1996, p. C6, from the *San Francisco Examiner.*

33. Kim Ratcliffe, "Five Girls Fight Back," *Seventeen*, July 1996, p. 118.

34. Maria Alicia Gaura, "Peer Harassment Suit Settled," *San Francisco Chronicle*, June 12, 1997, p. A19.

AFTERWORD TO THE PERENNIAL EDITION

1. Barbara Vobejda, "Study: More Teens Refrain from Sex," *The Washinton Post*, September 18, 1998, p.A2

2. "Teen Pregnancy Rate Continues to Decline," press release from the National Campaign to Prevent Teen Pregnancy, December 15, 1999.

3. Sheryl Gay Stolberg, "Birth Rate at New Low as Teen-Age Pregnancy Declines," *The New York Times*, April 29, 1999.

4. "Academic Freedom Survives Court Battle," *Censorship News*, a newsletter of the National Coalition Against Censorship (New York, NY), Spring 1999, p. 1.

5. Jodi Wilgoren, "Abstinence Is Focus of U.S. Sex Education," *The New York Times*, December 15, 1999, p. A18.

6. Christine Russell, "The 'Talk' with Kids Should Occur Early, Often," *The Washington Post*, April 6, 1999, p. C10.

7. Kaiser Family Foundation/MTV/*Teen People* National Survey of Teens on STD's, conducted in March and April, 1998. This was a random-sample national survey of 400 teens, ages fifteen to seventeen.

8. Judy Mann, "Wanted: A Realistic Attitude Toward Teen Sex," *The Washington Post*, January 27, 1999, p. C14.

APPENDIX A: WHAT TO DO
1. Nan Stein, "No Laughing Matter: Sexual Harassment in K-12 Schools," in Emilie Buchwald, Pamela R. Fletcher, and Martha Roth, eds., *Transforming a Rape Culture* (Minneapolis: Milkweed, 1993), p. 318.
2. Ibid., p. 327.
3. Nan Stein, "No Laughing Matter," p. 319; "What Do I Do If I Have Been Sexually Harassed?" *Teen Voices,* 2:3 (Fall 1993), p. 22.

ACKNOWLEDGMENTS

I could not have written this book without the girls and women who told me about their own lives. Many felt awkward sharing intimate details with me, a stranger, but decided that a bit of discomfort was worthwhile if it meant raising awareness about slut-bashing. I couldn't agree with them more.

I am fortunate to have many dear friends with sharp minds. I am particularly indebted to David Futrelle, who read and critiqued the entire manuscript in countless forms, but always with a fresh eye. David counseled me on everything from the structure of the book to the wisdom of using a four-letter word for a title. My special thanks go to DeDe Lahman, who first asked me to write about my high school reputation for *Seventeen*; she has been an indispensable and expert editor-on-call.

Once I undertook the research, Haviva Ner-David provided unflagging emotional support. Mala Mosher engaged me in provocative monthly discussions. Amy Richards went out of her way to clip and send me articles on the sexual double standard. Nan Stein generously shared with me information about the girls who sued their high schools for sexual harassment. Barrie Thorne provided me with an excellent reading list. Carol Diament was a role model of a serious thinker and writer. Doe Lang calmed my frazzled nerves and dispensed wise guidance. And Patricia Stush never failed to inspire me.

I want to express a special thank you to Jaclyn Geller and Sharon Loferski Engler, each of whom meticulously read the manuscript and engaged me in thoughtful discussions. I am grateful to Rachel Schwartz and Amy Zalman, who also carefully read the manuscript and urged me to rework certain passages. Robin Dionne, who also read the manuscript, offered many fresh, perceptive observations. Claire Needell-Hollander, the very first to work with me on this project, provided adept direction.

I thank my husband Jonathan for listening to me talk about slut-bashing for over three years and for nurturing me the many times my confidence became deflated or an important file was misplaced. Jonathan weighed every single sentence of this book with thorough (dare I say lawyerly?) consideration. I also thank my parents, Sheila Tanenbaum and Martin Tanenbaum, for their encouragement.

I am enormously grateful to Jennifer Lyons of Writers House, who has never wavered in her support of this project. Having Jennifer as an agent is like snagging a two-for-the-price-of-one deal, since she has provided essential editorial advice. Hannah Tinti, formerly of Writers House, has buoyed me with incisive guidance and consistent enthusiasm.

I am grateful for the expertise of everyone at Seven Stories Press, and particularly to associate publisher Jon Gilbert, publicity director Ruth Weiner, assistant editor Michael Manekin, and publicist Nicole Dewey. I also thank former editor Mikola De Roo for her early encouragement and advice. And how can I express my gratitude to Daniel Simon, editor and publisher extraordinaire? No matter what aspect of the book was under discussion, Dan was poised with advice as precise as a laser beam.

For the paperback edition of this book, I have been fortunate to work with a wonderful team of skilled and smart women: Sally Kim, my editor; Jennifer Hart, my marketing director; Diane Burrows, my academic promotion director; and Michelle Aielli, my publicist.

These acknowledgments would not be complete without a huge thank you to Barbara Seaman, always an advocate, friend, and confidante. Barbara championed this book when it was simply a modest proposal; her support was the adrenaline shot that allowed me to complete it.

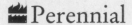 Perennial

Books by Leora Tanenbaum:

CATFIGHT
Rivalries Among Women—from Diets to Dating,
from the Boardroom to the Delivery Room
ISBN 0-06-052838-9 (coming Fall 2003 in paperback)

Part sociological study, part journalistic account of the American everywoman, *Catfight* explores the history and function of competition in society and the reasons why these covert, negative behaviors persist.

"An incisive exploration of a long-taboo subject—how and why women sabotage one another." —Gail Sheeby

SLUT!
Growing Up Female with a Bad Reputation
ISBN 0-06-095740-9 (paperback)

Girls may be labeled "sluts" for any number of reasons, often having nothing to do with sex. In this important account of the lives of young women who stand up to the destructive power of sexual labeling, Leora Tanenbaum weaves together three narrative threads—powerful oral histories of girls and women who tell us their personal stories, Tanenbaum's own story, and a cogent analysis of the underlying problem of sexual stereotyping.

"Tanenbaum has written an important and alarming book; it deserves serious attention and should encourage serious action." —*Women's Review of Books*